DICTIONARY
OF
SYMPTOMS

Text by A. Ward Gardner, M.D.

Introduction by
Winfred Van Atta

GRAMERCY PUBLISHING COMPANY

NEW YORK

Introductory Chapter by **Winfred Van Atta**
Director, Office of Public Interest
Columbia-Presbyterian Medical Center
New York City

Text by **Dr. A. Ward Gardner**

Consultant Editors **Dr. Reginald B. Cherry**
Director, Woodlands Health Clinic, Houston, Texas
Attending Physician,
Houston Northwest Medical Center

Dr. Lenore S. Katkin
Board Certified Specialist in Pediatrics
Associate Professor, Albert Einstein College of Medicine,
New York City

Dr. Glenn Patterson
Specialist in Internal Medicine and Family Practice
Attending Physician, Nyack General Hospital

Dr. Carl R. Wise
Board Certified Specialist in Internal Medicine
Medical Director of the Westchester Community
Health Plan
Former Vice President for Professional Services to
Patients, Columbia-Presbyterian Medical Center

Copyright © 1976 by The Hearst Corporation
All rights reserved
This 1982 edition is published by Gramercy Publishing Company,
distributed by Crown Publishers, Inc.,
by arrangement with Hearst Books.

Manufactured in the United States of America

h g f e d c b a

Library of Congress Cataloging in Publication Data

Gardner, A. Ward (Archibald Ward)
    Dictionary of symptoms.

    Reprint. Originally published: Good Housekeeping
dictionary of symptoms. New York: Grosset &
Dunlap, c1976.
    1. Symptomatology—Dictionaries.   2. Medicine,
Popular—Dictionaries.   I. Title.
RC69.G33   1982   616.07′2′0321   81-20208
ISBN: 0-517-369524   AACR2

Contents

Preface

Medical concepts and treatment techniques, diagnostic tools and laboratory tests, specific drugs for specific complaints, doctor and patient attitudes, and the costs and methods of paying for health care services have changed drastically during the past quarter century, but two elements in medical practice remain unchanged: the signs and symptoms of the diseases and abnormalities that afflict the human organism, and the way a doctor uses them to make an accurate diagnosis.

This book has been prepared to meet a specific need of today's intelligent adult who is concerned about his own health and the health of other members of his family. It is *not* a "Home Doctor Book" or "Family Medical Adviser," which is often improperly used for self-diagnosis and treatment, a most dangerous practice indeed. The purpose of this book is to help make you an informed and responsible patient, and it is best used in cooperation with your doctor. The text has been written by a practicing physician, then checked by a panel of distinguished specialists, which includes two internists, a pediatrician, a psychiatrist and a surgeon. The principal functions of this guide are:

1) To list in encyclopedic order the common and serious human diseases, along with the physical signs and symptoms that signal their presence. The scientific names that doctors use to describe them are given along with the common names and terms that make them understandable to you.

2) To impress you with the importance of recognizing the early signs and symptoms of disease and of reporting them in specific detail to your doctor.

3) To help you separate those common recurring disorders that run their course in a few days, with or without professional medical treatment, from those serious diseases which require immediate medical attention.

4) To spell out your responsibilities and obligations in the doctor-patient relationship and the doctor's responsibilities and obligations to you; to offer guides for choosing a doctor who is right for

you and your family and for judging his competence after you have found him; to help you best utilize his time and get the most value from the fees you pay for his services.

5) To explain how a doctor evaluates the signs and symptoms that you report to him and that he detects or observes, and the steps he takes, or should take, in performing a thorough physical examination—all essential for arriving at an accurate diagnosis.

6) To list and explain the laboratory, radiological and other sophisticated tests the doctor may order to confirm or rule out his tentative diagnosis, but more often to evaluate the present status of a disease or abnormality that he knows to be present in your body. The book also provides an extensive chapter on the most modern techniques of first aid and a special section on nursing the sick at home—features which add greatly to its value as a home guide.

What this book CAN do
· it can help you to find out about illnesses and medical problems.
· it can list some of the more likely possible causes of symptoms
· it can help you to pick out the likeliest cause of your symptoms

What this book CANNOT do
· make you into a doctor
· diagnose with certainty and assurance
· be right all or most of the time
· list every possibility

A layman's guide to the practice of medicine

Signs and Symptoms

A "sign," in medical parlance, is any physical manifestation of the body that can be observed, measured, felt, or even smelled, by an examining doctor. A "symptom" is the result of any variation in body functions that produces changed perception by the patient in terms of feeling. Signs and symptoms may be synonymous, such as a body rash that itches. Typical signs might be fever, vomiting, an altered walking gait, swelling, bad breath, skin discoloration, a coffee- or clay-colored stool, an abnormal blood pressure or heart rhythm, a distended abdomen, an enlarged liver that can be felt by the doctor. Typical symptoms might be pain in any of its many manifestations, dizziness, ringing in the ears, feelings of hopelessness and despondency, auditory and visual hallucinations, a lack of energy. Most often signs and symptoms are present in combinations, each of which has diagnostic value to the doctor, especially by the way a patient describes them, giving his own peculiar perception of them.

The cross-referencing within this guide permits you to locate a specific disease quickly, by both its scientific name and the signs and symptoms associated with it. Let us look at a specific example of a primary disease process, the signs and symptoms of which may be listed as specific disorders, each with its own peculiar signs and symptoms.

Arteriosclerosis (hardening of the arteries) is an incipient (silently and slowly developing) disease that may take twenty years, or longer, to produce the following conditions and symptoms: Angina Pectoris (sharp chest pain upon physical exertion); Hypertension (high blood pressure), Anterograde Amnesia (loss of memory for recent events), Dyspnea (shortness of breath, or oxygen hunger), Vertigo (dizziness, or a feeling of giddiness), Ischemia (depletion of blood supply to a part of the body), and many other signs and symptoms.

A good doctor might tell his patient that arteriosclerosis, and one of its most dangerous forms, Atherosclerosis (the formation of plaques in a major artery which impede or totally block blood flow) is thought to be of genetic origin (runs in families), but affects most of us in old age, and is due to the body's improper metabolism of Lipids (fat molecules in the blood). He would also point out that it develops more rapidly in men than women, that a complete and accurate family history is the most important element for early diagnosis, and that detected early it can be successfully treated before it results in catastrophic illnesses, such as heart attack and stroke. If questioned, he might describe the disease process something like this: As a person ages, his arteries harden and thicken, narrowing the pipeline that carries oxygenated blood to all organ systems of the body. As the pipeline narrows, the heart muscle must work harder to force blood through the narrowing passageway, which raises blood pressure. When blood to the overworked heart is depleted, its tissues cry for more oxygen and this is expressed in sharp chest pain. The lungs must then work harder to provide more oxygen, which results in quicker breathing and shortness of breath. If the arteries leading to, or circulating blood within, the brain, harden and clog, the memory system may be impaired, the patient may suffer dizzy spells, and various bodily functions may be altered. If the doctor detects advanced arteriosclerosis in you, or has evidence of early heart attack or stroke in members of your family, on either or both sides, he will be practicing the best traditions of preventive medicine if he advises you to warn close relatives, especially males over thirty, to be examined for this most dangerous of incipient diseases.

Obviously, in a book of this length, it is not always possible to go into such detail in describing the signs and symptoms of a disease process. The important thing is to have the necessary information to ask specific questions of your doctor and to understand why you should follow his instructions.

What kind of doctor are we talking about?
Except for brief mention of practitioners who are only licensed to practice a specific type of treatment, we are concerned in this book with the scientifically trained doctor who has graduated from an accredited college or school of medicine and has completed the required clinical training in an accredited teaching hospital to be licensed for the general practice of medicine. The general practitioner, often referred to as "Family Doctor" or "Primary Care Physician," will usually have finished a one-year

internship followed by at least a year of resident training in general medicine. To qualify as a board-certified specialist, or in one of the sub-specialties of medicine or surgery, he must complete from three to six years of resident training. Board certification in his specialty indicates that he has been examined by a board of certified specialists and found competent in the specialty or sub-specialty he will practice.

There is one other scientifically trained doctor practicing today: the osteopathic physician. Schools of osteopathy, once frowned upon by the medical establishment, now have educational and clinical training programs that compare favorably with those of many accredited medical schools and colleges. Qualified graduates of the better schools of osteopathy are now being accepted for intern and resident training in accredited medical teaching hospitals, and upon completion of such training may take the same examination for licensing that the M.D. graduate is given. When he passes, and most of them do, the O.D. graduate can use the M.D. as well as the O.D. degree after his name. All licensed osteopathic physicians can prescribe drugs legally and perform surgery. Like yesterday's Schools of Homeopathic Medicine, which have now been absorbed into the mainstream of scientific medicine, schools of osteopathy are expected to take the same course.

This cannot yet be said about Schools of Chiropractic. Their educational standards have been raised to meet the licensing requirements of many states, but their graduates cannot prescribe drugs legally or perform surgery. Although frequently helpful in treating certain disorders, it seems obvious that chiropractic manipulations and adjustments of the skeletal system, heat treatments, exercises, rest and diet therapy may be less than adequate for patients with undiagnosed systemic disease, psychological problems, or conditions requiring corrective surgery. Their fees may be comparable to those charged by medical doctors.

Patients should feel confident that most doctors in practice today, who have been adequately educated and clinically trained, do keep up with advancing medical knowledge and are competent to diagnose and treat most of your family's illnesses. If a doctor has a staff appointment and admitting privileges at an accredited hospital (one that is regularly inspected and approved by the Joint Commission for Hospital Accreditation), his patients should feel reassured of his competency, whether he is a generalist or specialist, and that, in a sense, you will have the benefit of his hospital's staff experience in rare and unusual diseases or serious injury, especially if it is also a teaching hospital engaged in training future doctors and nurses.

Good physicians who are dedicated to their profession and the welfare of their patients keep up with advancing medical knowledge, but there are less admirable reasons why doctors with accredited hospital staff appointments do keep up and are most likely to maintain high standards of practice. Three are offered here:

1) Such hospitals have peer review committees to assess the quality of performance of their staff members. If a doctor makes too many mistakes in diagnosis, performs too many operations that are proved needless by the tissue committee, attempts too many procedures that are beyond his competence, develops a problem with alcohol or drugs, or is found negligent in his responsibilities, he will be warned or restricted in what he can do. If he continues to follow the same road, he can lose his staff appointment. This may explain why some well educated and clinically trained doctors are limited to office practice, or practice some specialty that seldom requires hospitalization. It is not uncommon for such doctors to join in a group practice and sometimes establish their own proprietary hospital (operated for profit). Still others may move to some doctor-shortage area, often at the expense of a Citizens' Committee eager to bring a doctor, any kind of doctor, to their community. If you choose a doctor without hospital admitting privileges and you require hospitalization, he will probably refer you to another doctor who has such privileges and you, of course, will have to pay two fees.

2) Today, when government agencies pay a large percentage of all hospital and doctor costs, regular peer reviews of staff performances are mandatory.

3) Hospitals and doctors are now confronted with another grim reality: the high cost of malpractice insurance. Anesthesiologists and surgeons, the most vulnerable, now pay as much as $40,000 annually for such insurance. Teaching hospitals, which must provide such insurance for their salaried doctors, interns, residents and fellows, have had malpractice premium increases of up to 750% during the past two years. This has intensified the efforts of hospitals and doctors to identify and weed out those doctors who continue to make them liable for malpractice suits which may result in settlements running into hundreds of thousands of dollars.

Choosing a doctor who is right for you

From what has been said, it should be obvious that a primary consideration is that your doctor has a staff appointment and admitting privileges at an accredited hospital. A second consideration should be that his office and hospital are as close to your home as possible, to save time in cases of emergency and to save money. If you live at a distance, you waste time and money commuting and may have to add up to 25% to the cost of an office visit for parking. A third, perhaps the most important consideration, is choosing a doctor with whom you can feel comfortable, whose attitudes and methods give you confidence in his ability to help you. Although we live in the age of scientific medicine, the *art* of medical practice is still a vital force in successful treatment, especially of a frightened or timid patient, which includes most of us when we first go to a doctor for help.

Since the days of the shaman and the medicine man the afflicted have endowed their healers with supernatural powers, never questioning their methods or the reasons for what they do. The scientific doctor who emerged during the past century did little to discourage this false image. He continued—not always consciously—to cloak his profession in a shroud of mystery, using language and medical jargon that had precise meaning to other doctors, but remained as mysterious and incomprehensible to the average person as the ritual chant of a witch doctor exorcising demons and evil spirits. This attitude is now changing.

Some of today's doctors, especially those in surgery and its sub-specialities, are more committed to the science of medicine than its art, but most doctors have now learned that an informed patient, who is given the reasons for a treatment regimen, or a surgical procedure, is a more cooperative and responsive patient. You should always bear in mind, when choosing your doctor, that doctors, generally, are not much different from the rest of us in a success-oriented, materialistic society. They may be inherently lazy, selfish, acquisitive, eccentric, arrogant, obsessively ambitious for recognition, neglectful of their own families, and rude to colleagues and their own office staff. They can have any of the faults common to us all and still be good doctors. The difference lies in the centuries-old traditions of their profession and in their long years of carefully controlled schooling and clinical training, during which they learn to sublimate, re-direct or control basic attitudes, emotions and instincts when they are dealing with patients. Nonetheless, each human being, whose emotions and attitudes are peculiar to his own personality, has an uncanny instinct for sensing hostility, sham, or insincerity in another person. The doctor's looks, mannerisms and attitudes may remind a patient, often unconsciously, of a cruel parent, an overbearing sibling, an overdemanding teacher, or any of many persons with whom he has had unpleasant experiences. When this happens, the patient is likely to feel uncomfortable, even distrustful of that doctor, and the odds are against a successful relationship. So if you cannot feel comfortable with a doctor and have complete trust in his judgment, he is not the best doctor for you.

Many surveys among doctors indicate that they believe that individuals, and especially families, should have a primary care physician (general practitioner or family doctor). He will be able to diagnose and treat a majority of the illnesses and injuries of both parents and the children of a family. Equally important, he will serve as their medical "manager," referring them to the proper specialist when it is required, but he will provide aftercare when they are released by a surgeon, and will continue to participate in their treatment even while they are under a specialist's care.

How do you find such a physician?

You might start by calling the nearest accredited hospital, asking them to give you the names of two or three staff doctors who do general or family practice in, or near, your community. If you seek only a personal physician, you might ask for a board-certified internist, who is a specialist in internal medicine and usually limits his practice to adults. You might also ask your neighbors about their doctors. Most of them will tell you that their doctor is the best around, that you'll be lucky to get him, and that his fees are reasonable, of which only the last recommendation may be true. If there is no immediate need for a family doctor, you might write to the American Academy of Family Practice, 1740 West 92nd Street, Kansas City, Missouri, 64114, asking for the names of its diplomates practicing in your area. Such doctors have qualified as specialists in family practice, and are required to take periodic refresher courses in teaching hospitals to keep abreast of new developments in medicine. You might also call your local County Medical Society and ask for the names of family doctors, or any other specialist you might seek. The secretary will usually give you three names, but she goes through her list in order, and you'll get the names of those who are next in line. They may be the best or worst doctors in town.

If you wish to check the educational and clinical training credentials of any doctor you are considering, you can use a national physician directory that may be in your local library, or you can write to The American Medical Association, 535 Dearborn Street, Chicago, Illinois, 60610, for such information.

If you live in, or near, a large city where a major medical center is located, you might want to call their appointments supervisor, asking for the name of the doctor who might see you at the earliest date. He will give you the name of an internist, or a specialist if you ask for one, and you can be certain that he will be competent. The large medical center, or teaching hospital, is at the center of modern medicine, is usually affiliated with a University School of Medicine, and most of what is new in medicine will be available there. If the internist you get sees only adults, a qualified pediatrician or any other specialist you might need will be only a few floors away. You might want to assume the extra cost of traveling and parking, and perhaps the doctor's larger fee, by going to such an institution, but its staff and services will also be available to you, through your local doctor or accredited hospital, for those rare and unusual conditions which they are best equipped and staffed to treat. Many families once used their out-patient clinic for all medical services—and the city's poor still do—but there are many disadvantages in seeking such services today. You are not likely to see the same doctor twice in a row, you may wait your turn for hours, and you, or the third-party agency responsible for your medical bills, will pay as much for clinic services as would be paid for one of their doctors who sees private patients by appointment.

Most people seeking a family doctor usually start by making a visit by appointment, paying the doctor's usual fee, not returning if they do not like him. There is a better way. If you have obtained the names of two or three doctors who meet the qualifications you seek, call their offices and make appointments to see each, explaining to the appointments clerk, usually a nurse or secretary, that you are looking for a family physician and would like to come in and discuss this with the doctor at his convenience. Most family doctors will not charge for such a visit.

When you see each of your candidates, be prepared to ask them specific questions. *Will he/she treat all members of your family?*

Does he have admitting privileges at the nearest accredited hospital? Will he make house calls to see a bedridden patient, or in extreme emergencies? In the event of pregnancy, does he provide prenatal care and do the delivery, referring to the obstetrician only high-risk mothers with predictable complications that require a specialist's skills? What, if any, types of surgery does he perform? Does he, as a matter of routine, practice preventive medicine, sending notices for annual physical checkups, booster inoculations, repeat tests for breast and cervical cancer, allergy immunizations and other follow-up checks and tests that are due? Does he maintain office hours that will permit working members and school-age children to be seen without loss of work or school time? What are his fees for routine and special office visits? Does he charge for telephone consultations? And of special importance: *What doctor, or doctors, cover for him when he is away or not available?*

If you have questions about special problems peculiar to any member of your family, don't hesitate to ask them. Be aware during this "get-acquainted" interview that the doctor will be judging you, just as you are judging him, that just as you have a right to the doctor of your choice, the doctor has the right to reject or accept a patient. The good doctor will not resent your asking so many questions. On the contrary, he will respect you as a concerned, responsible person who does not take his doctor or his medical services lightly. It might be wise to offer to pay for this special visit. If the fee is waived, he will be telling you that he would like you and your family as his patients. If he sets his usual fee for the time given, he may be telling you otherwise or that he already has a full schedule. If so, this is the time to find out.

After you have interviewed your candidates and thought about them later, one is likely to stand out. This will be the best doctor for you and your family, because your feelings and attitudes will be passed along to the others.

Your responsibilities to your doctor

Once you have selected your doctor, you should understand that you are beginning one of the most delicate and intimate relationships you can enter into; that it will endure and become more rewarding only if each participant lives up to his responsibilities. At the beginning of the relationship, doctor and patient could almost be said to be adversaries. Each expects something of the other that he may not be able or willing to give immediately. The doctor, from experience, is aware of this stalemate situation and will make a special effort to break down the barriers that inhibit most new patients, but his success is dependent upon the patient's response to his overtures. Therefore, as an informed patient, anxious to get the most for the fees you are paying, consider ways in which you can help the doctor help you.

Start with this basic realization: Today's average family doctor, in addition to making hospital rounds and attending to his own business and family affairs, will see from 30 to 40 patients daily during regular office hours. He will give all the time he can possibly spare during a first visit to establish rapport with his patient, to take a complete personal and family history and perform a thorough physical examination, but on routine office visits he can give only 15 to 20 minutes to each patient, if he is to see all who depend upon him. If for no other reason than this, sit down at home and list answers to questions the doctor is most likely to ask, whether about yourself or another member of the family:

What signs and symptoms have brought you to me? How long have they been present? What parts of the body are affected? Have similar symptoms been present before and, if so, has a doctor treated them?

If there is pain, is it dull, sharp, throbbing, flashing, a vague ache? Is it constant or intermittent, more intense at certain times of day or when you do certain things? Does it originate in one place then spread to another?

Has there been fever? If so, for how long and in what ranges? Have there been chills or sweating? Have there been recent colds, sore throats, coughing, infected burns or lacerations, boils? Have you noticed spots or rashes? If there has been high fever in a child, has there been any sign of convulsions?

How are your bowel movements, regular, irregular, hard, loose, watery, and have you noticed any discolorations in your stools or urine? How is appetite? Do symptoms occur shortly after eating, or the eating of certain foods; do you get temporary relief after eating?

Do you have frequent headaches, dizzy spells, ringing in the ears, distortion of vision? Do you feel down in the dumps most of the time, or at certain times, or when you do certain things. Do you go to sleep easily, then awaken in the early hours of morning and find it impossible to go back to sleep?

There are as many variations of symptoms as there are patients. The above questions are given only as examples. By identifying your own signs and symptoms through the use of this book, you will know the questions your doctor is likely to be most concerned about and be prepared to answer them.

Unless your first visit is for a specific illness that requires immediate attention, your doctor's first interest will be in your personal and family medical history. You can help him immensely, and save him time, if you'll sit down at home and list specific details for yourself or your child. The personal medical history should include the following:

Circumstances of birth: full-term or premature · normal delivery or by caesarean section · complications such as infections, allergies or genetic defects.

Childhood diseases: list them all, especially the infectious contagious diseases, because the hearing or vision problems you have as an adult may date back to the measles you had as a child · chickenpox · rubella (German measles) · diphtheria · scarlet fever · polio · recurring ringworm infections · fever blisters · eye infections · rheumatic fever · convulsions · asthma, etc.

Inoculations and vaccinations: When given · follow-up booster shots.

Diseases and injuries in adulthood: list them by dates, starting with the most recent · names and addresses of doctors and surgeons who treated them · names and locations of hospitals in which you have been a patient.

The story of previous illnesses, injuries and treatments is of great importance in helping to decide what is the matter with the person today. Omissions of information here can lead to serious errors in diagnosis or to easily avoidable blunders.

Laboratory and X-ray tests: list them by dates, again starting with the most recent · names and addresses of hospitals and commercial laboratories in which they were made · X rays that you still might have (past laboratory test results and X rays are invaluable to your doctor; he may not have to repeat them if done recently, or he can use them as a baseline to determine what changes, if any, have taken place since they were made).

Drugs, special diets, exercises ordered by a doctor: names of drugs you are now taking, including those bought over the counter at a drugstore; if you don't know the names of prescribed drugs, take samples to the doctor · drugs to which you have reacted adversely, such as penicillin and other antibiotics, horse serum inoculations, tranquilizers and antidepressants, etc.

The family medical history on both sides, immediate and remote, are of utmost importance to your doctor. The following information, if known, should be listed.

Diseases and genetic abnormalities suffered by parents, grandparents, aunts and uncles, cousins, sisters and brothers · sudden deaths from heart attack, stroke or unknown causes, and age of victim at time of occurence · diabetes, asthma, hay fever, emphysema, cancer, tuberculosis · blood disorders such as hemophilia, leukemia, Hodgkin's disease, sickle-cell anemia, thalassemia (previously known as Cooley's or Mediterranean anemia) · mental disorders such as mongoloidism, chronic and intermittent depression, learning disabilities, schizophrenia, or any other problem that might have required psychiatric treatment or hospitalization.

Occupational history. Work is an important part of most people's lives. What a person does at work can often affect his health and may even be at the root of his present complaint. For example, people who have worked in dusty jobs can suffer from lung diseases. Many chemicals are hazardous on the skin and may be encountered at work. People who have sedentary occupations have more heart attacks than those whose work involves physical activity. Bartenders, hotel managers and business executives on the sales side tend to have higher than average alcohol consumption and from these groups there will be more problem drinkers and alcoholics.

If the foregoing seems overdrawn, it is presented for a reason. The more details you give your doctor about your personal and family history, the more he will be prepared to help you, especially in preventing or detecting and treating early those family diseases that can now be controlled, such as diabetes, high blood pressure, Hodgkin's disease, chronic and acute depression, and many others.

When you visit the doctor's office, and especially for a first visit, you are certain to be nervous, anxious and apprehensive. A good doctor will understand this and make every effort to put you at ease, but he will not often question you until he feels you are ready. Your instinct will be to avoid, as long as possible, the main reason for your visit, to talk about everything else but your medical problem, Don't do it, because you are paying for the doctor's time. If you've done your homework on histories and signs and symptoms, you'll be ready and the doctor will have the preliminary work done quickly, allowing him more time for a thorough physical examination.

In every step of the doctor-patient relationship, whatever the cost to you in embarrassment or lost self-esteem, you must be absolutely honest in answering his every question. You must not embellish, diminish or avoid reporting certain symptoms to excuse yourself or influence his diagnosis. First of all, he's bound to find out, and secondly nothing you say to him will be shocking, new, or surprising, or make him like you less; he's heard it all before, many times, and he will not share with anyone, except another doctor, the information you give him.

If the doctor orders laboratory tests, X rays or any of the new diagnostic procedures that are available today, believe that he is doing it for your own good, although he may order some tests for self-protection to avoid a future malpractice suit (family doctors are least likely to be sued for malpractice and most of them will order only tests essential to make or rule out a tentative diagnosis).

If he prescribes drugs, take them exactly as directed and report immediately any adverse side effects; he can prescribe another that you can tolerate and that will be as effective. If he orders periodic laboratory tests while you are taking certain powerful drugs, take them and at the time he sets, because he needs to know how to regulate the exact dosage, and the tests will tell him how much or how little is required for you. Keep all drugs out of the reach of children, and never under any circumstance, even though similar symptoms may be present, give or make available to another person a drug that has been prescribed for you or other members of your family. Many of the powerful new drugs change with age, can lose their potency or produce dangerous reactions. Destroy those left over after treatment is completed. If the doctor prescribes special diets, exercises, asks you to lose weight, stop smoking, reduce intake of alcohol, do what he says, no matter how difficult it may be. If he recommends immediate hospitalization for special tests, or for any reason, don't contest his decision.

If the doctor has done his job properly and you have done yours, you should leave his office feeling uplifted and reassured, relieved of much of the anxiety that has brought you to him, even though he has not yet made a specific diagnosis of your complaint. The following suggestions will, if followed, increase your doctor's respect and appreciation of you as a desirable patient, worthy of his best efforts:

· Never delay seeing him when new symptoms occur or old ones change.

· Follow his recommendations for preventing illness—inoculations, immunizations and booster shots for children, or for older people vulnerable to colds and influenza; annual checkups for adults, especially for breast and cervical cancer in women.

· If you are in pain, have a high fever, or have suffered severe injury, you have the right to an immediate appointment with your doctor, but try to fit your routine visits into his schedule. When you know that you cannot keep an appointment, notify the doctor's office as early as possible so that another patient can take your place.

· Limit requests for house calls to true emergencies. When you do ask the doctor to come, be prepared when you call him to give pertinent facts about the emergency: type of accident, the victim's signs and symptoms, the poison ingested, state of consciousness in a stroke or heart attack victim. If he asks you to meet him at a hospital emergency room or his office, don't argue but get there as quickly as possible. If he deems a house call necessary, he will know, if properly informed, what drugs and equipment to bring with him.

· Never see two or more doctors at the same time without their knowledge; they may be prescribing drugs that are incompatible, or you may be taking double doses of a drug that may have a different brand name and appearance but contains the same powerful ingredients.

What are the things patients do that annoy doctors most? The following examples have been taken from a survey made among doctors:

· The patient repeatedly fails to follow instructions. He does not take his medicine, or fails to take it as directed. He does not follow prescribed diets or recommendations for rest. He refuses to admit these oversights even when the doctor presents evidence given by other members of his family.

· He fails to keep appointments, or is late for them, abuses house call privileges, telephones unnecessarily, is rude and discourteous to the doctor and his employees; is a disruptive influence in the waiting room.

· He makes a nuisance of himself by demanding every new drug, test or treatment that he reads about or hears about.

· He fails or delays paying bills or repeatedly contests them, even though he knew the fee schedule in advance.

· A pediatrician said: "I resent most the mother who compares the treatment of her child to that of another, then demands the same, even though it is not indicated."

· A gynecologist said: "I urge my patients to come back at six-month intervals for routine tests of the cervix and breast for cancer. Most promise faithfully to return and then ignore my mail rem.nders. When will women ever learn that we do not need to solicit patients, but have only a genuine interest in protecting their health? There is nothing in my practice more tragic than a woman, adequately warned, who comes in two or three years after a negative Pap test with obvious evidence of cervical cancer. Caught in its preinvasive stage, it can be cured in ninety-nine out of a hundred women."

· An internist said: "It's hard to believe that a patient who spends his money and is genuinely concerned about his health will deliberately withhold important symptoms. Another type of patient will take the belligerent attitude that he is spending his money, so it's up to the doctor to find out what's wrong."

· A surgeon said: "I'm appalled when a patient has been referred to me and I find out that, either through fear of the procedure or resentment of the cost, he refuses to sign a consent form for surgery that may correct a crippling handicap or cure a chronic disorder that may require emergency surgery later, often in a place where a qualified surgeon is not readily available."

The doctor's responsibilities to you

Just as informed patients carefully select their doctors, good doctors are now becoming more careful in accepting good patients, and there is no patient shortage today.

A doctor is not legally or ethically required to accept a patient for treatment, except in a true emergency situation. If, on a first visit, a patient presents a wide variety of questionable symptoms and complaints, or is hostile and uncooperative, the doctor, before examining him or attempting treatment, can simply advise him to seek another doctor. However, if he completes the physical examination and orders a battery of tests, then tells the patient that is healthy and does not need treatment, he is not off the hook if the patient insists upon further examinations, treatments and tests. In such situations he will probably refer him to a specialist, perhaps a psychiatrist, which will usually get rid of him in a hurry.

When the doctor undertakes treatment, even in an emergency

situation, he is legally required to continue treatment for as long as it is needed. It matters not that the patient refuses to pay his fees, upsets the office and makes a nuisance of himself. He can sue and collect his fees, if the patient has resources, but he must continue to provide needed medical services until another doctor accepts the patient. If he refuses treatment, or fails to meet established standards of treatment, he can be sued on two counts: negligence and abandonment.

The responsible family doctor will not usually reject a co-operative patient whose very real symptoms are of emotional origin. If he did, he would lose a large number of his best patients, most of them needing his help as desperately as the organically ill. Repeated questionnaires and surveys among family doctors and general practitioners reveal that as many as half of the patients who come to them for treatment have signs and symptoms for which no pathological explanation can be found. After completing a thorough physical examination and a battery of tests to rule out organic disease, the doctor will usually learn by careful listening and indirect questioning that the patient has very real justification for his symptoms. He is simply expressing psychic pain in physical symptoms. The doctor may prescribe mild tranquilizers, or antidepressant drugs if true depression is suspected, but he knows from long experience that this patient's greatest need is a friendly ear and practical counseling. A woman may be unhappy in her job, her marriage, her children, her home. A man may be stuck in a job that he hates and cannot leave, has a staggering debt load, is drinking too much. Both patients may be able to cope with all of their problems most of the time, but some new crisis or burden is added to send them over the edge of emotional stability. They are sick, but not sick enough to be sent to a psychiatrist. The good family doctor, with patience and sympathy, will get to the root of the problem and can often offer practical advice. He knows that he'll be seeing these patients again when the next crisis develops, but he will not refer them until he recognizes the development of mental symptoms that a psychiatrist should evaluate and treat.

A hospital may refuse admission to a patient who cannot present evidence of adequate hospital insurance or ability to pay, but a good doctor will never deny services to the patient or family who cannot pay for them. He will usually make arrangements for large bills to be paid over a period of time, and he will help an indigent patient get needed financial assistance from the proper health agency for needed hospital care, office treatments and drugs.

The family doctor should refer to the specialist any patient who requires treatment beyond his competence to provide, or any patient who is organically ill and does not respond to his treatments after a reasonable period of time. He should not feel offended if the patient suggests that he'd like to get another doctor's opinion. If the patient is referred for major surgery, the primary care doctor should prepare the patient physically and psychologically for such a traumatic event, unless the need for surgery develops suddenly.

The surgeon will do his own examination and study past X rays and laboratory reports, ordering needed new tests. If he confirms your own doctor's recommendation for surgery, he will explain that you must sign a consent form authorizing the operation. Before you sign it, he should explain in detail both the risks and the benefits that may result from surgery. He should answer any questions you ask him: about his fee, the fees of the anesthesiologist, the radiologist and other specialists who might be called in for consultation. You can ask about the hospital's per diem rate, operating room charges, the cost of a private duty nurse, if needed. You can ask what the normal hospital stay will be and the recovery period at home before returning to work, if no complications develop. When it is elective surgery, which can wait a reasonable period of time, you should not hesitate to seek a second opinion from another surgeon of your own choosing. If he makes the same recommendations as the first one, you should feel sure that the operation is needed and go through with it.

A further word should be added about signing consent forms. Many intelligent laymen still do not know that any licensed M.D., whatever his training or facilities might be, can legally perform any and all operations, even brain and open-heart surgery. He can do it in his office, your home, or his clinic or proprietary hospital. He can be successfully sued for malpractice if he botches the job, but he cannot be held criminally liable for attempting surgery beyond his competence. That is why it is always wise to ask questions about your surgeon's training and experience in your type of operation, and to seek a second opinion before signing a consent form for major surgery. The recent news stories about the vast amount of unnecessary surgery being performed today have not been exaggerated.

If, after a period of treatment, a doctor finds he cannot develop rapport with a patient and anticipates growing dissatisfaction in the patient, he should carefully explain that another doctor might be better for him. He should make the patient understand that some doctors and patients are sometimes incompatible and cannot feel comfortable with each other, which is necessary for good medical treatment. If he recommends another doctor that he feels would be right for an individual patient, the patient should trust his judgment.

The good doctor will be as honest with a patient as he expects the patient to be with him, except when it might be to the disadvantage of the patient. For example, withholding the truth of a confirmed diagnosis of a painless, slowly progressive fatal disease, when he is certain that such knowledge would destroy the quality of life still left to the patient. He should, of course, tell a responsible member of the patient's family the truth.

The doctor should always make certain that another doctor is covering for him when he is away, even for a short period, and that the covering doctor's telephone number will be available to his patients through his office or an answering service.

The doctor should never be expected to criticize another doctor's management of a patient, even though the patient or members of his family may seek confirmation of their own doubts and dissatisfaction.

How the doctor makes his diagnosis

From the moment a patient enters his consultation room, the doctor will be gathering information important to making his diagnosis. The comparison that is sometimes made between a programmed computer and a doctor's mind as he evaluates signs and symptoms, personal and family history, and performs the physical examination, is an apt one in many respects, but computers can never take the place of a competent doctor. The doctor judges the whole patient, his emotional makeup, his tolerance to stress, pain and fear, his individual needs as a human being. He does not simply see him as a biological machine whose parts wear out or need adjustments.

As you enter a doctor's office and sit down to talk with him, he will be making judgments, based on your appearance. Your face may have a pinched look, your expression may reveal anxiety, fear, indifference, anger, apathy, be mask-like. The way you walk and sit, your manner of dressing, the jewelry you wear, how you use your hands or re-cross your legs, your hesitancy or eagerness to talk, all will have special meaning to him. From long experience, he will, subconsciously perhaps, have your emotional and personality makeup typed before he begins taking your medical history, and this judgment will influence the way he handles you. Nevertheless, if his "snap" judgment is wrong, he will change his approach as required.

He will first want the general symptoms that have brought you to him for this visit. You may complain of burning sensations in various parts of your body: head, throat, arms, chest, abdomen. Your complaint may be of feeling too hot, too cold, tired all the time, loss of appetite, low back pain, headaches. Whatever your signs and symptoms may be, he will encourage you to describe them in your own way. He will not, or should not, ask you specific leading questions that you can answer "yes" or "no," but should indirectly lead you to give details. Whatever your illness might be, wherever it is located, an experienced doctor will be able to make an accurate diagnosis in more than 50% of the patients he sees simply on the basis of their histories and the signs and symptoms they report and he observes. His physical examination will help him make an accurate diagnosis in another 25%, but it may require a battery of tests and X rays to pinpoint the diagnosis in the remaining 25%. He knows how to take a cluster of signs and symptoms which may be common to several diseases or abnormalities, then, one by one, he will rule out those that do not apply in your case, to reach a differential diagnosis. Laboratory and radiological tests will confirm, rule out, or help him evaluate the present status of your medical problem.

In a young, generally healthy person, the doctor will usually make only a cursory examination of the body's various organ systems, unless he detects or suspects serious systemic illness, but he will carefully examine that organ system in which your present problem is located.

Many doctors now question the need for a complete annual physical examination in young healthy adults, but if they find evidence of a chronic or developing disease in such patients they should set dates for periodic checkups. During the forties and early fifties all adults should have periodic physical examinations, men as they approach the age when hypertension, heart attack and stroke are most likely to develop, and women as they approach the menopause. A complete physical examination should be given at the first evidence of pregnancy, with regular periodic examinations until time of delivery. Large corporations, not necessarily notable for humanitarian concern for the individual employee or unnecessary expense on his behalf, usually pay for a complete medical evaluation of a new employee before hiring him, and of middle and top management personnel at periodic intervals. They are noted for keeping good cost statistics, so this practice must be worth the money.

The individual going to his personal physician will get the examination he requests and is prepared to pay for. The comprehensive examination, which may cost from $75 to $250, or more, depending upon the doctor and a patient's ability to pay, should include careful examination of each organ system and basic laboratory and X-ray tests, plus special tests that might be indicated by the medical history or physical findings. Few doctors go about making their examinations in the same way, but most of them will follow a course that includes the following:

General inspection of the body: its general contour, type of body build in relationship to age, height, weight, muscular and bone structure, size of chest and abdomen. The doctor will, from experience, quickly detect abnormalities in body movements and speech, and will notice swellings, such as edema of the ankles.

Head and neck: he will inspect the eyes, using an ophthalmoscope, perhaps applying drops to dilate the pupils so that he can see and evaluate blood vessels, which give him leads to serious illnesses that may be developing, especially diabetes, arteriosclerosis, and abnormal pressures within the skull. He will inspect the retina, the clearness of fluids within the eye. He will check for abnormalities of vision in each eye, and for abnormal pressure within the eyeball (glaucoma).

He will use an otoscope to inspect the ears, a light source instrument that has a speculum and mirror. He is able to visually inspect the ear canal back to the eardrum for excessive wax, insects and other foreign bodies, scars, infections, growths, drum puncture, normality of position. He may pull or manipulate the external ear to evaluate the middle ear and hearing mechanism. He will test hearing by the whispered or spoken word, then use special equipment or order tests, if he finds a loss of hearing.

By changing the speculum of his light instrument, the doctor will examine the nostrils to determine if the divider (septum) is straight or crooked, if the passages are obstructed, or if there are abnormal discolorations, evidence of infections or allergies, sinus problems or growths.

Using light, he will inspect the throat for infections, growths, condition of tonsils, the presence of spots, swelling, or any visible abnormalities. He will examine the external throat with his hands to detect thyroid or lymph gland enlargement.

While examining the internal throat, he will check other parts of the mouth, including teeth, tongue and mucus membranes, for abnormalities, discolorations and growths. He will at the same time be smelling your breath, for odours such as urine, feces, new cut hay, sweetness, or sourness, which can offer clues to systemic diseases. He will be interested in the color of the lips, if they are dry, drawn, deformed, puckered or have evidence of healed lesions or sores.

Chest: which includes heart, lungs and breasts. He will use his stethoscope to listen for abnormal heartbeats which may include murmurs, extra beats, irregular rhythms, or sounds like water tumbling or splashing. If severe abnormalities are found, he will order special tests immediately. He will also listen for the exchange of air in the lungs, detecting abnormalities that may also call for immediate special tests. Even before using his stethoscope he will examine your chest by percussion (thumping across your back and around the rib cage to elicit dull or resonant sounds), to determine if fluids have collected in the lungs or chest cavity. He will use a tape measure to establish adequacy or inadequacy of chest expansion, which is not only important to heart and lung functions, but may offer clues to other abnormalities. He will carefully examine the breasts of both men and women for growths and lumps, which, if found, should be biopsied (tissue samples taken by needle or a small incision) for examination under a microscope to confirm or rule out cancer. The doctor will examine the lymph glands under the arms for enlargement or nodes.

Abdomen: this part of the examination will usually include the genitalia (reproductive organs) and ano-rectal areas. He will observe the abdomen to make the following determinations: is it distended, rigid, flabby, fat, enlarged or bulging in certain areas? He will use his stethoscope to listen for normal and abnormal sounds of the bowel and intestinal tract. He will feel the liver to determine its size and condition, the same for the gallbladder and the spleen, if it can be found. Growths, obstructions and other abnormalities can be detected in this way. He will check for hernia, which is most often found in men, but may be present in women, and for lymph nodes in the groin.

The examination in men will include, if done properly, a careful evaluation of the prostate gland, penis and gonads. The rectal examination should be made with a proctoscope which can be inserted into the lower bowel. As it is slowly withdrawn, its light source will permit a careful observation of tissues. This is a most important part of the examination, because a majority of intestinal cancers and other growths occur in this area. He will feel and observe for hemorrhoids, fissures and test the sphincter muscle.

The pelvic examination in women requires the use of a speculum, which is inserted to spread the vaginal walls so that the vagina and cervix can be visually inspected and needed tests can be made. At this time a Pap smear from the cervix should be taken for pathological examination to detect evidence of early cancer. The doctor should then insert the finger of one hand into the vagina, then place the other hand on the abdominal wall. The finger and hand, working together, will permit him to determine the shape and location of the uterus, ovaries and tubes. The final step should be a proctoscopic examination of the ano-rectal region, as in men.

Neurological and skeletal examination: these examinations may be done together in routine investigations. The doctor will check all reflexes, the functioning of limbs and joints, back and neck. He will check for sensory perceptions, tremors, the overall coordination and balance of the body. Much of his neurological examination will have been included in his examination of the internal eyes and in the questions he asked during the history taking.

Skin: the doctor will carefully inspect the skin for coloration, expecially evidence of jaundice (yellowish), cyanosis (bluish), for paleness, redness, moisture, texture. He will look for moles, lesions, eruptions, scars, bruises, spots and rashes, lumps. He will carefully inspect the scalp and hair for abnormalities.

Routine tests: A thorough physical examination should also include the following routine tests:
Urinalysis. From this single test the doctor may be able to detect a malfunctioning kidney, diabetes, the slow formation of kidney stones and infections of the urinary tract. It can alert him to the possibility of gout, hardening of the arteries, and other systemic diseases.
Complete Blood Count. This gives the hemoglobin content (the protein to which oxygen is attached) and the red and white blood

cell counts, which, if abnormal, may denote the presence of anemia and infections.

Serum Cholesterol Count. This measures a fatty substance in the blood that is found in the plaques and linings of arteries when they harden and thicken. A normal count is from 150 to 200 milligrams per cent. People with counts between 260 and 300 milligrams per cent are considered borderline and should be watched. Counts above 300 may cause the doctor to order diets and drugs to lower it. People prone to cardiovascular disease should be especially careful.

Serum Tryglyceride Count. Tryclyceride is a combination of glycerol with three fatty acids in the blood. It is also found in combination with cholesterol in the arteries of patients with ateriosclerosis.

The Sedimentation Rate. This valuable routine test is not of specific value for any particular diagnosis, but it can indicate a state of good health, or the activity of some abnormal process within the body, such as arthritis, tuberculosis, and malignancies.

Electrocardiogram. If the doctor finds or suspects abnormal heart function, or the history suggests that it might develop, he should order this test. It measures the electrical potential across the heart muscle, and the results are printed out on graph-lined tapes. Every person has his own peculiar reading. The electrocardiogram is not dangerous or painful, nor is it used as a specific diagnostic test. However, used in combination with other tests, it is invaluable in diagnosing and treating heart disease. If a young man in his thirties, for example, has his normal electrocardiogram established, and there is a history of heart disease in his family, it will be used as the baseline for recording possible future changes in heart action. The *stress electrocardiogram* is usually given following a heart attack or when coronary disease is present, to evaluate the exercise stress limit a patient's heart can safely handle. He may walk up and down a set of steps, walk or run on a revolving belt that can be angled to simulate hill or stair climbing. By using the stress electrocardiogram, doctors have been able to permit many recovered heart attack victims to safely resume almost normal activities, even jogging, golf, tennis and other sports.

Specific tests for specific disorders

Infections of unknown origin may call for *culture studies.* These should be made of material swabbed from a sore throat or pus from any source to determine what germ is responsible, such as streptococcus or staphylococcus, which will determine the drug or drugs that are most effective against them. The untreated strep throat may lead to rheumatic fever and acute heart disorders in later life.

Abdominal abnormalities may call for *barium studies*. The patient swallows, or is given by enema, a milk-like substance that serves as a contrast medium for X rays, which may be taken from many angles, or for fluoroscopic examination. The trained radiologist will be able to evaluate normal and abnormal shadows that represent growths, ulcers, obstructions and other abnormalities.

There are several standard techniques used to evaluate the body's various organ systems, among which the following are most common:

Angiography, is a radiological technique in which a radiopaque substance is injected into a blood vessel, usually an artery, that leads to or from an organ, then a series of X-ray film is taken in rapid sequence as the contrast media flows through the organ's vascular system. This test is most often associated with the brain. It can detect the presence of tumors, atherosclerosis, and of an aneurysm. The latter is an abnormal bulging of a thin arterial wall, which, if ruptured, will lead to massive hemorrhage and death. Detected in time, it can be successfully corrected by surgery.

Pneumoencephalography. Cerebrospinal fluid is withdrawn from the spine and air is injected, permitting radiological examination of the brain's ventricles and the subarachnoid spaces.

Ultrasonography. This is a relatively new technique now in common use, especially for the internal examination of pregnant women, who should not be exposed to X rays. It operates on the same principle as the ultrasonic technique used by surface vessels to locate submerged submarines. Sounds of frequencies above 16,000 cycles per second are directed into the body and have different velocities in tissues which differ in density and elasticity from others. The ultrasonic echoes are picked up as they strike tissues and can be printed out to produce an image or photograph of an organ or of an abnormal tissue growth.

Radioactive Isotope Tests are now used to detect abnormalities in many parts of the body. For example, radioactive gold and sulfur colloid concentrate in the liver, red blood cells tagged with chromium 51 in the spleen, phosphorus 32 and strontium in the bones, radioactive iodine in the thyroid gland. When lodged in their specific targets, a scanner prints out a picture revealing abnormalities. The radiation in an organ scan is usually less than that received from standard X rays.

Mammography has greatly increased the radiologist's ability to detect and evaluate breast malignancies before they can be felt or diagnosed by other methods. It is a technique that uses very low energy radiation and supersensitive film to detect abnormalities.

Thermography is a relatively new technique that is proving useful in diagnosis. It depends upon catching, recording with a sensitive scanner, and interpreting the meaning of radiant heat thrown off by tissues affected by disease. Variations in skin temperature of the face, for example, can indicate the condition of blood vessels leading to the brain.

Fetal Monitoring is one of the very important new procedures now being carried out in advanced medical centers and teaching hospitals, and is important to every mother expecting a child. Early in pregnancy, cell samples can be taken from the amniotic cavity for genetic evaluation of the developing fetus. Such heart-rending genetic disorders as mongoloidism, sickle-cell anemia, thalassemia and many others can now be detected early, so that a pregnancy can be interrupted, if the mother chooses not to have such a child. To a family that is prone to this type of tragic genetic abnormality, which may be transmitted to only a small percentage of infants, those afraid to risk pregnancy can now usually feel reassured, by genetic testing, of having a normal healthy baby.

Computerized Axial Tomography is one of the most recent and exciting diagnostic techniques, which holds great potential for diagnosing cancer and other abnormalities, without the use of contrast materials, and without discomfort, hospitalization, or invasion of the body. This technique has linked the computer to an X-ray tube to take internal three-dimensional photographs in color. Most of the first such instruments made are now installed in a few major medical centers for diagnostic studies of the brain. They are replacing the often risky angiogram, which requires hospitalization, a team of radiologists and technicians, and is costly. With this new technique, the patient comes in, lies on a table and places his head in the instrument's cavity for about twenty minutes as the X-ray tube revolves around his head, photographing a thin slice of his brain with each revolution. This information is fed into the computer which prints out a three-dimensional picture that permits the doctor to look inside the brain for tumors and other abnormalities. The results are accurate in more than 90% of the patients examined and the errors, when made, are always on the good side, predicting an abnormal brain that may be normal. This error can be detected by an angiogram, which is always given in such cases.

Even more remarkable diagnostic facilities are being developed. A team of radiologists was recently awarded a grant by the National Cancer Institute to develop an advanced complete body scanner that will incorporate new concepts and features never before used. It is expected to be ready for testing in 1976 and its designers predict that it will be able to detect cancer and other abnormalities throughout the entire body long before symptoms occur or they can be detected by conventional methods. Because the percentage of cancer cures is increased greatly by early detection and treatment, the potential of this marvelous new diagnostic instrument to alleviate pain and suffering is incalculable.

It's always comforting for a lay person to read of new advances and developments in medicine, but it should always be remembered that the signs and symptoms of disease, and the way a doctor uses them to make the initial diagnosis will not change.

Symptoms

Abdominal distension

May be caused by overeating, by a lot of *gas in the bowel* giving rise to *flatulence*, by *fluid in the abdomen* (ascites), or by gross enlargement of any abdominal organ. A protuberant abdomen from *obesity*, or slack muscles, should not be mistaken for a distended abdomen, where the skin is tense and stretched. Flatulence may be accompanied by *colic*, by *diarrhea* and by *loud rumbling bowel sounds*. Abdominal distension due to gas will give rise to a drum-like sound if the abdomen is tapped with the finger. Fluid distension will not resonate, and tapping with the finger will give rise to very little sound. Gross enlargement of any abdominal organ can give rise to distension. This may be due, for example, to an ovarian cyst, to an enlarged spleen or an enlarged liver or to *cancer*. Severe malnutrition in children can cause the condition.

Abnormal

Describe the abnormality, and check further in the book.

Abortion

The expulsion of a nonviable fetus from the uterus. A nonviable fetus is one which is too young to survive on its own. Twenty-eight weeks of intrauterine life—counted from the first day of the last menstrual period—is usually assumed to be the youngest age at which a fetus can survive on its own. After this date the term "stillbirth" is used if the fetus does not survive. Abortions may be described as spontaneous when they occur on their own, or as induced when they occur as a result of operative or other interference. Induced abortions may be medically induced or may be criminal abortions.

"Abortion" and "miscarriage" mean the same thing, although the word miscarriage is generally reserved for spontaneous abortions before the twenty-eighth week.

Most spontaneous abortions occur at about the end of the third month of intrauterine life counted from the first day of the last menstrual period.

The biological reason for many of the miscarriages at three months appears to be related to malformation of the fetus or placenta.

The symptoms of an impending abortion will be cramping *pains in the lower abdomen* and perhaps a slight amount of *bleeding from the vagina.* Immediate rest in bed is necessary, and medical help should be arranged.

Abscess

The result of localized infection in the tissues. Most abscesses give rise to localized red, tender, throbbing swellings. These may discharge pus, or become a "blind boil" and resolve without escape of pus.

Abscesses can be caused by a wide variety of infective organisms and can occur in most parts of the body. Bacteria commonly causes abscesses, but abscesses may be caused by fungi, yeasts and amebae. A cold abscess—"cold" because there is no heat or redness around the swelling—is usually due to tuberculous infection.

A *carbuncle* is a special type of abscess.

Recurrent abscesses or carbuncles are common in people who suffer from *diabetes mellitus.*

Acariasis

Any disease caused by an acarus—a mite, or tick. *Scabies* is a common form of acariasis.

Achalasia

The term used to describe failure of relaxation or opening of a sphincter (valve). Failure of opening of the sphincter between the lower end of the esophagus and the stomach may lead to *difficulty in swallowing,* and is referred to as achalasia of the cardia—the cardia being the sphincter between the esophagus and the stomach. In this condition the esophagus may become very distended due to the obstruction at the lower end. The internal diameter may be three times the normal size.

See also *stenosis.*

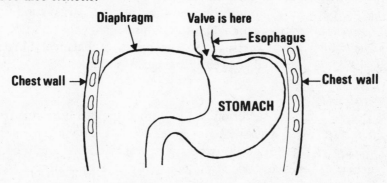

Aching See *pain* in part concerned.

Aching bones and joints See *fever · pain in joints*.

Achlorhydria
Absence of secretion of hydrochloric acid in the stomach. This is found with pernicious *anemia*. Individuals who have no acid in their stomach often suffer from *diarrhea*, because many organisms are killed by stomach acid in normal people.

Acid regurgitation
The appearance of sour acid in mouthfuls on burping or on lying down. The condition may be associated with a *hernia through the diaphragm* or with a *peptic ulcer*.

Acne
An inflammatory disease of the sweat glands. It may begin with *blackheads*. Then an infected red spot or pimple develops which may discharge some pus. Scars may be left as a result of these small *abscesses*. The disease usually begins in the teens a few years after puberty. The face, back of the neck and upper trunk are principally affected. In mild cases, the disease disappears within a few years, but it can persist for about twenty years. Oil acne results from the skin being exposed to lubricating or cutting oils through bad work habits allowing contamination, and through wearing oil soaked clothing. Oil acne usually affects the fronts of the thighs and the forearms. This form of acne is easily prevented.

Acoustic neurinoma
A *tumor* which affects the hearing nerve by pressing on it. The onset of a particular form of one-sided deafness—nerve *deafness* —in a person of middle age is suggestive of this condition. *Dizziness* may also occur if the tumor presses on that part of the nerve which sends messages to the organ of balance. Surgical treatment is indicated at as early a stage as possible.

Acromegaly
Is due to excess of secretion of the human growth hormone from the pituitary gland in the brain in an adult. Giants are produced if excess of the growth hormone is secreted before adulthood is reached. The excess secretion is usually due to a simple *tumor*

(adenoma) of the pituitary. The result is to produce a character-istic appearance in the sufferer: large hands, heavy bones and a protruding jaw, and all the features become coarser. If the disease progresses, *high blood pressure* and *pain in joints* due to arthritis develop.

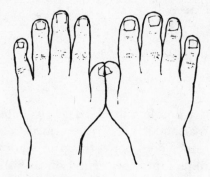

The hands in acromegaly

Acroparasthesia

Tingling ("pins and needles"). See *tingling of the hands and/or feet*.

Addison's disease

A disease caused by lack of the internal secretions of the adrenal (suprarenal) glands. It is characterized by *weakness,* and by increased pigmentation of the skin (see *disorders of pigmentation of the skin*). Brown patches or *spots in the mouth* may be found. In the early stages of the disease when weakness is beginning, the disease may be mistaken for neurotic behavior or for the general-ized weakness associated with other diseases such as tuberculosis and malignant *tumors.*

Adrenal glands

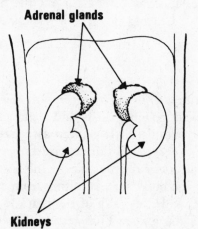

The site of the adrenal glands

Kidneys

Agitation   See *anxiety · confusion · depression · psychosis.*

Agoraphobia   See *phobic anxiety.*

Air sickness   See *motion sickness.*

Alcohol induced pain   See *pain after drinking alcohol.*

Alcoholism

The usual first symptoms of problem drinking or alcoholism are social and not medical. An alcoholic may be described as anyone who, because of alcohol, either does not turn up to work or has trouble at work. Most sufferers find this definition distasteful to them and reject it at first. But, if and when they come to look back on it, they will agree that it highlighted the borderline between social drinking and problem drinking. Later, the social effects will be loss of job, or family, absence of control over drinking, of self-control and of self-respect. Finally the sufferer cares about nothing but where the next drink comes from. Unfortunately most alcoholics are not prepared to recognize the early stages of addiction, and so have to suffer the later stages.
The medical effects of alcoholism, such as liver damage, are late effects. Anyone who thinks that he may have problem drinking or alcoholism should contact both his doctor and Alcoholics Anonymous (AA) for help. Once alcoholism is well established it is difficult to cure without considerable help from others. Stopping is the only successful way of shaking off the habit of any drug, including alcohol. Cutting down is a useless form of self-deception.

Allergic rhinitis

A form of *running nose* due to *allergies. Hay fever,* which is due to pollen allergy, is a form, and pollens, dusts and dandruff from animals can give rise to this complaint. It is often associated with *itchy eyes,* and sometimes *red eyes.* Children who have allergic rhinitis will often have a *nose crease* running across the nose at the junction of the soft tip and the bony part, resulting from pushing the tip of the nose upwards with the palm of the hand to relieve irritation and to wipe away discharge. This gesture is known as the "allergic salute," and any child who makes it is suffering from allergic rhinitis.

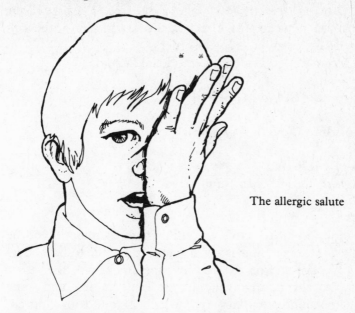

The allergic salute

Allergic salute   See *allergic rhinitis*.

Allergies

Reactions of the body to certain substances which may be introduced into the body or onto the skin. Acute allergic responses to such foods as shellfish and strawberries, to such drugs as penicillin or to stings from bees and wasps may result in sudden *urticaria*, or may even cause swellings of the face, eyelids, lips or throat. These swellings, or angioneurotic edema, can create a serious medical emergency if the swelling occurs in the throat or larynx, because the swelling can lead to choking and asphyxia.

Allergies can cause the skin to react to a substance or substances with which it has been in contact. This is often known as atopic dermatitis. The usual reaction is characterized by *itching* and irritation, and by redness of the skin with tiny yellowish blisters at the worst-affected areas. The *target organ* in allergies can vary. The causes of atopic dermatitis are very numerous, and include plants, glues, chemicals of all kinds, penicillin, nickel (often in watch straps) and many other substances.

Hay fever, or *allergic rhinitis,* is another common form of allergic illness, often brought on by pollen and dust. *Asthma* and *wheezing* may often be allergic in origin, associated with pollen, house dust and house mites, and with chemicals such as diisocyanates in lacquers and paints.

Allergies may also be involved in eye diseases, diseases of the bowel, and reactions to drugs and medicines. *Atopy* is the collective name for many allergic disorders.

Allergies are often aggravated by emotional factors.

Alopecia areata See *loss of hair.*

Alopecia totalis Total *loss of hair.*

Alteration of the voice

See *hoarseness · loss of voice · difficulty in speaking.*

Amblyopia

Dimness of vision or defective vision in which examination of the eye reveals no disease. This is often found to be due to immoderate use of alcohol and/or tobacco by pipe smokers. Other toxic substances can also be involved, such as lead, quinine and some drugs and medicines. A "lazy eye" which is found in children, especially in those who have *squinting eyes* (strabismus) or who have had a squint corrected, is properly known as amblyopia ex anopsia—a form of suppression of the visual image so that *double vision* is prevented. Amblyopia may also be associated with *nystagmus,* a rapid and very small sideways movement of the eyes followed by a slower movement back. Nystagmus may be continuous, or may only occur at times, or may appear on looking in certain directions.

Amenorrhea

Amenorrhea means absence of menstruation. Four main groups of amenorrhea can be described:

ABSENCE OF MENSTRUATION DUE TO A CONGENITAL DISORDER. The causes include:

absence of the essential organs · underdeveloped reproductive organs · abnormal cervix, vagina or hymen so that the menses cannot escape. In these circumstances the menses accumulate within the uterus (hematometra), tubes (hematosalpinx) or vagina (hematocolpos).

ACQUIRED AMENORRHEA DUE TO CLOSURE OF THE VAGINA OR CERVIX may occur following pelvic injury or after operation.

NORMAL OR PHYSIOLOGICAL AMENORRHEA. Menstrual periods are

normally absent before puberty, after the menopause, during pregnancy, and during the period when a woman breast feeds a baby—that is, during lactation. When menstruation has started, the commonest reason for a missed menstrual period in any woman who has been sexually active is pregnancy. Until this obvious possibility has been eliminated by pregnancy testing if need be, it is probably unnecessary in apparently healthy women to look much further.

AMENORRHEA ASSOCIATED WITH GENERAL DISEASE OR WITH DISEASE OF THE REPRODUCTIVE ORGANS. Any serious general disease which saps the general strength and vitality of a woman can lead to amenorrhea. Among the possible causes are *anemia · leukemia · Hodgkin's disease ·* tuberculosis *· diabetes ·* nephritis · serious heart disease *· cirrhosis of the liver ·* malignant *tumors.* Some diseases of the endocrine glands will alter the states of the internal secretions produced by them. Among these possibilities can be listed *hyperthyroidism · hypothyroidism ·* diseases of the pituitary gland *· Addison's disease* of the suprarenal gland · disorders of the ovary.

Emotional causes of amenorrhea can include fear of pregnancy and emotional upset such as bereavement. Some forms of mental disease may also be associated with amenorrhea.

Anorexia nervosa is usually accompanied by amenorrhea when the loss of weight becomes marked.

Amnesia   See *loss of memory*.

Anemia

Literally, "lack of blood," a term generally used to describe lack of red blood cells. There are many varieties. The symptoms of anemia include *breathlessness · tiredness · pallor · yellowness of the skin · palpitations · angina pectoris. Spoon-shaped nails* may be found in association with anemia. A smooth tongue or a *sore tongue* may also be associated with anemia.

Anesthesia   See *loss of feeling*.

Aneurysm

A swelling in an artery which increases its internal diameter and finally greatly weakens the vessel wall. An aneurysm of the aorta is a possible cause of *pain in the chest* or *pain in the abdomen*. The usual reason for an aneurysm of the aorta is late *syphilis*. Another form of aneurysm is a dissecting aneurysm, in which the blood in the aorta gets between the layers of the aorta and, under the normal pressure of blood flow, dissects the walls. This occurs in Marfan's syndrome and in arteriosclerosis.

Angina pectoris

The *pain in the chest* which arises when the heart muscle has an insufficient supply of blood—thus, angina pectoris usually indicates that the person has *ischemic heart disease* or *anamia*. The *ischemia* may be due to narrowing of the arteries, or may be due to total cutting off of blood supply to a part of the heart as a result of a *thrombus* in the coronary arteries that supply blood to the heart. This results in a *coronary thrombosis*.

Angina pectoris is felt as a pain in the sternal area. Typically the

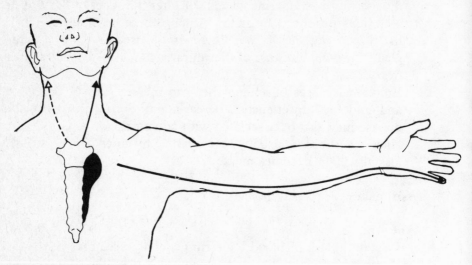

Position and spread of pain in angina dectoris

pain is felt as a dull, boring or pressing sensation which begins on exertion and increases if the exertion continues, forcing the person to stop. After a few minutes' rest, the pain disappears and the person can walk slowly. The pain is usually felt at the left edge of the upper sternum, but may extend downwards along it. If the pain is more severe, it may radiate up the neck to the jaw, usually on the left side, but possibly also on the right.

The pain may also be felt in the shoulder down the inside of the left arm as far as the elbow. Angina pectoris is often said to be the cry of the heart muscle for more oxygen.

The important point to note about angina is that the pain is produced by exertion or excitement and disappears on rest. It is not always possible to deduce from the kind of pain, or from its duration or severity, which form of ischemic heart disease is involved: angina of effort due to narrowing of arteries, or a coronary thrombosis due to blocking of arteries. An *electrocardiogram* and other investigations will be necessary. *Arteriosclerosis* and *pain in the leg* from intermittent claudication are associated with angina pectoris. Cigarette smoking is associated with angina pectoris and ischemic heart disease.

Angioneurotic edema   See *allergies · urticaria.*

Ankylosing spondylitis
A disease of the spine of unknown origin which ultimately results in stiffness of the spine. The disease affects men almost exclusively, and usually begins between the ages of twenty and thirty. Treatment can only ensure that the spine stiffens in a straight position of good function and not in a hunchback deformity. Sometimes the disease is associated with eye trouble in the form of iritis and iridocyclitis. The disease may be confused in the early stages with *rheumatoid arthritis* and *psoriatic arthropathy.*

Anorexia nervosa
A condition almost always of adolescent and younger women in which the individual cuts down on the amount she eats or almost gives up eating entirely. Young men are very occasional sufferers. There is often a history of emotional upset before the girl or young women stops eating normally. As she eats less and less, her weight drops, her menstrual periods stop and sexual feelings are reduced. Some of these young women may almost starve themselves to death—and a few indeed do. All the features of starvation are to be found. The precise causes of stopping eating or of eating less are unknown. Treatment must therefore concentrate on the emotional problems and on encouraging the young woman to eat and to keep eating. This can be very difficult for all concerned.
Of those who have suffered from this disease about half eventually regain normal weight and half remain thin in varying degrees from slight to emaciated.

Anosmia   See *loss of sense of smell.*

Antimetabolic drugs See *cancer.*

Anxiety

Is a normal reaction to any stressful situation. It becomes abnormal if prolonged in duration or if it is *phobic anxiety.* Slight anxiety states can lead to jumpiness and irritability. More severe attacks lead to concentration on the source of the anxiety to the exclusion of other thoughts and interests, and to *disorders of sleep* until exhaustion occurs.

Anxiety which is prolonged in duration or which is phobic is a form of illness which requires skilled medical help. These states will not disappear if left alone.

Apathy See *depression · tiredness.*

Appendicitis

Commonest in the age group 10–25 years but can occur at any point from infancy to old age. In many cases the first symptoms are of *pain in the abdomen,* which may be *colic* and felt as *pain around the umbilicus.*

At this stage the person may lose his appetite, and may have a slight *fever* (raised body temperature). As the illness develops, the pain moves from the center to the right lower quarter of the abdomen and may be accompanied by *nausea* and *vomiting.*

Any abdominal pain which is accompanied by fever, nausea and vomiting should be seen early by a doctor.

Pain which moves from the center to the right lower abdomen is usually due to appendicitis.

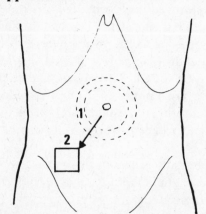

Appendicitis—1. Appendicitis begins as central pain
2. The pain moves to this area

Appetite, excessive   See *excessive appetite*.

Appetite, poor   See *poor appetite*.

Arteriosclerosis
A condition in which the walls of the artery become thickened, hard and inelastic. This results in a narrowing of the internal diameter of the artery. Blood flow through the artery is thus reduced. The effects of generalized arteriosclerosis are felt most in organs and tissues particularly dependent on a good blood and oxygen supply. The heart muscle is one such tissue. *Angina pectoris* and *ischemic heart disease* are consequences of depleted blood supply through the coronary arteries, which supply blood to the heart muscle. The brain is also very susceptible to any deficiency of blood supply. The *loss of memory* seen in older people is usually due to defective blood supply to the brain. Arteriosclerosis affecting the kidneys can lead to *high blood pressure* in an attempt to get sufficient blood flow through the kidneys.

Arthritis, infective   See *septic arthritis*.

Arthritis, septic   See *septic arthritis*.

Ascites   See *fluid in the abdomen*.

Asthma
A condition characterized by *wheezing* and *difficulty in breathing*. The condition fluctuates—sometimes the sufferer has a very bad attack of wheezing, and at others he is free of symptoms and breathlessness. The condition often runs in families, and is associated with other diseases such as *hay fever, allergic rhinitis, eczema, migraine* and *allergies*. The overall name for this group of diseases is *atopy*. Asthma can be brought on by allergens, by infections, by emotional and psychological factors, and by non-specific lung irritation such as cold air, cigarette smoke and irritant gasses.
In asthma, the smooth muscle which encircles the bronchi and bronchioles contracts and thus narrows the tubes. This results in wheezing and difficulty in breathing.
These remarks apply to bronchial asthma—usually referred to simply as asthma. However, there is one other form of asthma,

called cardiac asthma, which usually occurs at night in bed in middle-aged or elderly people. It is due to left-sided heart failure.

Asymmetry of the chest

Slight asymmetry is normal and healthy. Greater degrees of asymmetry are unusual, and should be seen by a doctor for assessment. The causes can range from congenital abnormalities to chest diseases.

Asymmetry of the head

Slight asymmetry is normal and healthy in adults and babies. Few of us are completely symmetrical. After a baby is born, the head is often molded as a consequence of passing from the uterus. This will usually right itself within days. Greater asymmetry is not normal, and should be seen by a doctor for assessment.

Atherosclerosis

A form of *arteriosclerosis* in which fatty substances are laid down in the arteries and their inner layers become tough and sinewy.

Atopic dermatitis   See *eczema · allergies · atopy*.

Atopy

The collective name for the inherited disorders of *asthma, allergic rhinitis* and *hay fever, eczema* and some forms of *urticaria,* which occur separately, together or in various combinations in individuals and families. In about four out of five cases another member of the family has one of these diseases, so that the condition is an inherited familial disorder. The conditions are often triggered off by *allergies* or infections. *Asthma* is occasionally precipitated by exercise. *Stress,* especially emotional stress, may bring on any of these atopic diseases.

There is some evidence that potentially atopic and allergic children—that is children of parents who have or have had atopy in any form—will benefit by being kept away from anything which is known to produce allergy during the first six months of life. In effect this means that the infant should be breast fed for the first six months of life, because this will avoid cow's milk, which is the commonest allergen to which infants are exposed in quantity. Care should also be taken to avoid other allergy producers, such as feathers, pets—for example cats, dogs and birds—and dust from house mites.

Audiogram See *audiometer*.

Audiometer
An instrument used to test hearing. Audiometry is usually carried out with sounds of different frequencies (pitches) to determine what can be heard at each frequency. The amplitude of the signal (loudness) is increased until the person can hear the sound, and the lowest level at which he can hear each sound is recorded to plot the audiogram. The nature and extent of *deafness* can thus be measured and recorded.

Baby fat See *obesity*.

Backache
A condition which may be associated with *fever* or *tiredness,* or with disease or injury.
Diseases which can cause backache include *ankylosing spondylitis, osteoporosis, tumors* in the spine, and pains which are felt to be in the back and are related to diseases of the lungs, kidneys or abdominal organs. Disease or injury to the intervertebral disk may cause both backache and a *pain in the leg* which is often referred to as *sciatica.* This pain is due to the nerves being trapped by the collapsed disk at the exit from the spinal cord. Pain and *loss of feeling* may both be present in the leg when there is a "slipped disk."
Obesity will always tend to make any backache worse because of the extra weight carried.
Muscular aches in the back may follow unaccustomed effort in lifting and bending.
Always check for a *cloudy urine* if backache is accompanied by fever.

Bad breath (halitosis)

The causes usually fall into five main groups which include:

INFECTIONS of the mouth, teeth, tongue, pharynx, nose and nasal sinuses. The infection itself causes the bad breath.

SEPTIC CONDITIONS in the mouth, such as a *Vincent's infection, tonsillitis* and chronic *sinusitis* which result in a *postnasal drip* of purulent material into the pharynx are also commonly found to be causes of bad breath.

INFECTIONS IN THE LUNG. In this case the bad breath will usually be associated with an excess of thick, infected or foul sputum from such causes as *bronchitis, bronchiectasis* or lung abscess.

SOME SERIOUS DISEASES OF THE STOMACH, LIVER AND INTESTINE such as *cancers* and *cirrhosis of the liver* may also be associated with bad breath. In these cases, the illness itself will usually be very obvious, and the bad breath will only be regarded as a part of the serious general illness.

Very occasionally more serious conditions such as cancer which can cause painless ulcers in the esophagus and pharynx may give rise to bad breath.

A sweet smell in the breath due to acetone may be found both in *diabetes* and in people who have not been eating because of illness or because of strict dieting.

Smoking tobacco, eating certain things such as garlic, onions, or drinking alcohol can all give rise to breath which is objectionable to others.

By far the commonest causes of bad breath are those associated with poor oral hygiene and bad teeth.

Bad dreams   See *nightmares.*

Bad smells

May be experienced in connection with *bad breath, body odor* or *hallucinations.*

Balanitis

Causes symptoms of irritation around the end of the penis and under the foreskin. The end of the penis may appear a mottled red color and there may be some slight discharge behind the foreskin. *Candidosis* and bacterial infections can cause balanitis. *Diabetes mellitus* is often a predisposing cause.

Baldness   See *loss of hair.*

48

Barrel chest

Used to describe the appearance of the chest when the back to front diameter is larger or is equal to the side to side measurement. It is associated particularly with *emphysema*. The condition is also seen in association with chronic bronchitis.

Being sick   See vomiting.

Bent back   See *curvature of the spine.*

Biliary colic

Colic which arises in the bile ducts. The pain is felt in the upper right quarter of the abdomen, and is usually situated under the rib margin about halfway out. The pain may extend around or through to the lower end of the right shoulder blade. In severe

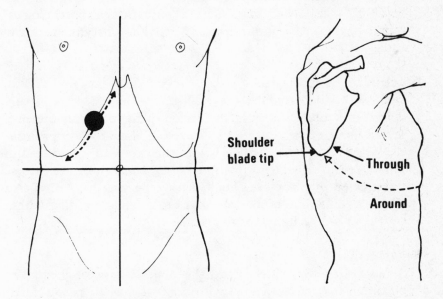

The site and paths of pain in biliary colic

pain, the spread may even be to most of the right upper quarter of the abdomen, around and through to the back and upwards towards the right shoulder. The person will usually be *rolling about with abdominal pain,* and may suffer from *nausea,* may *vomit,* and in some cases will have *fever.* Biliary colic is usually associated with *gallstones. Jaundice* may occur if there is obstruction to the outflow of bile.

Bilious attack

A term used to describe an attack of *nausea* which may go on to *vomiting* green bile. Minor attacks of *migraine,* which are associated with *nausea* and dizziness and perhaps also with vomiting, may also be described by sufferers as bilious attacks. *Infection of the gallbladder* and *stones in the gallbladder* are often the cause of true bilious attacks, although the early stages of *jaundice* from any cause can precipitate bilious attacks. Overeating and overdrinking may also cause these symptoms.

Birthmarks

Can be of many varieties from "stork marks" to brown moles, and from red blotches to "port wine stains." All should be seen by a doctor, because without an exact diagnosis of the variety concerned it is very difficult to advise parents on any sensible course of action. Most birthmarks, if they are not large in area or on the face, will cause neither physical nor psychological trouble, and some will disappear if left without treatment of any kind.

Black eye

Due to bleeding around the eyeball under the lids. It is usually caused by a blunt injury in the region of the eye. Any violence severe enough to produce a black eye can also produce a *detachment of the retina* or bleeding within the eye. Both could lead to *blurred vision,* visual deterioration, partial *blindness* or even worse if untreated. A black eye should always be seen by a physician within a short time of its occurrence to exclude bleeding within the eye or a detachment of the retina.

Blackheads

A small black plug which blocks the mouth of a sweat gland. The condition may be associated with *acne,* or may be produced by bad work habits when using lubricating or cutting oils. Wearing oil soaked overalls or clothing will lead to oily plugs being formed in the mouths of sweat glands. This condition is usually seen on the fronts of the thighs, and develops into oil acne, a condition produced by plugging of sweat glands. Oil acne can be easily prevented by avoiding oil exposure on the skin.

The medical name for a blackhead is a comedo.

Blackout See *fainting.*

Black specks before the eyes

Can be seen by anyone with normal healthy eyes who looks at a blue sky or at a white or light colored wall. These spots move, and cannot be brought into focus. They are of no significance. If a large spot is always in one place, this may be due to an old scar or to some opacity developing in the eye. Help should be sought in this case if the condition is of recent origin.

See also *spots before the eyes*.

Black stools (melena)

This condition is usually due to bleeding from the stomach, abdomen, or the upper part of the bowel. The black color is due to digested blood. Bleeding into the bowel at or near the rectum will result in bright red bleeding from the rectum.

Black stools are often rather tarry and sticky. Occasionally black stools and recognizable blood may be seen together. They can occur from swallowing blood after a nosebleed or after a tooth socket has bled following extraction of the tooth.

Black stools may be found after *vomiting blood*. Aspirin may cause bleeding from the stomach, and can thus also give rise to vomiting blood or to black stools.

The common causes of bleeding in the stomach and duodenum are gastric and duodenal ulcers (*peptic ulcers*) or *cancer* in these parts. Sometimes *varicose veins* in the esophagus can bleed. These esophageal varices are often found in association with *cirrhosis of the liver*, especially in people who have alcoholic cirrhosis of the liver as a result of heavy drinking or *alcoholism*.

Injury to the chest and abdomen may also lead to bleeding and to black stools. Some fruits, for example black cherries and blueberries, may lead to dark or black stools, and iron-containing medicines or charcoal can also result in black stools.

Black tongue

May be seen in heavy smokers or in others at times. It is thought to be due to a fungus growing on the tongue. The condition is not serious, though its appearance may alarm the sufferer.

Black vomit

Black "coffee grounds" vomit is due to the presence of digested blood in the vomit. For the causes of this, see *vomiting blood* and *vomiting*. *Black stools* may also occur at the same time.

Bleeding disorders   See *hemophilia · leukemia · purpura · scurvy*.

Bleeding from the ear passage
The causes include · injuries to the ear · injuries to the head · *infection in the ear passage · infection in the middle ear*.
If any child or adult has blood coming out of the ear passage as a result of injury, the person should be seen by a doctor to be certain that the eardrum is not damaged. In head injuries, bleeding from the ear usually means that the skull has been fractured or that the eardrum has been torn as a result of the violence. All head injuries which cause unconsciousness for however short a time should be examined, since there may be underlying brain damage or a fracture of the skull (see *concussion*). Infections in the ear passage and the middle ear will usually be accompanied by *earache*. A discharge of pus, often mixed with a little blood, may signal the breaking of an *abscess* or the rupture of the eardrum in middle ear infections. See *discharge from the ear*.

Bleeding from the gums
See *bleeding from the mouth   infected gums*.

Bleeding from the mouth
The commonest causes of slight bleeding from the mouth are minor *trauma*—in which case the cause will be obvious—and *infected gums* (gingivitis). Other causes will include local conditions which can give rise to *ulcers in the mouth* and thus bleeding from the ulcer. Blood from other situations may find its way into the mouth and appear as bleeding. However, further investigation should show whether the blood originated in the nose or nasal sinuses, since this will usually result also in nose bleeding. Blood in the mouth can also appear as a result of bleeding from the pharynx, esophagus, stomach and duodenum. Bleeding from the pharynx will usually be vomited, see *vomiting blood*. Blood from the trachea, bronchi and lungs will be coughed up or spat out— see *coughing or spitting blood*.
General diseases which can cause bleeding in the mouth will include *purpura, leukemia, hemophilia* and *scurvy* (vitamin C deficiency).

Bleeding from the nose
Commonly associated with *trauma*. It may also commonly follow the rupture of a small blood vessel in the nose for no ascertainable reason.

Nosebleeds may be associated with local disease in the nose, such as a bad cold, *hay fever, allergic rhinitis,* a nasal polyp or other disease of the lining of the nose, including, though rarely, malignant disease. The commonest serious cause of a nosebleed is *high or raised blood pressure.* Other general causes include heart failure, *uremia,* and general bleeding disorders such as *purpura leukemia hemophilia scurvy.*

Bleeding from the rectum

Obvious bright red bleeding from the anus or blood-streaked stools can be due to conditions at the anus such as *hemorrhoids* (piles), an anal fissure, an *abscess* or to *trauma.*

Bleeding from the rectum and colon can cause blood to appear from the anus. *Cancers* of the rectum and bowel can give rise to bleeding. One common mistake is to assume that because a person has, or has had, hemorrhoids that bleeding is from these. Because of this, many cancers of the rectum are not diagnosed until a needlessly late stage. Anyone with bleeding from the anus should see a doctor at once so that examination can reveal the reason for the bleeding. Any cause of inflammation in the bowel such as *ulcerative colitis* can also cause bleeding. Bacterial infections of the bowel such as typhoid fever may also be responsible. Many of these diseases may be associated with *diarrhea.* Some causes of bleeding will be associated with *pain in the abdomen.* This will include some of the causes of *intestinal obstruction* and *diverticular disease.* Bleeding disorders such as *leukemia, purpura* and *hemophilia* may also give rise to blood being passed. See also *black stools* (melena).

Bleeding from the vagina

May be normal menstruation or may be associated with irregular menstruation (*metrorrhagia*).

Blood from the vagina can arise from a surface lesion at the vulva or from anywhere within the vagina and uterus. Bleeding after sexual intercourse will usually indicate a surface lesion in the vagina or at the cervix. This may be the first sign of a *cancer* of the cervix. A *prolapse of the vagina and uterus* may also cause vaginal bleeding, usually as a result of ulceration of the cervix. Bleeding from the vagina can also be related to infections, some of which are *sexually transmitted diseases.* Foreign bodies, vaginal pessaries or tampons can cause bleeding. Any bleeding which is not clearly menstrual should always be carefully investigated by a doctor.

Any bleeding which occurs after the *menopause* should be suspected of being due to cancer until proved otherwise. General causes of bleeding such as *leukemia* may be associated with vaginal bleeding.

Simple polyps of the uterus can also be a cause of bleeding.

Bleeding under the skin

Can be caused by injury and by general causes of bleeding such as *leukemia · purpura · hemophilia · scurvy* (vitamin C deficiency).

Blemishes on the skin

See *abscess · acne · birthmarks · disorders of pigmentation of the skin*.

Blepharitis   See *red eyelids*.

Blindness of sudden onset in one eye

The causes include · *detachment of the retina* · sudden cessation of blood supply to the back of the eye due to cut off of the artery or vein by a *thrombus* (clot) · bleeding into the eye, usually into the vitreous humor · acute *glaucoma* · injury to the optic nerve associated with a fracture of the skull or compression of the optic nerve due to bleeding · retrobulbar neuritis (see *pain in the eye*) *migraine*. See also *blurred vision*.

Blisters on the skin (bullae)

The causes may include · friction blisters · burns and scalds · cold injury and frostbite · *impetigo* · pemphigus or pemphigoid · severe *urticaria* · erythema multiforme · dermatitis herpetiformis · cheiropompholyx.

Pemphigus and pemphigoid are diseases of the skin which are associated with blisters. Erythema multiforme is an illness of children or young adults associated with sensitivity to organisms —for example hemolytic streptococci—which cause feverish illnesses such as *sore throats,* or with sensitivity to drugs, especially aspirin, salicylates and penicillin. The skin shows circular red spots, often with a yellow center called "target lesions." These may become blistery in the central yellow area. Dermatitis herpetiformis is a disease which commonly affects middle-aged men and which produces redness and blistering of the skin. In many cases the underlying cause is thought to be malabasorption from the small bowel or gluten sensitivity. A gluten-free diet as given for celiac disease may often benefit the sufferers.

Cheiropompholyx is the name given to acute dermatitis of the hands and feet which results in blister formation by the running together of many tiny vesicles under the thick skin of the palms and the soles. The cause of the underlying acute dermatitis must be sought.

Blocked nose

Can be caused by any of the conditions listed under *running nose,* or by a nasal polyp, nasal *cancer* or *tumor.* In young children, large adenoids are probably the commonest cause of a blocked nose not also a running nose. In young adults, *sinusitis* and *allergic rhinitis* are common. A stuffy nose may also be found in hypothyroidism. In young children beads, nuts or other foreign bodies may be a cause of a blocked nose.

Blood from the nipple

Or a yellow serous discharge may be a sign of a duct papilloma or an intraduct *cancer.* Both may be felt as a small swelling at or very near the nipple. There is no way of distinguishing one from the other except to remove the part for diagnosis.

Blood in the stool   See *bleeding from the rectum.*

Blood in the urine

Large amounts of blood are easy to recognize because the urine turns red. Clots may be found. Smaller amounts of blood make the urine orange and slightly turbid. A very small amount of blood is not detectable as such by looking at the urine, although it may cause a *cloudy urine.* Special tests are needed. Blood in the urine can arise from the kidneys, ureters, bladder or urethra. In males, the blood may come from the prostate, seminal vesicles or other parts of the genital tract. In females, blood in the urine may come from disease of the neighboring organs such as the uterus, vagina or rectum, or may be mistakenly thought to be in the urine. Certain bleeding disorders such as *leukemia, purpura* and *hemophilia* can also cause blood in the urine. Acute fevers and excessive exercise are also recognized as less common causes.

DISEASES OF THE KIDNEY which can cause blood in the urine include nephritis   kidney infections   simple and malignant *tumors*   a variety of other causes.

BLEEDING FROM THE URETERS is likely to be caused by *stones* and *cancer* (see *ureteric colic*).

BLEEDING FROM THE BLADDER can result from *cystitis* (inflammation of the bladder, due to infection), from simple and malignant *tumors*, from *stones*, from injury and from parasites called schistosoma (bilharzia) found in certain warm countries whose eggs injure the bladder.

BLEEDING FROM THE URETHRA may result from injury, from infection, from damage by a stone or gravel or from a simple or malignant *tumor* which gives rise to bleeding.

All cases of blood in the urine require medical investigation to determine the cause of the bleeding and so treat the condition correctly.

Blood in vomit   See *vomiting blood*.

Blood pressure   See *high or raised blood pressure*.

Bloodshot eye   See *redness of the eye.*.

Bloodstained vomit   See *vomiting blood*.

Blue lips   See *blueness of the skin*.

Blueness of the skin (cyanosis)

Blueness is due to lack of oxygen in the area where blueness shows. The condition may be found all over the body, when it is known as systemic cyanosis, or may only affect one part, local cyanosis.

Systemic cyanosis, when small in amount, is usually most easily detected in the lips, in the tips of the ears and in the nail beds. Small amounts of blueness can be detected by comparing lip and nail fold color with others in a good light.

SYSTEMIC CYANOSIS is associated with diseases of the upper respiratory tract or lungs in which not enough oxygen can enter the body. *Diphtheria · pneumonia · pneumoconiosis · swellings in the neck* which can cause *stridor* and obstruction can all cause cyanosis. An acute *pneumothorax · a pulmonary embolism · chronic bronchitis · bronchopneumonia* are other possible causes. Blueness may occur during an acute attack of *asthma*. Congenital heart disease, or heart failure—for example, as a result of *coronary thrombosis*—are common causes of blueness, because the blood is not circulated fast enough and all the oxygen in it gets absorbed. This leads to blueness.

LOCAL CYANOSIS is due to circulatory stagnation or failure in the affected part. Cold is a common cause of circulatory shutdown, and can cause cyanosis. Arteriosclerosis and *diabetes mellitus* may be associated with circulatory failure in the extremeties, especially the toes. Any *thrombosis* or *embolism* can lead to local cyanosis. The reason for the blueness should be sought in the underlying cause after finding out whether the cyanosis is systemic or local. *Chilblains* and *white cold fingers* may be associated with local blueness as circulation returns to the affected areas.

Blueness of the whites of the eyes
This is found in people who suffer from an inherited condition called fragilitas ossium. As the name suggests, their bones are brittle and break easily. Some members of affected families may have normal whites in the eyes. It is only those with blueness of the eyes who suffer from brittle bones. The condition is rare.

Blurred vision
Can be caused by foreign bodies in the eye · refractive errors · blunt *trauma* to the eye · iritis · *glaucoma* · *cataract* · bleeding into the eye · diseases of the vitreous humor · diseases of the choroid and retina · *detachment of the retina*. Full eye examination will be required to find out why vision is blurred.
An occasional cause of transient blurred vision is *migraine*. See also *blindness of sudden onset in one eye* · *black eye*.

Blushing
Usually *redness of the face* associated with repressed emotion or excitement. It should not be confused with *flushing* of the face.

Body odor
Can arise in three main ways:
LACK OF NORMAL WASHING AND CLEANING OF THE PERSON AND CLOTHING. All that is usually necessary, in the absence of excessive sweating, in order to prevent body odor is to shower, bath or wash all over on a daily basis, and to change into clean clothes frequently. Body odor is generated from stale perspiration by bacterial action, and washing with soap and water will remove stale sweat from the skin. If clothes are changed and washed frequently, no accumulation of stale perspiration will occur, and no body odor will be generated. It may be useful after showering or bathing to use an underarm antiperspirant to cut down sweat

production, so that clothes do not get sticky. A little talcum (dusting) powder may also help to keep the skin more comfortable and dry, especially in areas where *intertrigo* may develop, such as under the arms, in the crotch and groin, and under the breasts.

FUNGUS INFECTIONS OF THE FEET. Sometimes fungus infections of the feet can cause the production of a very disagreeable odor. No amount of washing or bathing will eliminate the condition unless the basic fungus infection is tackled and eradicated. This is a matter for a doctor.

MENSTRUATION. Body odor from menstruation can usually be eliminated by frequent changing of sanitary protection, adequate showering, and washing of clothes. Women who have heavy periods can be advised to use internal sanitary protection in the form of a tampon, because it is only menses in contact with air that can give rise to odor. Vaginal deodorants should not be used, because they are no substitute for the advice given above, and because they can often cause irritation.

Boil   See *abscess*.

Boil in the ear   See *infection in the ear passage*.

Bornholm disease (epidemic myalgia)
Due to infection with coxsackie B virus. Children and young adults are most often affected. The illness is characterized by fever and by *pain in the chest* which can be quite severe and tends to occur in attacks or spasms. The attacks usually last for only a few days. Muscular pains may also be felt. Complete recovery is usual inside two weeks. The disease is named after the Danish island of Bornholm on which epidemic myalgia was first identified and described.

Bowel movement   See *stools · constipation · diarrhea*.

Bowel sounds, loud and rumbling
See *loud rumbling bowel sounds*.

Bow legs
Seen in normal healthy babies, in children who have rickets, and in older people who suffer from *Paget's disease* (osteitis deformans).

Bradycardia See *slow heartbeat*.

Breat pain See *pain in the (female) breast · pain in the chest*.

Breast, tender See *tightness in the breast and nipples*.

Breast, tight See *tightness in the breast and nipples*.

Breath-holding
Attacks may be found in children around the age of one year or older. It usually occurs when the child is upset angry, frustrated, or suddenly frightened. The child takes in a big breath as if he were going to shout, and then stops breathing. If the breath is held long enough, *fainting* may occur, and even a slight *fit or convulsion* may follow. The best way to deal with a breath-holding attack is as soon as the child has taken the big breath to hook the index finger over the back of the tongue and pull the tongue forward. This will always make the child breathe again. Action must be swift because if breath holding is allowed, the jaw tightens, the teeth clench, and the attack cannot be prevented. The prevention of breath-holding attacks must deal with the cause of the child's anger, frustration or fright.

Breathing difficulties See *difficulty in breathing*.

Breathlessness See *difficulty in breathing*.

Brittle bones
Found in certain families as a result of a disease called fragilitas ossium. Sufferers can be recognized because of *blueness of the whites of the eyes* and because they experience many *fractures,* often as a result of only minor *trauma*.

Brittle hair
May be found in *hypothyroidism* and *alopecia areata*. See also *loss of hair*.

Broken bone See *fracture*.

Bronchial asthma See *asthma*.

Bronchiectasis

Means enlargement of the bronchi—the tubes are wider than normal. This dilation is usually irregular and uneven. The result is that there are dead spaces in the tubes in where infected material can collect. This leads to: lung infections · *bad breath* · *difficulty in breathing* · *infected sputum* · *spitting of blood* · generalized ill health.

Bronchitis

In children it may occur as acute bronchitis or as bronchitis with bronchopneumonia. Most young children with a bad cold will have some degree of bronchitis associated with it. The illness, however, is a short-term one.

Adults generally suffer from chronic bronchitis and *emphysema*—the two are often closely associated. Chronic bronchitis is a disease related to breathing contaminated or dirty air. In more than nine out of ten cases of chronic bronchitis the basic cause is smoking, which is also associated with increased illness and death rates from *ischemic heart disease* and *cancer* of the bronchus (lung cancer). Work in dusty occupations may also be associated with a few cases of chronic bronchitis. General atmospheric pollution is only a very minor contributor to the causes of chronic bronchitis.

Brown patches in the mouth   See *Addison's disease.*

Brown patches in the skin

See *disorders of pigmentation of the skin.*

Bruise

Due to bleeding under the skin. The usual cause is trauma. Brusing may also appear in bleeding disorders associated with *leukemia* · *purpura* · *hemophilia* · *scurvy.*

Bulky stools   See *constipation.*

Bunion

A swelling of the joint between the foot and the big toe which often causes *pain in the feet.* It is usually due to *osteoarthritis,* though *gout* can also be a cause. Other causes of *pain in joints* may also have to be considered.

Burning pain behind the sternum (breast bone)
See *hernia through the diaphragm · reflex esophagitis*.

Burning pain on urinating   See *pain on urination*.

Bursitis
A bursa is a small sac like a collapsed balloon containing a small amount of lubricating fluid. Bursae are found near joints and provide a smooth glide between bony prominences and the overlying structures. The bursae can fill up with an excess of fluid or become infected, and will thus cause symptoms of an *abscess* or of a *swelling near joints*. Sometimes bursitis is due to *trauma*. Bleeding can also occur in a bursa, thus causing it to swell. *Swelling of the knee* may be due to bursitis. Because bursae sometimes are in direct communication with joints, anything which can cause *swelling in joints* can also cause bursitis. This is often seen around the knee, where there are a number of bursae.

Buzzing in the ear   See *tinnitus*.

Cancer
Not one disease but many. The term "cancer" is used to describe malignant *tumors* which can arise in many parts of the body. Simple tumors will only spread locally by direct extension and growth. The characteristic of a malignant tumor is that it can spread from the primary source both locally, by infiltrating the tissues in which it is growing, and systemically, by a process of detachment of cells which seed themselves into other tissues. This systemic or secondary spread is often first via the lymphatics to the adjacent lymph nodes, where it causes *swelling of the lymph nodes*. For example, a skin cancer on the hand could spread to the lymph nodes under the arm. The second common method of systemic spread is via the blood stream. This can result in secondary spread to almost any site in the body. Tumors which arise by secondary spread are known as metastases and the process is referred to as metastatic spread. Cancers are usually destructive of the tissues in which they grow. The effects will therefore vary greatly according to the site of the primary growth and the number and sites of any metastases.

The aims of treatment in cancer are to detect a primary tumor as early as possible so that it can be destroyed before metastatic spread occurs. In addition to surgery to remove the cancer, radiotherapy may be used to destroy the cancer.

Radiotherapy aims to destroy the tumor by irradiation with X rays, gamma rays or other suitable forms of radiation. Unfortunately radiotherapy will also affect normal tissues, and so the method has to be used with skill to attack the tumor while minimizing the damage to normal tissues.

Chemotherapy is also used in the treatment of cancer. Drugs which attack dividing growing cells are used. These drugs are classified as nucleotoxic when they attack the cell nucleus, radiomimetic when they imitate radiation, and antimetabolic when they interfere with the normal processes which go on within the cell. Chemotherapy and radiotherapy may be used together. Some cancers are hormone sensitive, for example some cancers of the breast, cancer of the prostate and cancer of the thyroid. The difficulty with hormones is in giving a dose which suppresses the tumor but which does not produce hormone effects of an unwanted kind. For example, in cancer of the prostate the hormone given is a female one, stilbestrol. This can cause breast development in a man.

The word cancer has been used here in the broadest sense of any malignant tumor. Strictly, the term is used to describe only tumors of epithelial tissue, and does not include sarcoma, *leukemia, Hodgkin's disease,* malignant *melanoma* and a number of other malignant tumors. However, the general points made here will apply to all these conditions.

Candidosis
See *vaginal candidosis · thrush · balanitis · itching of the skin · swelling of the nailfold · ridges and furrows on the nails · diabetes mellitus.*

Carbuncle
A special kind of *abscess* usually associated with a staphylococcal infection of hair follicles, sweat glands and the surrounding areas. It usually discharges pus through several openings. Carbuncles are commonly found on the back of the neck. They are often painful and produce a tense red swelling at the site. Incision of the carbuncle may be necessary to allow escape of pus. Sometimes a scar remains.

Cardiac asthma   See *asthma.*

Carpal tunnel syndrome   See *tingling in the hands.*

Cartilage trouble   See *displaced or torn knee cartilage.*

Cataract
An opacity in the lens of an eye. It may give rise to dimness of vision or *blurred vision* in the early stages, and may later cause partial *blindness.*

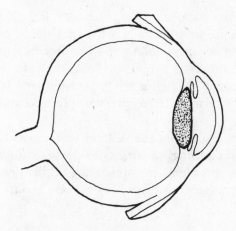

A cataract is an opacity in the lens of the eye

Catarrh
Can follow any condition which causes a *running nose. Allergic rhinitis, hay fever* and *sinusitis* are the commonest conditions which lead to catarrh. *Coughing* up *phlegm* may be mistaken for or associated with catarrh. A *postnasal drip* is often found in association with catarrh and sinusitis.

Cauliflower ear
Due to *trauma* to the ear cartilage. When the cartilage heals, it joins with lumpiness around the injured area, thus giving rise to the cauliflower appearance. The swellings caused by *gout* (tophi) in the ear cartilage should not be mistaken for a cauliflower ear.

Cervical rib
An extra "rib" in the neck. It may give rise to symptoms of *tingling in the hands* or *drooping of the eyelid* due to *Horner's syndrome.*

Cherry spots on the skin

A cherry spot is a tiny circular red spot which does not blanch on pressure. These spots usually appear in people over the age of about 35 years. They have no significance as far as is known at present.

They should not be confused with red spots which come and go in a *rash* or with red *birthmarks*.

Chest pain   See *pain in the chest*.

Chilblains (perniosis)

Bluish, slightly swollen areas which occur on the hands, legs and feet during and after exposure to cold. When the part becomes warm, intense *itching of the skin* may follow. Bad chilblains can ulcerate. The only known remedy is protection from the cold to prevent the condition. Ulcerated chilblains are treated similarly to any wound of the body surface in order to prevent infection and to encourage healing.

Often one of the main problems is that the sufferer will not wear suitable weatherproof warm clothing, or forgets to do so. Vanity has been known to be a problem in preventing chilblains, especially in younger women. See also *blueness of the skin · white-cold fingers*.

Chill

A sudden fit of shivering or chilling, usually associated with a raised body temperature. It may also accompany any feverish illness. Sometimes when the body temperature has been raised for some time, a chill may herald either a further rise in temperature or, if accompanied by much perspiration, a reduction in body temperature. A chill may be mistaken for a *fit,* on account of the *shaking* and *shivering*. See also *feeling cold · fever*.

Cholecystitis   See *infection of the gallbladder*.

Chordee

The name given to a sideways curved erection of the penis which is accompanied by pain and by a *urethral discharge,* usually from *gonorrhea*. Another cause of a curved erection is Peyronie's disease, in which nodules are found in the penis. It is these nodules which cause the curvature. Peyronie's disease is sometimes found in association with *Dupuytren's contracture*. In young boys, chordee is a congenital binding down of the penis which does not allow full erection. It is sometimes associated with hypospadius, a condition in which the opening of the urinary tract is not at the tip of the penis. Both these problems require medical evaluation and surgical treatment.

Circles around lights
Haloes or rainbows, if seen, may be due to *glaucoma*.

Cirrhosis of the liver
Will give rise to symptoms of *jaundice, varicose veins* in the esophagus, *melena* and general ill health. A common cause is heavy drinking and *alcoholism*.

Claudication   See *pain in the leg*.

Claustrophobia   See *phobic anxiety*.

Clawing of the fingers
May be associated with diseases of the nervous system which cause muscle wasting in the hands or with *Dupuytren's contracture*. Medical advice should always be sought in these conditions.

Clicking in joints
May be a normal phenomenon when the joint has been at rest for some time. Most people can make their finger joints click. However, clicking may also be a sign of unevenness of the joint surface and may be associated with *pain in joints* and *swelling in joints*. Clicking in the knee is usually associated with a *displaced or torn knee cartilage*. Clicking in the jaw which may be heard as quite a sharp crack just in front of the ear, can also be caused by displacement of cartilage in the joint between the jaw and the skull. *Grating in joints* may also be found in association with clicking.

Clicking in the knee   See *displaced or torn knee cartilage*.

Cloudy urine
In general, turbid or cloudy urines are probably abnormal. Clear urines are generally—but not always—normal. Infected urines are usually turbid or cloudy. Small amounts of protein (albumin) and any amount of glucose (sugar) can be found in clear urines.

Some kidney infections which cause protein to be present in the urine may thus not be detected by looking at the urine, and *diabetes* which causes glucose to be present in the urine will not be detectable by cloudiness. On the other hand, phosphates are found in the urines of healthy people, and will cause cloudiness. Acetic acid (vinegar) added to the urine will dissolve phosphates. See also *blood in the urine · frequency of urination · pain on urination.*

Some *sexually transmitted diseases* can cause a cloudy urine.

Clubbing of the fingers

A condition in which the nails are curved or bowed away from the nail bed in the line of the finger. This can be demonstrated by putting the fingers together at the last knuckle. A "window" will show in normal fingers. In clubbed fingers there will be a "V" at the finger tips. The earliest sign of clubbing is obliteration of the window, often best seen in the ring fingers.

Finger clubbing is associated with any condition which causes insufficient oxygen in the blood—for example, chronic chest and heart diseases. Finger clubbing may be found with *blueness of the skin.* Sometimes finger clubbing is found without any known cause.

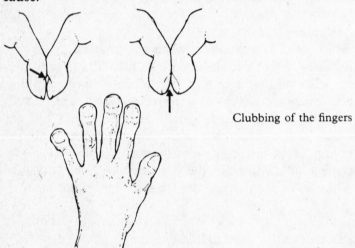

Clubbing of the fingers

Cold   See *running nose · fever · feeling cold · hypothermia.*

Cold, sensitivity to   See *feeling cold.*

Cold sore   See *herpesvirus.*

Cold spot See *herpesvirus.*

Colic

A sharp abdominal pain. When it arises from the small and large intestines, the pain comes and goes, is cramp-like in character, and can reach quite a severe intensity. When the pain is severe, the patient usually wants to curl up or bend forward. It may come and go within thirty seconds, or it may take as long as five minutes to pass · Pain arising from the bowel is associated with a strong contraction of the circular muscle coat of the bowel, or with stretching by gas. Colic can be very severe in intestinal obstruction and in bad *diarrhea.* Colic can also occur in the bile ducts giving rise to *biliary colic,* in the ureters giving rise to *ureteric colic* and in the uterus giving rise to premenstrual and *menstrual cramps.* Colic of any kind if severe will usually cause the person to be *rolling about with abdominal pain.*

Colitis See *irritable bowel syndrome.*

Collapse See *fainting · fits · heat stroke · stroke.*

Coloboma

A congenital disorder of the eye which can give rise to an irregular keyhole-shaped pupil, among other defects.

Color blindness See *defective color vision.*

Comedo A *blackhead.* It may be associated with *acne.*

Compulsions

Compulsive behavior occurs when a person feels that he has to do or not do certain things. The person usually recognizes that the impulse to behave in this way is irrational, but must nevertheless indulge the behavior. For example, having locked the front door of the house, the person will feel obliged to walk back to the house and recheck that the door is really locked and that the key was the right one. Compulsive behavior is a symptom of *obsessional states.*

Concussion

Term used to describe brain injury that results in sudden loss of consciousness, followed by recovery. "Knockout" is a common name for concussion. Immediately after the moment of injury, the person will suffer from *loss of consciousness* but will then, in the absence of other complications, recover. The rate of recovery depends on the severity of the original *trouma*.

Concussion may be associated with later bleeding inside the skull from the same blow that caused the concussion. Any loss of consciousness after apparent recovery is a dangerous and serious sign of continued bleeding inside the skull with consequent compression of the brain. Only an urgent operation to decompress the brain and remove the clot may save the person's life.

Frequent concussions suffered by boxers lead to a "punch drunk" condition.

Confusion

Feelings of confusion may be a part of *loss of memory* or may be associated with strong *anxiety* or excitement. Concentration may become difficult. Older people can become confused easily if they have unusual or upsetting events in their lives. If confusion is other than temporary, medical help should be sought.

The condition is often associated with the loss of blood supply to the brain due to *arteriosclerosis*.

Congestion of the lungs   See *bronchitis · bronchiectasis*.

Congestion of the nose   See *stuffy nose*.

Conjunctivitis

Infection of the conjunctiva, the clear "skin" that lines the inner surfaces of the eyelids and the front of the white of the eye. The usual symptom of conjunctivitis is a slight sticky discharge from the eyes which collects in the corners of the eyes and may make the lids stick together. The infection usually makes the eye feel gritty or sandy, and there is frequently also itching and irritation. It is often seen to cause *redness of the eye*. Most conjunctivitis gets better quickly with appropriate treatment.

Constipation

A term which is properly used to describe hard, dry and infrequent bowel movements. There may or may not be *pain on passing a bowel movement*. But constipation also describes a bowel neurosis or bowel fixation in which the subject adheres to the idea that the bowels, like an alarm clock, should sound off regularly every twenty-four hours. A moment's reflection would indicate that the signal to drink is thirst, that the signal to urinate is given by a full bladder, and that the signal to empty the bowel is given when the bowel is full. Then, and only then, should it be emptied. It also follows that the amount of food residue depends largely on what is eaten—some foods have a high residue, and some very little. The bowels will thus tend to accumulate food residue at different rates according to what, both quantitatively and qualitatively, is eaten. The longer the residue stays in the large intestine, the drier it becomes. Small volumes of residue will not trigger off the need to empty the bowels, and the movements will become more dry. The answer is therefore to increase the food residue if constipation (or bowel neurosis) is troublesome. This can most easily be accomplished by eating natural unprocessed bran in suitable quantities.

Constipation and change of bowel habits may be a result of obstruction of the large intestine. Cancer may be a possibility, as may hypothyroidism. In children, constipation frequently occurs as a resistance to toilet training at about two years of age. Rarely, a congenital absence of nerve cells in the colon (Hirschsprung's disease) may cause constipation · Any acute change in bowel habits should be discussed with a physician.

Convulsions   See *fits and convulsions · fainting*.

Corns
Areas of skin thickening where friction occurs. Typically they are seen on the upper surfaces of the toes and on the soles of the feet behind the base of the toes. Corns can cause *pain in the feet*.

Coronary thrombosis
Describes a *thrombosis* in the coronary arteries, which supply blood to the heart muscle. When the blood supply is cut off to a small part of the heart, the person will usually complain of *angina pectoris*, which is a particular kind of *pain in the chest* felt mainly on exertion. If the cut-off of blood is to slightly larger areas, the pain may come on at rest, and may be felt, like angina pectoris, to the left of the upper part of the sternum, up both sides of the neck to the jaw but more especially on the left, into the left shoulder and down the inside of the left arm.
General collapse will be apparent if the coronary thrombosis cuts off blood supply to large areas of the heart.

Irregular heartbeat may occur because the conduction of the electrical impulse to tell the heart when to beat may be interfered with as a result of damage to the blood supply. A tiny coronary thrombosis may produce vary little in the way of symptoms and may only be recognized if an *electrocardiogram* is taken. These small coronary thromboses may also be mistaken for *indigestion,* because the person feels discomfort after a heavy meal. This is because the pressure of a full stomach impinges upon the action of the heart by pressure through the diaphragm, and it is under these conditions that the *ischemic heart disease* gives rise to symptoms.

Coughing

May be due to a very large variety of conditions, some of which will be associated with *fever · foul sputum · spitting of blood · pain in the chest · stridor · hoarseness* or a *running nose.*

Cigarette smoking, chronic *bronchitis,* chest colds and influenza are probably the commonest causes of coughing. *Bronchiectasis,* bronchial *cancer* (a "lung cancer") pneumonia, tuberculosis, heart or kidney failure causing congestion in the lungs by fluid accumulation, and habit coughs are other possible causes.

Dry, irritating coughs at their worst at night may be related to a change of temperature in the bedroom, or may follow a cold. Any cough which is accompanied by other symptoms or which does not clear up inside a week should be investigated by a doctor.

Coughing or spitting blood

Should always be carefully distinguished from vomiting blood, because the causes will differ. Coughing or spitting blood is usually associated with conditions of the respiratory system affecting the larynx, trachea, bronchi and lungs. Occasionally, other chest diseases may produce this result. On the other hand, *vomiting blood* is usually associated with conditions of the digestive system affecting the esophagus, stomach, duodenum or liver.

Blood coughed up is usually small in amount and bright red. Because the blood is mixed with sputum it is often frothy. There is often an association with chest illness and *pain in the chest.* Vomited blood is often greater in amount and dark red. The blood may be mixed with recognizable food in vomit, and there is no frothiness. There may be an association with *indigestion* or *pain in the upper abdomen. Black stools* may follow vomiting blood. The commonest causes of coughing or spitting blood in young people are infections—pneumonias and tuberculosis. In older people, especially those who smoke cigarettes, the commonest cause of spitting up blood is a bronchial cancer ("lung cancer"). The causes of coughing or spitting blood include *trauma* · pneumonia · *hydatid cyst* · chronic *bronchitis* · *bronchiectasis* · *cancer* of the bronchus ("lung cancer") pulmonary *embolism*. The causes of embolism include rheumatic heart disease (which can cause valvular narrowing such as mitral stenosis) and *deep vein thrombosis* in the legs after illness or operations.

Systemic diseases which cause bleeding are *leukemia* · *purpura* · *hemophilia* · *scurvy*.

Cracked lips

Often follow a bad cold or *herpesvirus* infection. Simple remedies such as cold cream will usually be sufficient. However, if any crack does not heal within a week, or if an *ulcer on the lip* develops, medical help is necessary.

Cracked nipple

Can develop when breast-feeding. A doctor will advise on how this condition should be treated. Cracking occurring at any other time should be carefully examined by a doctor to exclude *cancer*. See also *discharge from the nipple*.

Cracked teeth

If a tooth is broken, this should be seen at once by a dentist so that he can, if possible, save the rest of the tooth. Cracks due to *trauma* should be seen soon for the same reason. Small fissures in teeth are probably due to decay and will require treatment by the dentist to prevent worsening. *Toothache* may be present if teeth are cracked.

Cramp in the legs

Can occur after unaccustomed exercise or in bed at night for no known reason. A special form of cramp called "claudication" occurs when a person has a deficient blood supply to the leg muscles. After walking for a little while, *pain in the leg* develops. This passes off on resting. Medical investigation is required to determine the reason for the deficiency of blood supply through the arteries. Claudication may be associated with *arteriosclerosis* and *ischemic heart disease*.

Creaking in joints   See *grating in joints · osteoarthritis.*

Creaking under the skin
May be likened to the feeling in a chamois leather, is found in association with pain or movement in two main conditions, either when bleeding has occured under the skin and the clot is a few days old, or in association with tenosynovitis, a disease of tendon sheaths. When tenosynovitis is present, any movement will cause pain and wash-leather creaking. The condition is usually precipitated by unaccustomed exercise or by performing a particular movement repeatedly, such as in sawing or hammering. A hand laid flat over the painful area will detect the typical wash-leather creak on movement. Tenosynovitis usually requires little more than rest, time and simple pain relief by heat and/or analgesic tablets. If the activity that provoked the complaint continues, the condition will take much longer to clear up.

Crease in the nose   See *nose crease · allergic rhinitis.*

Cross eyes   See *squinting eyes.*

Croup
Acute inflammation of the mucous membranes of the larynx, trachea and bronchi due to infection. *Wheezing, stridor* and *difficulty in breathing* will usually be present. Any child who has *fever* and croup should always be seen soon by a doctor.

Crusts on the skin   See *impetigo · seborrheic dermatitis.*

Crying   See *depression.*

Curvature of the spine
This term is used only when the spinal curve is in an abnormal direction or when a normal curve is exaggerated. The normal spine curves in a back to front direction, but not from side to side. An exaggerated backward curve which gives rise to a hunchback deformity is called a kyphosis. This is due to collapse of one or more vertebrae, which can be brought about by disease, often tuberculosis, or by injury.
A forward curve is called a lordosis. This results usually from muscular weakness, and may be associated with any lesion or disease which causes muscle weakness, such as poliomyelitis.

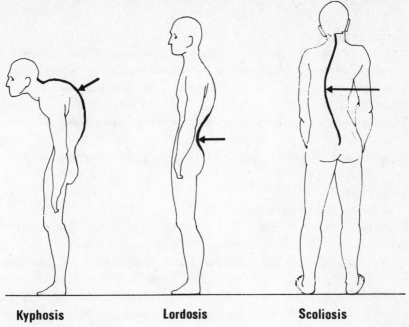

| Kyphosis | Lordosis | Scoliosis |

Curvature of the spine

Some people have curvature of the spine in the absence of any disease, and this is a condition with which they have usually grown up. If the curvature is detected early enough it may be possible to straighten it. Braces may be required.
Scolliosis is a sideways curve of the spine.

Cyanosis   See *blueness of the skin.*

Cyst
A swelling with a liquid or semiliquid center. A common cause is a blocked sweat gland, which gives rise to a sebaceous cyst. Cysts cause *swellings which can occur anywhere in the body.*

Cystitis   See *infection of the bladder.*

Dandruff See *scaly skin · seborrheic dermatitis.*

Dark urine
May be associated with *jaundice.* However, if the weather is warm, it may simply be a rather concentrated normal urine because of fluid loss in perspiration. See also *cloudy urine.*

Dead fingers See *white-cold fingers · Raynaud's syndrome.*

Dead hand See *white-cold fingers · Raynaud's syndrome.*

Deafness
Can be total or partial.
Partial deafness of slow onset is usually more apparent to others than it is to the sufferer—so that if a person thinks he may be becoming deaf, he should ask family and friends if they have noticed any difficulty in communication. The causes of deafness include *wax in the ear,* and other conditions which can block the ear passage, such as an *abscess* or a discharge, damage to the ear drum from trauma or *infection in the ear passage,* blocking of the eustachian tube—for example, from a cold, *infection in the middle ear, otosclerosis,* damage to the organ or hearing—for example, from *noise induced hearing loss, familial early deafness* which is an early wearing out of the organ of hearing, and conditions of the hearing nerve which prevent the impulses in the nerve from reaching the brain. The commonest cause of this is an *acoustic neurinoma.* In children who have heard normally, the commonest causes of deafness are associated with infections in the nose, throat and ear. Babies who have any apparent hearing difficulty should always be seen by an expert, since there are educational as well as medical problems. Such problems need to be diagnosed and assessed at as early an age as possible, so that suitable plans can be made for the child's future.
Children who do not speak or make imitative speech sounds should be suspected of a hearing difficulty.
An essential part of the management of any form of deafness which is other than transient is to assess the hearing by means of an *audiometer.* Sounds of different loudness (intensity) and pitch (frequency) are used to determine at what loudness each different pitch can just be heard. With this and other information it is possible to diagnose the cause of the deafness and to know if a hearing aid may be of use.

Debility See *tiredness*.

Deep vein thrombosis
Causes *pain in the leg*, and gives rise to swelling in the affected leg and ankle due to the impaired circulation. An *embolus* may be detached from the leg bringing about a *pulmonary embolism*. See also *swelling of the ankle*.

Defective color vision
An inherited disorder of varying severity which affects males commonly and females very rarely. About one male in twelve has some degree of defect varying from slight to severe. Simple tests are available to detect defective color vision. Very few people indeed are color-blind—that is, have no perception of colors at all. The most common form of defective color vision involves the colors red and green. Because defective color vision is generally an inherited disorder, it tends to occur in families. No treatment can affect the condition.
Visual acuity, the ability to see things in the distance or near at hand, whether well or badly, is totally unrelated to color vision.

Deformity See *dislocation · fracture · curvature of the spine* and/ or part of body affected.

Delirium See *fainting · fits · heat stroke · stroke*.

Delusions
False opinions which cannot be corrected by logical argument. For example, a person may see a group of people talking, and may be able to hear the hum of conversation, but not actually hear the words. He becomes convinced, however, that they are talking about him, when in fact they are not. But no explanation or argument will convince him otherwise.
Delusions may be associated with *hallucinations,* though hallucinations are usually indicative of a more serious level of disorder of perception found in *psychosis*. Mild delusions, often mixed up with some *confusion,* are common in old people whose blood supply to the brain is diminished because of *arteriosclerosis*. In younger people however, delusions may often point to early psychosis or a disorder of the brain arising from disease. Expert medical help will be necessary.

Depression

Two main forms are usually described:

DEPRESSION ARISING FROM EXTERNAL EVENTS AND SITUATIONS. A good example of this kind of depression is seen following the death of a much loved member of that family. This is known as a situational or exogenous depression. In these cases the reason for the depression is obvious or becomes obvious if reasons are sought.

DEPRESSION ARISING FROM WITHIN THE PERSON. In so-called endogenous depression there is no apparent reason for the depression. This form of depression is most common in those of middle age and may last for some years.

The symptoms of depression are blueness of mood, lack of interest in life, crying and moping, and one of the *disorders of sleep*, which is usually early waking if no added *anxiety* is present. More severe depression leads to feelings of total hopelessness, suicidal thoughts, suicidal gestures, *loss of weight*, withdrawal into self, non-responsiveness, and suicide. Mild transitory depression may be experienced by a few women associated with *premenstrual tension*. Sometimes depression may be associated with diseases such as *hypothyroidism*.

Detachment of the retina

Usually produced by blunt violence to the eye. Shortsighted eyes are particularly vulnerable. Any *black eye* may also have a detachment—and it is therefore important that all black eyes are examined as soon as possible to exclude the possibility of detachment of the retina or bleeding within the eye. Once the retina is detached from the back of the eye it will lose its blood supply if not reattached. This leads to an area of blindness corresponding to the amount of detached retina. Large areas of detachment will cause sudden *blindness* or sudden serious *loss of vision*. Small areas of detachment may give rise to blurred vision, but in some people such minor damage is not noticed, and gives rise to no symptoms at all. If the detachment is diagnosed immediately, it can often be spotwelded back using a laser beam, or it can be reattached in an operation, thus restoring normal vision.

Diabetes

There are two forms: *diabetes insipidus*, which is rare, and *diabetes mellitus*, which is the common form.

Diabetes insipidus

A rare form of diabetes caused by disease of the posterior part of the pituitary gland. It affects children and young people. It is characterized by frequent urination and by thirst and frequent drinking to compensate for the fluid loss thus occasioned. Provided the condition is not related to a tumor of the pituitary gland, the outlook with modern treatment is good, and the sufferer should live a normal lifespan.

Diabetes mellitus ("sugar diabetes")

A condition resulting from a deficiency or absence of insulin secretion from the pancreas. This results in raised blood glucose ("sugar") levels. Diabetes mellitus is often found in those who have another member of the family suffering from the disease. In children and young adults the condition often appears quite suddenly after an infectious illness.

The usual symptoms of diabetes mellitus are *frequency of urination* with *thirst* and frequent drinking to compensate for the fluid loss. *Tiredness,* getting up at night to urinate and *loss of weight* are usually found in children. Children often show these signs of diabetes for the first time following an infectious illness.

In adults the symptoms of diabetes mellitus may include *defective vision* because the disease affects the eye, *tiredness,* muscular weakness especially in the thighs, pins and needles in the limbs and *itching of the skin* especially in the genital area so that women complain of itching or *irritation of the vulva* and vagina and men complain of irritation around the end of the penis and under the foreskin *(balanitis).*

Sometimes recurrent boils, styes, *candidosis* or other infection may be the first symptoms of diabetes. Testing of the blood and urine for glucose will be necessary to establish the diagnosis.

Most children and young adults will need some insulin to control their blood sugar in addition to a high protein, low carbohydrate diet, which is the cornerstone of managing the disease. Failure to regulate the insulin and the diet correctly can lead to loss of consciousness from too low or too high a blood glucose level (*hypoglycemia* too low; *hyperglycemia* too high a blood glucose level).

Most adults who suffer from diabetes are middle aged and suffer from *obesity.* Diet and medication will usually control their disease. The major problem with diabetes is that it is present for life. The person has to come to terms with changes in life style, such as regular meals, to suit the disability, or the consequences may be serious.

Diaper rash

This condition in babies is due to prolonged contact with urine and feces. When stale urine decomposes, it produces ammonia. This is alkaline, and is the main cause of the skin redness. Irritation and fecal soiling may also make the rash worse. Infrequently, diaper rash can also be due to a bacterial or fungal infection of the skin in the diaper area. Frequent changes of diapers and exposure to the air will usually resolve a diaper rash. Where bacterial or fungal agents are involved, medications are required to eliminate the infectious agent.

Diaphragmatic hernia

See *hernia through the diaphragm into the chest*.

Diarrhea

The frequent passage of loose stools. Diarrhea is rare in breast-fed babies, and in bottle-fed babies is usually due to unsuitable feeding (too much fat or sugar are common causes) or to gastroenteritis, which is an infection of the bowel. Gastroenteritis will show as diarrhea and *vomiting*, with *fever* and general symptom of illness. It can be serious in young babies, and quickly leads to dehydration on account of the fluid lost both from diarrhea and from vomiting. Urgent medical treatment is necessary.

In older children and adults, diarrhea can be of two main kinds: DIARRHEA OF SUDDEN ONSET can result from unsuitable food such as green apples, or "food poisoning," when the food eaten is contaminated by bacteria or contains some toxic substance. This often begins with diarrhea, sometimes severe, which may also be accompanied by *nausea, vomiting, colic* and *fever* (raised body temperature). Dehydration will follow, due to loss of fluid in the diarrhea and vomit, unless copious drinks are given and retained. If fluids are not retained, they must be replaced intravenously. Cholera is a tropical disease with intense diarrhea leading to dehydration. Drugs and medicines may also cause diarrhea.

DIARRHEA AS A LONGER-TERM SYMPTOM may be related to operations such as a gastrectomy, a vagotomy or a gastroenterostomy. Crohn's disease (of unknown origin) causes symptoms of diarrhea, malnutrition and malabsorption. The disease is usually discovered in the 20–30 year age group. Intestinal parasites of many kinds can cause diarrhea. Amebic dysentery is one such common parasitic disease. Tropical illnesses of various kinds are associated with diarrhea. So also are *diverticular disease of the colon* · *ulcerative colitis* · *cancer* of the bowel · *allergies* · poisons and drugs · the *irritable bowel syndrome*.

Difficulty in breathing (dyspnea)

Often described as shortness of breath and may come on suddenly, or slowly on exertion. There are numerous possible causes, some of which are given below.

NARROWING, BLOCKING AND OBSTRUCTION OF THE AIR PASSAGES, caused by narrowing or blocking of the larynx and trachea may be due to *diphtheria* · acute laryngotracheitis (*croup*) · swelling of the larynx due to *allergies* · foreign bodies lodged in the airway · paralysis of the vocal cords · cysts or *tumors* in the pharynx · cysts, tumors or *swelling in the neck* · cysts, tumors or *swelling of the thyroid* · and *lymph nodes* from many conditions, including *Hodgkin's disease*. Narrowing or blocking of the bronchi and bronchioles may be due to acute *bronchitis* · *asthma* · lodging of a foreign body · bronchopneumonia · *cancer* of the bronchus ("lung cancer") · and other causes listed below.

EXTENSIVE LUNG DISEASE, caused by *emphysema* · *bronchitis* and bronchopneumonia · *pneumoconiosis* · *sarcoidosis* · cystic disease of the lung · *bronchiectasis* · *pneumonia* · *tuberculosis* · pulmonary *embolism* and *cancer* of the bronchus ("lung cancer").

CAUSES IN THE CHEST WHICH AFFECT THE LUNG include collapse of the lung due to *pneumothorax,* pleural effusion and hemothorax (blood in the pleural space) · paralysis of the diaphragm · spinal abnormalities which interfere with chest movement, particularly *kyphosis* (hunchback deformity) · large swellings inside the chest which compress the lungs, for example a greatly enlarged heart, an *aneurysm* of the aorta and cysts and tumors · *hernia through the diaphragm* into the chest (diaphragmatic hernia) · gross abdominal distension causing pressure upwards through the diaphragm.

HEART DISEASE OR FAILURE from congenital heart disease · *ischemic heart disease* (coronary thrombosis) · rheumatic heart disease leading to valvular disease such as mitral stenosis and aortic regurgitation · subacute bacterial endocarditis and *high blood pressure* (hypertension).

ANEMIA OF ANY KIND

PAINFUL CONDITIONS such as *Bornholm disease* · fractured ribs · *pleurisy* or *pleural effusion* · *pneumothorax*.

OTHER CONDITIONS including being out of condition following illness or general debility, or not "in training" · increasing age · chronic *bronchitis* · *ischemic heart disease* (which may be associated with cigarette smoking) · *hysteria* · the effects of high altitude.

The commoner causes of sudden difficulty in breathing in children and in adults are: in children, *croup* and laryngeal infections · inhaled foreign body · acute bronchitis · *asthma* or pneumonia. Where these illnesses are of an infectious nature, *fever* and illness will be apparent. In adults, the condition may be due to swelling in the throat and larynx associated with *allergies*. Pneumonia and asthma are also common causes. Sudden heart failure for any reason can trigger off difficulty in breathing, as can a sudden collapse of a lung due to a *pneumothorax,* any infection, or bronchial (lung) cancer. Occasionally, lung cysts may rupture to give rise to sudden shortness of breath.

The common causes of difficulty in breathing of slower onset which may show first as breathlessness on exertion and later as breathlessness at rest, are: in children, congenital heart disease; in young adults, rheumatic heart disease, asthma and bronchitis; and in middle-aged and older people, bronchitis · emphysema · ischemic heart disease · cancer of the bronchus ("lung cancer") and anemias.

Difficulty in seeing   See *defective vision.*

Difficulty in sleeping   See *disorders of sleep.*

Difficulty in speaking

May be due to simple conditions such as a dry mouth or a painful condition of the tongue, or to a disorder in the nervous system. A speech difficulty in the nervous system may stem from an inability to recall words from memory, associated with *loss of memory,* or it may lie in transmitting the messages to the parts of the body concerned with phonation—that is, with making the sounds. *Stroke,* often related to *high blood pressure,* and cerebral *thrombosis* in an older person, are probably the commonest causes of speech difficulty arising in the brain. Conditions which cause *hoarseness* or which affect the vocal cords or their nerve supply can also cause speech difficulty.

Difficulty in swallowing (dysphagia)

May be associated WITH PAIN. The causes include: *soreness in the mouth* (stomatitis), a *sore tongue*, a *sore throat* including *tonsillitis* and *quinsy* (peritonsillar abscess), and acute laryngitis.

WITH OBSTRUCTION. The causes include: a narrowing of the esophagus due to injury, or from swallowing acid or other corrosive substance, a foreign body in the esophagus, a *cancer* of the esophagus or a cancer of the stomach invading the lower end of the esophagus, a *cyst* or *tumor* in the chest which compresses the esophagus from the outside. Esophageal pouches filled with food which may narrow or obstruct the esophagus. See also *swellings in the neck*.

WITH DISEASE OR DISORDER OF THE NERVOUS SYSTEM. *Hysteria* is a possible cause of nervous difficulty in swallowing. Paralysis of the soft palate may occur after diphtheria. This leads to difficulty in swallowing and food and drink trickling out through the nose, because the back of the throat is not sealed off during swallowing. Many diseases of the nervous system may affect the nerves which control swallowing. *Myasthenia gravis* and poliomyelitis may be mentioned as examples.

OTHER CAUSES include: cleft palate or holes in the roof of the mouth from destructive *ulcers in the mouth* due to *syphilis* or *cancer,* inability to use the tongue because of infection, swelling or paralysis, a very dry mouth (xerostoma), *achalasia* of the esophagus, iron-deficiency *anemia*. This latter condition is nearly always found in women, and is known as the Paterson and Brown Kelly syndrome or as the Plummer-Vinson syndrome.

Difficulty in urinating

See *urine leaking or dribbling · weak or poor stream when urinating · enlargement of the prostate · stress incontinence · multiple sclerosis.*

Dimness of vision   See *defective vision.*

Diphtheria

A disease caused by corynebacterium diphtheriae, which is now uncommon. The disease begins as a throat infection with a *sore throat,* a raised pulse rate, fever and *difficulty in breathing.* The infecting organism produces a toxin which can cause paralysis of the muscles of the larynx and pharynx or elsewhere. The toxin also can affect the heart. Fortunately immunization against the disease is effective. All infants and children need to be immunized against diphtheria.

Diplopia   See *double vision.*

Discharge from the ear
The causes include: *wax in the ear · infection in the ear passage · infection in the middle ear.* Discharge in children, if associated with pain, fever and general upset, should always be a reason for seeking immediate medical attention, because the child may have a middle-ear infection.

Discharge from the nipple
A discharge from the nipple is normally found during pregnancy, and before, during and shortly after feeding. All other discharges must be regarded as abnormal. Discharges may be yellow and serous, or there may be *blood from the nipple.* Medical attention should be sought at once for any abnormal discharge, because it may be an early sign of breast cancer. See also *pain in the breast.*

Discharge from the penis   See *urethral discharge.*

Discharge from the vagina   See *vaginal discharge.*

Disk trouble   See *backache* and *sciatica.*

Dislocation
Occurs when a bone has been displaced from its normal position at a joint. The symptoms of dislocations are similar to those of broken bones, and are often associated with *fractures.*
Never attempt to reduce a dislocation, because you may be trying to manipulate a fracture. Until an X ray has been taken no one can be sure. If you suspect a fracture or a dislocation because of pain, swelling, unusual shape or position of the joint and bones, or inability to use the joint normally, then an X ray is necessary.

Disordered thinking
See *anxiety · confusion · depression · loss of memory · psychosis.*

Disorders of balance   See *dizziness.*

Disorders of pigmentation of the skin

INCREASED BROWN PIGMENTATION. Freckles and increased brown pigmentation during pregnancy are normal variations in skin pigmentation. The pigment will mostly disappear. Sometimes an increase in pigmentation may occur in an area of skin which is healing after an injury or burn. This will also usually revert to normal.

Some perfumes and medicines contain substances which sensitize the skin to sunlight, and thus lead to increased pigmentation. Abnormal brownness may appear in *Addison's disease* of the adrenal gland, in chronic infections such as bacterial endocarditis, in association with the wasting found with malignant disease, and occasionally in *hyperthyroidism*. Exposure to pitch or tar can sensitize the skin to sunlight and lead to increased pigmentation.

DECREASED BROWN PIGMENTATION. Irregular patches of depigmentation are found in a common condition called vitiligo. The cells which produce pigment cease to function in certain areas, and the result is a white patch of irregular shape. In dark-skinned people this will be noticed at once, but in fair-skinned individuals the condition may not be noticed until sunburn makes the rest of the skin darker and the depigmented area shows up. The areas may come and go in size.

Depigmentation may also be found in the scaly patches of *psoriasis,* in the scars associated with severe destruction of areas of skin following on boils and abscesses, or in diseases such as *syphilis* and leprosy. A rare inherited disorder called albinism is associated with total lack of pigment. The condition is easily recognized by white hair and pink eyes.

OTHER SKIN PIGMENTATION can be produced by *jaundice,* by drugs, by pigment from eating vegetables such as carrots, by metals such as iron, mercury, and silver which may be deposited under the skin, and by nevi, moles and *warts* which are pigmented. A local area of dark brown pigmentation which appears suddenly and spreads may be a malignant *melanoma,* a condition which requires urgent diagnosis and treatment. Simple senile keratoses are rough mid-brown pigmented patches which appear on the the skin of older people. Red pigmented areas on the skin are usually due to nevi. The strawberry mark seen in babies is an area of dilated blood vessels. Similar red or reddish-purple nevi are seen in adults who have a cavernous hemangioma—an area of dilated blood vessels under the skin. In very young babies blotchy red marks often known as "stork marks" are seen on the back of the neck and on the face and head. These marks usually disappear in the first year.

See also *blueness of the skin*.

Disorders of sleep

Insomnia refers to inadequate sleep or sleep of poor quality. This begs the question of what is adequate, because individuals differ greatly in what they believe to be enough. In general terms, a person who feels that he is getting enough sleep probably is, regardless of the number of hours shown by the clock. The causes of insomnia include: disturbances of regular routine · shift work · pain and discomfort · *anxiety* · other emotional problems · psychiatric disorders.

Anxiety is a great disturber of sleep. The characteristic pattern is difficulty in getting to sleep, light sleeping in the early part of night, and difficulty in staying asleep. Eventually, exhaustion will occur, and the sufferer then sleeps. The treatment in these cases must be directed toward the anxiety, and not to the symptom of not sleeping. *Early waking* is a symptom of *depression*. The mildly depressed person will tend to wake slightly early; the very depressed person will wake very early and will lie awake or get up, because he realizes that he cannot sleep any more.

Falling asleep in the middle of the day or when working may be due to overtiredness, or may be a form of *narcolepsy* requiring medical investigation.

Disorders of urination

See *urine leaking or dribbling · weak or poor stream when urinating · enlargement of the prostate · stress incontinence · fistula · multiple sclerosis*.

Displaced or torn knee cartilage

The source of injury in displaced or torn knee cartilages is nearly always the same: the person's knee is slightly bent, and in this position a rotary strain is applied to the joint. The effect is to grind the cartilage between the lower end of the thigh bone (femur) and the top of the shin bone (tibia), on which the cartilage is mounted. This rotary straining force will split, tear or displace the cartilage. *Pain in the knee* will usually be felt at once, and may be followed shortly by *swelling of the knee* joint. If the cartilage is displaced inward between the bone ends, locking of the knee may occur. Locking is inability to move the joint and is usually due to extreme pain. In most cases if locking occurs, the knee is locked in a very slightly bent position, not far from straight. Any attempts to straighten the joint are accompanied by sharp severe pain. A further small increase in bending the knee may be possible. Medical help will be needed to deal with this condition. Tears of smaller amounts which do not give rise to locking may cause a good deal of pain and swelling in the joint, and may be accompanied by a click on certain movements or every time the joint is straightened.

Any knee which is other than slightly swollen and painful should be examined by a doctor, and will probably need to be X rayed to see whether there are fractures or loose bodies or diseases in the joint. Badly torn knee cartilages will have to be removed surgically from the joint.

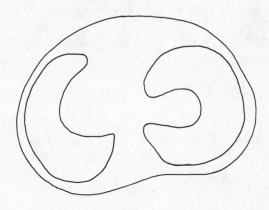

The knee cartilages on the top of the shin bone

Disseminated sclerosis   See *multiple sclerosis.*

Distended abdomen   See *abdominal distension.*

Distension   See *swelling.*

Diverticular disease

Of the colon occurs mainly in people over thirty years of age. Many have diverticula, which are little pouches on the large bowel. Only a few, however, have symptoms as a result. The common symptoms are *diarrhea · colic ·* slight fever · *pain in the abdomen,* usually the lower abdomen. Sometimes *mucus in the stools* may be seen.

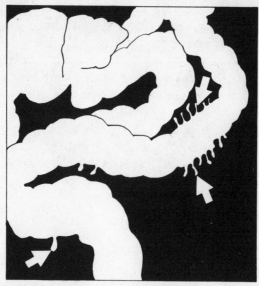

X ray (barium) enema showing diverticular disease (arrowed) of lower part of large bowel.

Dizziness

Due to disorders of the balance mechanism. *Infection in the middle ear* can affect the organ of balance. Head injuries may also damage the organ of balance, the nerve to it or the parts of the brain concerned with balance. Brain disease from *multiple sclerosis, thrombosis, embolism* or *tumors,* or nerve disease from *acoustic neurinoma,* may all cause dizziness. *Menière's disease, motion sickness* and *migraine* are possible causes. Certain drugs, such as aspirin and salicylates, quinine and streptomycin, can cause dizziness. Alcohol in excess is well known in this connection. *Anemia, high blood pressure, fainting* and any state associated with low blood pressure may also cause dizziness.

Double vision (diplopia)

Normally of two kinds. Closing each eye in turn will establish whether the cause of double vision is present only in one eye, or occurs when both eyes are open.

DOUBLE VISION FROM ONE EYE CAN ARISE FROM a dislocation of the lens · an early cataract (a lens opacity) · slight astigmatism · corneal opacities or irregularities · *detachment of the retina* · serious brain disorders.

DOUBLE VISION FROM BOTH EYES CAN ARISE FROM paralysis or weakness of the muscles which move the eyes. Because the eyes will not always move evenly and together, the images from each eye will not be fused in the brain. Displacement of an eye as a result of pressure on or behind the eye from an *abscess,* blood clot, cyst or *tumor* can cause double vision. Disease or other disorder of the nerves behind the eye or of the parts of the brain which deal with vision can result in improper functioning, and therefore in failure to perceive the images from both eyes. Many brain diseases such as *meningitis, multiple sclerosis, syphilis* and others, and conditions arising from injury, bleeding, *thrombosis* or *tumors* can interfere with nerve and brain function.

Transient double vision may occur in *migraine.*

Dribbling from the mouth   See *Parkinson's disease · nausea.*

Dribbling of urine   See *urine leaking or dribbling.*

Drinking excessively   See *alcoholism · thirst.*

Drip at the back of the throat   See *postnasal drip.*

Drooping of the eyelid(s)

May be simply due to *tiredness* or to muscular fatigue in old age. Some people are born with droopiness in one or both eyelids. *Myasthenia gravis,* a general muscular disease, may also affect the muscles of the eyelids. Sometimes in fact the first sign of this condition is drooping of the eyelids. Other muscular disorders can also produce drooping.

A one-sided slight droop of an eyelid is found in *Horner's syndrome,* which is caused by pressure on the sympathetic nervous system. The pupil of the eye is smaller on the affected side. Among the causes of pressure giving rise to Horner's syndrome are: lung *tumor · aneurysm* of the aorta · *cancer* of the thyroid · *cervical ribs* (see also *unequal pupils*). Anything that can affect the nerves behind the eye can also produce drooping of the eyelid. This includes bleeding, diseases of the nervous system and tumors. Thickening of the eyelids seen in *hypothyroidism* (myxedema) may be mistaken for drooping.

Edema and *swelling of the eyelids* can cause drooping.

Dropsy   See *edema.*

Drowsiness   See *disorders of sleep · narcolepsy · uremia.*

Dry skin   See *scaly skin.*

Dry stools   See *constipation.*

Duodenal ulcer   See *peptic ulcer.*

Dupuytren's contracture
A condition found mainly in men which causes the tissues under the skin of the palms of the hands (the palmar fascia) to thicken and contract. When this happens, the ring and little fingers are flexed towards the palms. Later, all the fingers may be affected. The thickened palmar fascia may be felt in the palm at the base of each finger. In more advanced disease the underlying structures may stick out. Early surgical treatment is advisable, so that finger movement can be retained. The condition is occasionally associated with *Peyronie's disease.*

Dysmenorrhea
Painful menstruation. This may or may not be associated with *premenstrual tension.*
Painful periods often occur for a few years after menstruation has started. The cause is unknown, and in most cases examination reveals no abnormality. The girl feels a *pain in the lower abdomen* which is usually *colic* in type. The pain tends to begin just after the period has started and usually lasts up to two days. In some cases, the pain begins just before the period starts. Generally the condition improves with age, and often disappears after child-bearing. There is no evidence that health education or attitudes to sex and reproduction affect the condition.
Occasionally, after years of painless periods, there may be pain on menstruation. This is sometimes due to pelvic infection or to lesions of the uterus. A doctor should always be consulted in these cases.

Dyspepsia   See *indigestion.*

Dysphagia   See *difficulty in swallowing.*

Dyspnea   See *difficulty in breathing.*

Earache

The causes include: *infection in the ear passage · infection in the middle ear.* Any earache which keeps a child awake and is accompanied by general upset or by *fever* is a signal to see a doctor, because the child may have a middle ear infection.

Pain in the ear could also be *referred pain* from the tongue or jaw, and may be related to *toothache.* Any *discharge from the ear—* often pus—may be accompanied by relief of pain. Sometimes *bleeding from the ear* occurs at the same time.

Ear bleeding   See *bleeding from the ear.*

Early waking   See *disorders of sleep.*

Ear passage infection

See *infection in the ear passage* and *infection in the middle ear.*

ECG   See *electrocardiograph.*

Ectopic pregnancy

A pregnancy which occurs outside of the normal site in the uterus. The fertilized ovum may embed itself in the tube and give rise to a tubal pregnancy. The tube will not be able to sustain a pregnancy, and will usually rupture at about two and a half to three months after the date of the *missed menstrual period.* The general symptoms of early pregnancy such as *morning sickness, nausea, vomiting* and *swelling of the breasts* will occur. Severe internal bleeding and vomiting may result from a ruptured tube following a tubal pregnancy.

Eczema (atopic dermatitis)

A skin disease associated with *atopy.* It can begin early in life, from about the age of three months. It generally starts on the face and behind the knees and in front of the elbows, and is usually very itchy. *Itching of the skin* is a prominent symptom. In older children and adults, the disease is usually confined to the backs of the knees and around the ankles and the fronts of the wrists and elbows. See also *varicose eczema.*

Edema

The swelling caused by systemic or local fluid retention.

Systemic fluid retention will be associated with heart failure, kidney disease and malnutrition. The swelling will usually be noticed first on the ankles or around the lower back if the person is lying down for long. Ankle swelling is affected by standing, and will therefore usually be present more at night than in the morning.

Edema can be recognized by pitting on pressure—if a finger tip is pressed firmly into the area for about ten seconds and then removed, an indentation or pit will remain.

Local causes of edema are inflammation associated with an *abscess, carbuncle* or other infection. *Trauma* may cause swelling, but this is most often due to bleeding and not to other fluid.

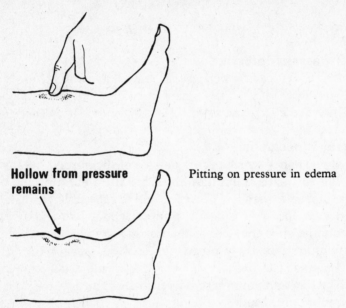

Hollow from pressure remains

Pitting on pressure in edema

EKG   See *electrocardiograph.*

Electrocardiogram   See *electrocardiograph*

Electrocardiograph

An instrument used to measure the amplitude and direction of the small electrical impulses associated with heartbeat. It is, in fact, a very sensitive galvanometer. The person whose heart currents are being recorded feels nothing except the placement of the electrodes, which are used to make a connection with the electrocardiograph. It can almost be compared to having a photograph taken—the person should suffer no pain or discomfort. The electrical impulses are recorded on a moving paper, and the result is the electrocardiogram (ECG or EKG), which will show whether electrical conduction is normal. If the conduction is abnormal, the nature and pattern of disease can be inferred. Any injury to the heart muscle or malformation of the heart may be reflected in the electrocardiogram. *Ischemic heart disease* and *angina pectoris* are conditions which an electrocardiogram can help in diagnosing. Alterations in the rhythm of heartbeat can also be detected. Among these are fibrillation and heart block. A *pacemaker* may correct the abnormal rhythm of heart block. The electrocardiogram is therefore a valuable aid in cardiac diagnosis.

Embolism

The process of obstructing a blood vessel, usually an artery, by a transported solid (an *embolus*). The embolus is commonly a blood clot, but may be any solid transported material. Fat embolism may occur after fractures, due to dislodgement of fat globules from the bone marrow. Other emboli can arise from the heart, especially from the edges of diseased heart valves. If these emboli come from the left side of the heart, the emboli may lodge in the arteries of the brain, causing a *stroke*.

Embolus

Generally any solid material circulating in the blood which may obstruct a blood vessel in which it lodges. For example, a common embolus arises by detachment from a blood clot, or *thrombus*, in a vein see *deep vein thrombus*. If there is *thrombosis* in a leg vein, then any embolus will go through increasingly large veins on its way to the heart, and then, after passing through the heart, will have to pass through increasingly small vessels on its way through the lung. As a result, the embolus will lodge in a blood vessel in the lung, giving rise to a pulmonary *embolism*.

Emotional stress   See *stress*.

Emphysema

A condition of over-inflation of the lungs, in which the air sacs become distended, the fine bronchioles become thinned, and finally the architecture of the lungs is destroyed. It is a very common cause both of breathlessness and of *difficulty in breathing*, most frequent among middle-aged and older men.

Empyema   A *pleural effusion* consisting of pus.

Enlarged glands   See *swelling of the lymph nodes*.

Enlargement of the head
See *Paget's disease*. In babies, enlargement of the head is usually due to hydrocephalus (water on the brain).

Enlargement of the prostate
Found to some extent in most men over middle age. Most men will have no symptoms, but in some cases the enlargement causes symptoms by obstructing the outflow of urine at the bladder neck and by causing *frequency of urination*. Most enlargement of the prostate is benign, but in some cases the enlargement is due to *cancer* of the prostate. A decreased or poor flow rate is noticed when urinating—it takes longer to empty the bladder. This is almost a test of age. As the obstruction at the neck of the bladder increases, frequency of urination develops. *Urgency of urination* and *infection in the bladder* may also be found in association with enlargement of the prostate.
Most enlargement is dealt with by an operation which takes away excess tissue by operating either through the penis or through the bladder.

Epidemic myalgia   See *Bornholm disease*.

Epidermophytosis   See *fungus infection of the skin*.

Epilepsy
A disease characterized by *fits* (convulsions) accompanied by transient loss of consciousness.
During the fit the person will twitch and move in an involuntary manner. The color may change toward blueness due to breath-holding at the beginning of the attack, when all the muscles are tense. Then, as twitching begins, the person will breathe again and normal color will be restored. The fits usually last quite a short time, from about one to four minutes, and during it consciousness is lost. The person then lies quietly and recovers. The tongue may be bitten and urine may be passed during the fit. The patient has a *loss of memory* for the short period of time before the fit began and may appear rather confused just after the fit. Epileptic fits can be quite severe, with much twitching, lasting

about five minutes (grand mal), or very severe, in which one fit runs into the next before the person has recovered from the last. (This condition is known as status epilepticus.) On the other hand, very minor fits will have hardly any twitching, or even none at all, and may only be apparent as minor and transient episodes of loss of consciousness with small memory gaps just before the loss of consciousness began (petit mal).

Epiphora   See *watery eyes*.

Erection, curved   See *chordee*.

Erection, failure   See *impotence*.

Erythema nodosum   See *rheumatic fever*.

Excessive appetite
Appears normally in boys, and sometimes in girls, around puberty. There is a tremendous growth spurt at this time, and the appetite grows to take care of the physical needs of growth. This is healthy and natural.
Some people who suffer from *obesity* seem unable to leave food alone, although most will say that they do not eat much in spite of evidence to the contrary. Occasionally in early *diabetes* an abnormal craving for food may be found. Emotional disturbances may also lead people to eat more as a substitute for other kinds of satisfaction, or even as a means of growing obese for protection against social or sexual pressures.

Excessive menstruation   See *monorrhagia*.

Excessive salivation   See *Parkinson's disease · nausea*.

Excessive sweating
Occurs most usually when the weather is hot, or in warm and extremely humid atmospheres when perspiration cannot readily evaporate.
Any *fever* or rise of body temperature can be accompanied by excessive sweating, so that any feverish illness must be considered as a cause. Tuberculosis of the lungs sometimes gives rise to "night sweats," in which the person wakes up bathed in perspiration and has to change clothing and bedlinen to be comfortable.

Local excessive sweating on the face and forehead, on the palms of the hands and the soles of the feet, and under the arms, may be found in some families, or may be found in people who are emotionally tense. If excessive sweating is foul-smelling, this is because of secondary bacterial infection of stale sweat. This can give rise to *body odor*. *Prickly heat* is a skin rash associated with excessive sweating in tropical conditions. It causes intense itching.

Hypoglycemia is an occasional cause of excessive sweating.

Exophthalmos   See *staring or protruding eyes.*

Eye, bloodshot   See *redness of the eye · black eye.*

Eye, itchy   See *itchy eye.*

Eyelashes, loss of   See *loss of eyelashes.*

Eyelids, puffy   See *swelling of the eyelids.*

Eyelids, red   See *red eyelids.*

Eye, painful   See *pain in the eye.*

Eyes, black specks in front of   See *black specks before the eyes.*

Eye, sticky   See *sticky eye.*

Eyestrain
A vague term used to express dissatisfaction with the working of the eyes in the absence of any redness or serious visual disturbance. The commonest problems found on examination of the eyes are simple errors of refraction, such as mild degrees of astigmatism and the need for reading glasses which affects most middle-aged people. With increasing age, the ability to focus the eyes on nearby objects in order to carry out tasks such as threading a needle or reading very fine print becomes increasingly difficult. The condition of "eyestrain" is usually felt when the person is tired, and not when he is feeling fit and fresh. It would therefore be wise to check on causes of *tiredness* or strain as well as having the eyes examined.

Failing vision See *defective vision*.

Failure to conceive See *infertility*.

Fainting

Loss of consciousness, usually for a short period of time. Fainting is often accompanied by feelings of weakness and dizziness. Most cases of fainting are not associated with serious medical conditions, and often represent nothing more than a form of escape from painful or unpleasant physical or emotional situations. However, some conditions accompanied by transient loss of consciousness may have a more underlying serious medical problem.

OBVIOUS CAUSES:

Emotional. Fainting can follow some emotional shock or a severe or very tense situation. In more susceptible people, the emotional levels required for fainting may be lower than in others.

Exhaustion. Fairly severe degrees of tiredness or exhaustion are usually required to produce fainting. Examples are prolonged lack of sleep, standing for long periods, severe physical exertion and stress leading to exhaustion, tiredness associated with a debilitating illness or after an operation, or excessive working hours.

Excessive heat or cold. *Heat exhaustion* is a well-known and dangerous condition resulting from a rise in basal body temperature while working in very hot conditions. Extreme cold leading to *hypothermia*, when the body core temperature falls, can lead to loss of consciousness. Old people and babies in inadequately heated surroundings can easily suffer from hypothermia.

Pain. Severe pain will cause fainting in many people. Certain particular injuries, such as a blow on the knee cap or testicles, can cause very severe pain leading to fainting.

Injury, including burns. Severe general injuries, especially with blood loss, can lead to loss of consciousness. Head injuries with *concussion* may bring about loss of consciousness.

Sudden or severe bleeding. Any loss of blood from the circulation, particularly if it is sudden or considerable in amount, will lead to a lowering of blood pressure, and thus to fainting. The blood loss may show (external bleeding), in which case the cause will be obvious. However, if the blood loss does not show (internal bleeding), the reason for the faint may not be apparent.

Bleeding from a *peptic ulcer* is a fairly common cause. The blood loss may show if the blood is vomited, or may appear later as *melena*. Nosebleeds, bleeding after injuries (external or internal), and bleeding from the uterus may all cause fainting. A rupture of the spleen or liver can cause serious internal bleeding and thus cause fainting.

Gassing. Many substances can produce loss of consciousness, which may be transient or prolonged. Among them are gasoline, carbon monoxide, car exhaust fumes, and hydrogen sulfide.

OTHER CAUSES:

Medical conditions affecting the heart, such as a *coronary thrombosis,* a sudden alteration in heat rhythm, and especially *heart block.*

Medical conditions in the abdomen associated with sudden events which themselves can cause fainting. These conditions are perforated *gastric or duodenal ulcers* which will usually be very painful · ruptured *ectopic (tubal) pregnancy* in which fainting may be associated both with bleeding and with pain · a strangulated *hernia* · acute pancreatitis · *intestinal obstruction.*

Medical conditions within the chest associated with sudden events. These will include a sudden *pneumothorax* · a pulmonary *embolism* · acute *pneumonia.*

Anemia. Any cause of *anemia* can give rise to fainting. The mechanism of fainting is probably connected with the poor supply of oxygenated blood to the brain.

Drugs and medicines. Insulin overdoses leading to *hypoglycemia* can cause loss of consciousness. Many other drugs, especially those given to lower blood pressure or to affect the heart, can bring about fainting.

FURTHER CAUSES include: *epilepsy* · early pregnancy · indigestion and flatulence · disease of the brain and of the cerebral blood vessels, including *tumors* inside the skull · *meningitis* · disturbances of balance with or without *middle ear infection* · *hysteria* · *breath holding* in young children · *overbreathing.*

Falling   See *epilepsy · fainting.*

Falling hair   See *loss of hair.*

Familial early deafness
A form of inherited *deafness* which usually begins around the age of forty. In simple terms, the organ of hearing appears to

wear out sooner in these people, and the sufferer of forty has the hearing of a person of eighty. This condition needs to be distinguished from *otosclerosis*. Unfortunately, familial early deafness is not amenable to treatment. A hearing aid may help slightly. Learning lip reading while some hearing remains may be the best way to deal with the problem if total hearing loss appears inevitable.

Fast heartbeat (tachycardia)

Can occur normally after exercise and during excitement of any kind. Pregnancy is also associated with faster heart rates. *Fever* is a common cause of a raised rate of heartbeat, and in these cases, the reason for the raised body temperature must be sought. *Hyperthyroidism* can also be a frequent cause of a fast heartbeat. *Anemia* and blood loss will raise the heart rate, as will pain or serious sudden illness or injury. *Ischemic heart disease,* especially if it causes coronary thrombosis, can result in fast heart rates. An occasional reason for very fast heart rates (140 per minute) is paroxysmal tachycardia, in which the heart rate can suddenly change from normal to very fast and back again without apparent reason. The condition may not be dangerous or significant. In paroxysmal tachycardia normal heart rate can sometimes be regained by blowing hard against a closed nose and mouth for about three to five seconds.

Fast pulse   See *fast heartbeat*.

Fatness   See *obesity*.

Fear

See *anxiety · phobic anxiety · confusion · depression · psychosis.*

Feeling cold

May occur as the body temperature rises in *fever* for any reason. This is often described as a *chill*. Extreme degrees of *tiredness* are usually accompanied by feeling cold. Lack of food can also lead to this feeling, as may *hypothyroidism*. The latter is especially noticeable when others do not feel cold in similar circumstances. *Hypothermia* produced by chilling will also cause feeling cold.

Feeling hot

Will usually be associated with *fever* in the absence of a hot environment. The temperature should always be checked with a thermometer.

Feeling sick See *nausea.*

Feelings of persecution See *delusions · schizophrenia.*

Femoral hernia See *hernia.*

Fever (raised body temperature)
Can give rise to symptoms of shivering, *headache,* general feelings of being unwell, aching bones and joints, and *excessive sweating.* Short spells of fever are common in children with upper respiratory infections, such as colds and *tonsillitis,* with the infectious illnesses of childhood such as measles, German measles and chicken pox, and with urinary infections, which are often much less obvious unless the urine is inspected and tested. Since infectious illnesses are accompanied by fever, it is only by looking at the other features of the illness that the diagnosis can be established.
The geography of disease is particularly important in adults with unexplained fever. Recent visits to foreign places may be related to the symptoms. People who have visited tropical countries should always tell their doctor if they become ill shortly afterwards, otherwise important diagnoses may be overlooked. The commonest causes of fevers in adults vary considerably, but are most generally colds and influenza.
If an individual has a fever and the explanation is not obvious after two or three days, then medical advice is needed, because the list of possibilities is vast and the cause can only be identified after examination and investigation. Any fever of 101 °F (39 °C) or over in a child or adult should generally be a reason for seeking medical attention. Babies and young children may have a *fit or convulsion* simply as a result of a high body temperature. See also *chill.*

Fever, glandular See *mononucleosis.*

Finger, inability to straighten See *mallet finger · trigger finger.*

Fistula
An abnormal connection between two hollow spaces or organs in

the body. A fistula can occur, for example, between the bladder and the vagina (a vesico-vaginal fistula). This can lead to *urine leaking or dribbling* from the vagina.

Fits and convulsions

A fit or convulsion—the terms have the same meaning—is characterized by involuntary movements of the whole body, or of only parts of it. The movements appear and then stop. The fit may sometimes be accompanied by loss of consciousness (*fainting*). A fit may conceivably be mistaken for the shivering rigors which occur in association with feverish illnesses and with raised body temperature. Other mistaken causes are the muscle spasms seen in *tetanus* and *tetany*. By far the commonest cause of fits without any obvious illnesses or injuries is epilepsy.

The causes of fits and convulsions at any age include: *epilepsy* · congenital injury or disease of the brain · head injuries · infection inside the skull from a brain abscess, *meningitis, sinusitis, infection in the middle ear,* encephalitis from any cause and cerebral malaria · cysts or *tumors* inside the skull (for example brain tumors), secondary tumors spread from elsewhere in the body, tumors of the blood vessels in the brain (angiomata), and *hydatid cysts* (from tapeworms) · diseases of the blood vessels inside the skull causing bleeding, *thrombosis* and *embolism* · *heatstroke* from working in very hot places and from failure of the heat regulating mechanism in the brain · toxic states arising from *uremia,* gassing and poisoning from a variety of sources, including alcohol and smoking · *hypoglycemia* (low blood glucose) from any cause including insulin overdose, lack of food and disease of the pancreas, especially a *tumor* · *hysteria,* in which the fits usually have an audience, and seldom occur when the individual is alone. The causes of fits and convulsions in infants and young children include any general or serious infection, such as gastroenteritis, childhood fevers, ear infections, pneumonia and urinary infections. Any cause of moderate or high fever may result in a fit or convulsion in babies and young children.

Flat feet

People who have flat feet are usually made that way—it is a congenital disorder. When it gives rise to symptoms, they are usually of *pain in the feet* on standing and walking.

Flatulence

Abdominal distension by gas. The distension may give rise to *colic.* Gas may be passed upwards via the mouth or downwards. Air swallowing as a habit may contribute to the amount of gas present. *Indigestion* may be a contributory factor. A *hernia through the diaphragm* and a *cancer* of the stomach are conceivable causes. If the flatulence is worse after fatty foods, cholecystitis or *stones in the gallbladder* may be suspected. *Intestinal obstruction* can give rise to extreme degrees of flatulence accompanied by loud rumbling bowel sounds in the abdomen.

Tapping the abdomen with the finger will result in drum-like taps if the *abdominal distension* is due to gas.

Flickering of the eyelid

Usually caused by irregular involuntary contraction of the muscles in the eyelids when a person is feeling tired. This condition disappears when the person is rested and is, in these circumstances, nothing more or less than a symptom of *tiredness.* Another cause is a *tic. Drooping of the eyelid(s)* may also occur.

Flooding in menstruation   See *menorrhagia.*

Fluid in the abdomen

Will result in *abdominal distension.* An abdomen distended by fluid will produce very little sound when tapped with the finger. *Flatulence,* when the abdomen is full of gas, gives a drum-like sound on tapping. *Colic* and *diarrhea* will probably be present if the abdomen is distended by gas, but will probably be absent if fluid is present. Fluid may be present in the abdomen as part of general fluid accumulation in kidney disease and kidney failure, and in heart disease with heart failure. Severe *anemias, Hodgkin's disease* and *leukemia* are other possible systemic causes. Local causes are usually related to serious disease within the abdomen. *Cancer* of any abdominal organ with secondary spread is a possible reason for fluid in the abdomen. Severe malnutrition is also a cause.

Flushing

Of the face after eating may be connected with *rosacea.* Redness associated with drinking is usually due simply to the relaxation of the walls of the small blood vessels induced by alcohol. Blushing, which is redness of the face associated with emotion, should

100

not be confused with flushing or other causes of *redness of the face* which are more constant.

In women, flushing of the face may be a part of the generalized "hot flashes" that are a part of the *menopause*.

Flushing may be associated with any cause of *fever* and with *hypoglycemia*. *Trigeminal neuralgia* may be a cause of one-sided flushing of the face.

Fluttering in the chest   See *palpitations · pain in the chest.*

Food sticking after swallowing
Usually indicates narrowing or obstruction in the esophagus. In older people *cancer* of the esophagus can be a cause. In younger people congenital abnormalities in the esophagus, *achalasia* of the cardia, and any other cause of narrowing, such as after burns of the esophagus, must be considered.

Foot ulcer   See *ulcer of the foot.*

Forgetfulness   See *loss of memory.*

Foul sputum   See *infected sputum.*

Fracture
Taking an X ray is the only sure way of knowing whether a bone is broken. However, when any part of the body has been subjected to a heavy blow or other force and is painful, misshapen, swollen and cannot be used normally, it should be assumed that the bone is broken until proved otherwise. A fracture may be found with a *dislocation*. Obviously broken bones may be easy to spot, but slight cracks without displacement may be very difficult to recognize. Sometimes undiagnosed fractures can give rise to disunited bones which can cause considerable trouble later. A good example of this is a scaphoid fracture in the wrist that has not united. The safe rule is to take X rays every time a broken bone is suspected, otherwise fractures will not be recognized and treated, and problems may result.

Fractures may be associated with disease of the bones, for example in *osteoporosis* and *Paget's disease.*

Frequency of urination
The causes include: infection of the bladder, ureters and kidney

stones or gravel · disorders of the neck of the bladder from disease there, such as infectious ulcers or cancer · in men, disorders of the prostate, including prostatitis, *enlargement of the prostate,* and *cancer* · in women, disorders of the bladder region that may cause pressure on the bladder leading to frequency of urination, also *"honeymoon cystitis"* and prolapse of the vagina and uterus · *diabetes.*

In any discussion of frequency of urination it is important to establish whether the frequency occurs every five minutes or every half hour, and to note whether it is affected by lying down or other change of position. It is also useful to know whether the frequency is only by day, or whether it occurs by night too. *Urgency of urination* often accompanies frequency. In all cases the urine should be examined to establish whether there is any *infection of the bladder* or *blood in the urine.* Many other tests may also be required. In old men, *enlargement of the prostate* is a common cause of frequency of urination. Enlargement of the prostate is often found together with infection of the bladder.

Because urinary infection is a common cause of frequency of urination, the temperature should always be checked. Urinary infections of sudden onset often follow *diarrhea* or diarrhea and *vomiting* (acute enteritis).

Frigidity

Means coldness, lack of sexual feelings and absence of interest in sexual intercourse. The term is usually used to describe a set of sexual problems in females. In males, *impotence* is the more usual term.

Frigidity in females may occur with one partner but not another, or it may be an ever-present condition. *Vaginismus* may be associated with frigidity. Pain on attempted sexual intercourse may precipitate or prolong frigidity. Lack of proper stimulation is particularly apt to lead to lack of response in females. It should be emphasized that lack of sexual response is a problem for both the individuals concerned. It is not simply a problem the female has.

Frozen shoulder

A term used to describe a stiff shoulder in which movement is limited, often severely. The shoulder may be so stiff that the hand cannot be raised much above shoulder level. It may be due to *trauma* or may be related to calcification in the tendon of one of the muscles (the supraspinatus) that acts on the shoulder. The condition is often associated with severe *pain in the shoulder.* Medical treatment is necessary to prevent the shoulder from becoming permanently stiff.

Fungus infection of the skin (epidermophytosis)
Commonly affects situations where two skin surfaces are in contact, and where the skin is moist. Fungus will not live on a dry skin. Fungus infection is found between the toes, in the groin and crotch area (tinea cruris), between the cheeks of the buttocks, and, in women, under the breast. The condition causes red and *scaly skin* with *itching of the skin.*
Intertrigo may be related to fungus infection of the skin or to candidosis. Ringworm is a type of fungus infection in which circular lesions are found on the skin. The lesions heal in the center but spread outward from the edge of the circle where there is redness and scaly skin.

Furred tongue
Smoking commonly produces furring, especially on the back half of the tongue. Characteristically, this varies in color from a dirty white through shades of yellowness to brown. In children, furring of the tongue is often associated with feverish illnesses. In adults, furring may be found in association with diseases of the esophagus, stomach, liver and bowel.

Gallstones   See *stones in the gallbladder.*

Gas in the bowel
Can cause *pain in the abdomen,* and occasionally *swelling in the abdomen.* Gas is produced mainly from carbohydrates, which are found in starchy food and sugar. Illnesses associated with *diarrhea* can also cause discomfort from gas in the bowel. In *intestinal obstruction* gas formation may be excessive due to food staying in one place; the gas cannot be passed downward because of the obstruction. This can give rise to abdominal distension from gas in the bowel.

Gastric ulcer   See *peptic ulcer.*

Genital ulcers

Any ulcers which occur at or near the genitals. Possible causes include: *syphilis · herpesvirus infection ·* other *sexually transmitted diseases.* Other conditions which can give rise to genital ulcers are *skin ulcers,* pimples or spots which can affect any part of the body, and skin *cancer.*

genital warts (condylomata acuminata)

A *sexually transmitted disease* caused by a virus infection. The warts are found on the external genitalia of both sexes, and around the anus, thighs and pubic region. Most of the warts are found in moist places. Genital warts must be distinguished from the warty growths found in the secondary stage of *syphilis* (condylomata lata) and, in older people, from warty *cancer.*

The interval between sexual contact and the appearance of a genital wart can be about one to six months, but more usually about two months. The warts begin as tiny raised red or pink pinhead-sized spots which grow upward into the typical stemmed cauliflower shape. They may vary in size from very small (about $\frac{1}{10}$ inch) to four inches or more (a few millimeters to 10 centimeters or more). Genital warts usually respond well to treatment.

Giddiness   See *dizziness.*

Gingivitis   See *infected gums.*

Glands, enlarged   See *swelling of the lymph nodes.*

Glands, swollen   See *swelling of the lymph nodes.*

Glaucoma

An increase in the pressure within the eyeball. It is commonly said to be due to lack of proper drainage of the aqueous fluid of the eye rather than to excess production of the fluid itself. There are two main kinds of glaucoma. The first comes on rapidly and is accompanied by severe pain in the eye and by impaired vision. The eye has a large pupil, the cornea is not crystal-clear, but looks misty, the eye has ciliary redness (see *redness of the eye*), and if felt gently through closed lids will feel hard by comparison with a normal eye because of the rise of pressure. A person should compare the feeling of one eye with the other, or the affected eye with another person's eye if there is any suspicion of glaucoma. The attack may be accompanied by pain sufficiently severe to prostrate the sufferer and make him vomit.

Attacks normally begin during the hours of sleep or darkness, when the pupil is large. The person sees halos around lights or rainbows such as a normal person sees when mist is present—and for the same reason—except that the mist is in the eye of the sufferer. The attack may settle naturally or only after medical treatment. Glaucoma will always result in visual deterioration if untreated.

The second form of glaucoma is undramatic and produces very few symptoms until visual deterioration is noted. However, the eye may feel hard for some years due to the rise in pressure.

Glossy tongue See *sore tongue.*

Goiter See *swelling of the thyroid.*

Gonorrhea

A *sexually transmitted disease* that causes a *urethral discharge* in males usually within forty-eight hours if the man has not been previously infected. In men who have experienced previous infections, the interval will be longer and may even extend up to twenty-one days. Gonorrhea can give rise to epididymitis, and infections of the epididymus. A late complication of gonorrhea in men can be a narrowing, or stricture, of the urethra. This can give rise to *difficulty in urination.*

In women, gonorrhea will often give rise to no symptoms of any kind. The only way a sufferer will know she has the disease is either to be specially examined by a doctor who is looking carefully for gonorrhea, or to be told by a man with whom she has had sexual contact that she has infected him. In other cases the woman may experience burning *pain on urination* or may suffer from a *vaginal discharge.* Gonorrhea may cause infection in the fallopian tubes, called *salpingitis.* This can give rise to sharp *pain in the abdomen.* Salpingitis may result in blocking of the fallopian tubes, and can thus produce sterility.

Gonorrhea should always be treated as soon as possible to prevent complications.

Gout

A disease of the uric acid metabolism which affects the joints, producing *pain in joints, swelling in joints* and extreme degrees of tenderness in some cases. Characteristically, gout attacks the joint between the great toe and the foot, most often on the right. Gout also causes swellings called tophi, which appear around affected joints and in the cartilage of the ear, where they should not be mistaken for a *cauliflower ear*.

Gout of sudden onset gives rise to a very painful joint with red shiny skin over it which is hot, swollen and tender. *Fever* may be present. Gout of slower onset causes painful joints, particularly in the feet, ankles, hands, wrists, and elbows, but other joints may be affected. Tophi do not generally appear until the disease has been present for about ten years. Measuring the plasma urates (the level of uric acid in blood) is a diagnostic test for gout.

Grand mal   See *epilepsy*.

Grating in joints

Found when the surface lining of a joint becomes worn and uneven. *Clicking in joints* may also be found. Grating is commonly associated with *osteoarthritis,* but may be found in other conditions which cause *pain in joints* and *swelling of joints.*

Gravel or stones in the urine

If a person passes gravel or a stone in the urine, it should be recovered so that the doctor can then have the gravel or stone analyzed as part of his investigations into the disease. The suspected urine specimen should be put into a container before flushing it down the toilet or urination should take place through a fine nylon sieve. Gravel or stones may give rise to *pain on urination, urgency of urination, frequency of urination, blood in the urine* and *ureteric colic.*

Gray hair

A normal part of aging in many people. In some families, grayness may occur in the 20–30 age group. Grayness of hair is unrelated to *loss of hair* and baldness. A few people have gray streaks in their hair. When the bald patches of alopecia areata are recovering, white or gray patches may be found. See *loss of hair.*

Greasy scales

On the skin are found in *seborrheic dermatitis.*

Greasy skin   See *seborrheic dermatitis · acne · scaly skin.*

Green vomit
  Bile-stained vomit, which can occur in any severe *vomiting,* or
  may be associated with diseases of the gallbladder and bile ducts,
  or with *intestinal obstruction.* See also *infection of the gallbladder ·
  bilious attack.*

Gritty feeling in the eye   See *conjunctivitis.*

Gumboil   See *swelling of the face.*

Gums, bleeding   See *bleeding from the mouth.*

Gums, infected   See *infected gums.*

Gums, painful   See *painful gums.*

Hair, brittle and dull   See *hypothyroidism.*

Hairiness   See *increased hair on the body.*

Halitosis   See *bad breath.*

Hallucination
  A disorder of perception, in which a person sees, hears, feels,
  smells or tastes things which are not in fact present. For example,
  a person may hear the voices of people talking about him when
  no one is about. Hallucinations occur in serious mental illnesses
  such as *schizophrenia* or other psychosis. They can also occur in
  the toxic confusional states which are associated with *alcoholism,
  uremia,* and use of hallucinogenic drugs. Hallucinations may also
  be found in some disorders of the brain, associated with diseases
  such as *syphilis* or with brain tumors. *Epilepsy* associated with the
  temporal lobes may sometimes be a cause. Anyone suffering from
  hallucinations for the first time, or when the cause is not well
  recognized and understood, is in urgent need of medical assessment and help.

Halos around lights may be seen by a person who has *glaucoma.*

Hangover

A term used to describe the collection of symptoms which include stomach irritation, dehydration, *nausea*, fatigue and *headache*. These are due to overindulgence in alcohol, and possibly also to lack of sleep. Treatment is directed toward the symptoms, which can usually be mitigated by rest, by aspirin or a substitute to relieve pain, by vitamin C tablets and by copious fluid replacement. The fluid should be non-alcoholic in nature.

Frequent hangovers are probably a sign of addiction to alcohol, and should warn the person that problem drinking and *alcoholism* are probably present.

Hard of hearing   See *deafness*.

Hard stools   See *constipation*.

Hay fever

A form of *allergic rhinitis* which is due to pollen allergy. It is usually associated with *atopy*.

Headache

This common symptom is associated with so many diseases and so many emotional states that it can present great diagnostic difficulties, even to experienced neurologists and physicians. In most cases headache is not a symptom of major importance, and any headache which responds to simple treatment with soluble aspirin or aspirin substitute, for example, is probably not of much significance.

Headache frequently accompanies the general feeling of being off color and unwell in such simple illnesses as the common cold. It may also be one of the many symptoms of an emotional illness. But it can sometimes be the first and only symptom of serious or grave disease. For this reason an accurate diagnostic assessment of headache is an important matter and must be performed carefully.

If a headache is one of many symptoms in any illness, the diagnosis of that illness will be easier if all the symptoms are assessed together with the headache. No two headaches are the same, but if previously the person has had similar headaches under similar conditions, the causes are also likely to be similar or related.

It is important to pay close attention to the character, location, time of occurrence and duration of the pain. Headaches may be constant, or may vary in intensity. They may also have peaks of pain without clear headache-free intervals between the pains. Certain actions may make the headache better or worse, and certain positions may increase or alleviate the pain. All these points must be considered in addition to the usual questions about whether the headache is part of a general illness, and whether the sufferer's temperature is raised or is normal.

A headache which persists or becomes worse in bed at night or which awakens a person suggests that the headache is related to a disease of the brain or its coverings, the meninges. Any headache which awakens a person should always be taken as an indication for an early visit to a physician.

LOCATION. Certain important features of well-defined types of headaches can be useful in diagnosing the causes. For example, headaches due to *migraine* are nearly always one-sided (left or right), and are sometimes confined to the back or the front half of that side of the head.

Headaches associated with *tumors, abscesses* and middle-ear disease will also tend to be localized on one or other side of the head. Frontal headaches are most often seen in association with frontal *sinusitis* or as an after-effect of malaria. Headaches associated with kidney disease are usually at the front or at the back of the head. These headaches also tend to occur in the morning.

TIME OF DAY may also give important clues. Morning headaches in kidney disease and headaches which awaken a person in the night due to serious brain or meningeal disease have already been mentioned. Morning headaches also occur in diseases of the nasal sinuses, because lying down permits retention of secretion in the sinuses and drainage is worse in that position. Morning headaches may also be due to stuffy bedrooms. Evening headaches are often the results of mental and emotional stress. They are an expression of a difficult day or an unhappy life situation and may often be associated with *eyestrain*. Headaches can further be divided into several main classes.

HEADACHE WITH FEVER AND/OR GENERAL ILLNESS. The causes may include: any feverish illness, such as a common cold, influenza, measles, gastroenteritis or *diarrhea/vomiting* type illnesses · typhoid fever, paratyphoid fever · malaria and other tropical illnesses · *abscesses* or septic illnesses which cause fever · *meningitis* · other general illnesses.

HEADACHE WITHOUT FEVER OR SYMPTOMS OF GENERAL ILLNESS

includes a number of major subdivisions: headache without fever or symptoms of general illness associated with diseases of the head and neck. The causes may include: diseases of the brain, such as an *abscess*, late *syphilis, cysts* or *tumors*, simple or malignant encephalitis from any cause and *multiple sclerosis* · diseases of affections of the blood vessels inside the skull, causing bleeding, *thrombosis, embolism, aneurysm* and *arteriosclerosis* · diseases of the meninges (without fever) such as *meningitis* and *cysts* or *tumors* which may simple or malignant · diseases or affections of the skull bones, for example, infection following *sinusitis* or mastoiditis, late *syphilis* and *cyst* or *tumours* which may be simple or malignant · diseases or injuries outside of the bony skull, such as rheumatism or neuritis in the muscles and nerves of the neck, *trigeminal neuralgia, herpes zoster, osteoarthritis* and *spondylitis* (disk lesions) of the neck · diseases of the eye, ear, nose and throat, for example *eyestrain,* iritis, *glaucoma* and *infection in the middle ear.*

Headache without fever or symptoms of general illness associated with diseases in the body elsewhere than the head and neck. The causes may include *uremia,* gout, *diabetes, high blood pressure,* low blood pressure and digestive disorders such as dyspepsia or "hunger headache." *Uremia* is a condition in which the blood urea is raised due to kidney failure. Headaches from this cause and from high blood pressure are probably the most important in this group. "Hunger headache," as its name suggests, can occur when a person does not eat at regular intervals or when he is hungry. Most sufferers can recognize the stages. "Hunger headaches" may be associated with a lowered blood glucose level (hypoglycemia).

The cure is simple and obvious—eat.

Headache without fever or symptoms of general illness related to emotional and other illness. The emotional and psychiatric causes may include emotional illness of all kinds: *anxiety* · mental strain and worry · disorders of sleep and exhaustion. Other causes of headache will include: *migraine* · *travel sickness* · menstruation · "*eyestrain*" · the after-effects of head injuries · sunstroke · *allergies.*

Headaches after head injuries. These headaches may occur after head injuries, particularly after injuries which cause loss of consciousness.

Head asymmetrical

See *asymmetry of head.*

Hearing loss See *deafness · noise induced hearing loss*.

Heart attack See *coronary thrombosis · angina pectoris*.

Heartbeat, irregular See *irregular heartbeat*.

Heartbeat, slow See *slow heartbeat*.

Heart block

A condition in which the electrical impulse that controls the contraction of the various parts of the heart fails to travel along the normal track. As a result, the atria and the ventricles of the heart do not contract in the usual ordered way—first the atria and then the ventricles. Instead, the ventricles contract very slowly, and usually only when they are full of blood. The ventricular rate, and therefore the pulse rate, may be as low as thirty beats per minute. As a result, the brain receives a deficient supply of oxygenated blood and *fainting* occurs. About three seconds of interruption of blood supply to the brain are all that is necessary to produce feelings of faintness, and about five seconds will lead to loss of consciousness. Heart block may be the result of *ischemic heart disease*. A pacemaker will usually remedy the condition.

Heartburn See *indigestion*.

Heart failure

Can cause symptoms of *difficulty in breathing* or *palpitations*. It may also be associated with *angina pectoris,* with *swelling of the ankles,* and with *high blood pressure*.

Heart, pain in See *angina pectoris · pain in the chest*.

Heat exhaustion

A condition caused by working in hot environments in which a serious loss of water and salts takes place.

Heatstroke

A serious emergency in which the body core temperature rises because heat regulation by the brain fails. The temperature should be measured at once, and if it is above about 102°F (39°C) urgent cooling is necessary.

Heberden's nodes See *osteoarthritis*.

Hematuria See *blood in the urine*.

Hemophilia

A sex-linked bleeding disorder which affects only males but is carried by females. In about one-quarter of hemophiliacs there is no family history of the disease. When bleeding occurs in hemophiliacs, it is difficult to stop, because the blood does not clot readily. For the same reason minor *trauma* can cause severe bleeding which is most often seen in and around joints. Serious and crippling disabilities can follow. Bleeding from anywhere can occur easily, and *blood in the urine* and melena are often noted. Any minor operation or tooth extraction can be a serious event in the life of a hemophiliac, but these traumas are now treated by the transfusion of specific blood fractions (cryoglobulins) which contain certain clotting fractions.

Hemorrhoids (piles)

Enlarged veins around the anus. External piles can be seen and felt below the anal sphincter. Internal piles may also occur above the sphincter. Hemorrhoids are a common cause of *bleeding from the rectum*. If the blood clots in an external pile, the thrombosed pile is usually painful, and is felt as a small *swelling at the anus*. Occasionally internal piles prolapse (come down) through the anal sphicter. This can be very painful.
Bleeding from the rectum should never be assumed to be due to piles, because a cancer of the rectum and hemorrhoids often occur together. Medical examination is always necessary when bleeding from the anus is a symptom. Hemorrhoids may be a cause of fecal *soiling*.

Hemothorax

A *pleural effusion* of blood or a pleural effusion containing blood.

Hernia

A protrusion of an organ or part of an organ out of the cavity which it normally occupies. Common sites for hernias from the abdomen are at the umbilicus (navel) in babies and around the umbilicus in elderly people, in the inguinal region in men and the femoral region in women, and through the diaphragm in both sexes.

UMBILICAL HERNIA, seen as a protrusion of the navel in babies, usually requires no treatment. It should disappear as the child grows. Those not gone by the time the child is 4 or 5, however, may require an operation.

PARA-UMBILICAL HERNIA, or hernia around the umbilicus, occurs in older people. A swelling or lump appears in the area. An operation may be desirable or necessary.

INGUINAL HERNIA ("rupture") is the common form of hernia in men. It produces a lump in the groin, and possibly in the scrotum as well. Inguinal hernia is also common in babies of both sexes, though more especially boys.

FEMORAL HERNIA is seen mainly in women and produces a lump low in the groin at the top of the thigh.

HERNIA THROUGH THE DIAPHRAGM INTO THE CHEST is found in both sexes.

A complication of any hernia can be the pinching of whatever has protruded. This may be complicated by twisting, thus cutting off blood supply of the parts involved, and by *intestinal obstruction*. An immediate operation may become necessary. See also *swellings in the groin and crotch area*.

Hernia through the diaphragm into the chest (hiatus or diaphragmatic hernia)

Associated with weakness at the point where the esophagus passes through the diaphragm. As a result of this weakness, the upper part of the stomach, or even all the stomach, can protrude into the chest cavity. When this occurs, the normal valve action at the lower end of the esophagus between it and the stomach is lost. The stomach contents, which are acid, can then leak into

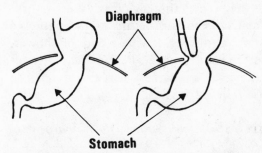

Two kinds of hernia through the diaphragm

the lower end or even further up the esophagus, and cause pain, which may be noticed especially if the person lies down, or bends

113

forward, or has a full stomach and slouches in a chair. In these positions a squirt of acid stomach contents can be shot into the esophagus, which does not have an acid-resistant lining. If this happens often, the lower end of the esophagus becomes permanently irritated, and perhaps scarred by the acid—a condition called *reflux esophagitis*. The pain of reflux esophagitis is usually felt to come from under the lower half of the sternum, often along the right edge of the bone. The pain is burning in character, and is temporarily relieved by alkaline medication.

Herpesvirus

A virus which, in one form, gives rise to cold spots or cold sores on the lips, and in another form causes *genital ulcers*. The genital ulcers are usually very painful, unlike those ulcers caused by *syphilis* or skin *cancer* in the genital area.

Herpes zoster (shingles)

Appears as a rash which affects small areas of the body. It is caused by the same virus that causes chicken pox. If the skin area affected includes the eye, herpes zoster of the cornea (ophthalmic herpes zoster) can occur. This is a serious problem, because the disease, in addition to affecting vision by causing cloudiness of the cornea, can also cause much pain in the eye.

The rash of shingles is blistery, beginning with small red blotches which become raised and form small blisters. The blisters may merge to form larger ones. As the rash fades, there may be destruction of the affected skin. Some people experience considerable pain after herpes zoster in the form of post-herpetic neuralgia. Sometimes the pain of herpes zoster appears about ten days before the rash, although twenty-four hours is more usual. An occasional clue to the nature of the pain is that it will be made worse by heat when having a bath or shower, or if attempts are made to relieve it by heat. Pain made worse by heat is in fact sufficiently unusual to suggest herpes zoster. The pain of most conditions is relieved by heat.

Hiatus hernia   See *hernia through the diaphragm into the chest*.

Hiccup (hiccough)

Can be a distressing symptom if it persists. Some cases of hiccupping may be due to heavy eating, to gas in the stomach or bowel, or even to excessive laughter. Other, less common causes can be described under two headings:

BRAIN IRRITATION arising from any condition which affects the brain, such as encephalitis · bleeding · *cysts* · *tumors* · diseases of the brain coverings such as *meningitis*. Illnesses with *fever* may also irritate the brain, and toxic conditions such as *uremia* due to kidney failure may lead to hiccupping. The causes of kidney failure must be sought—an *enlarged prostate* is a common reason in older men and acute nephritis is common in younger people.

IRRITATION OF THE PHRENIC NERVE OR DIAPHRAGM can arise from any pressure on the nerve along its course from the brain to the diaphragm. *Swelling of the lymph nodes* in the chest secondary to chest conditions such as pneumonia or tuberculosis, enlargement of the heart, or diseases which press on the diaphragm such as stomach and liver tumors may all give rise to hiccupping.

High or raised blood pressure

May be associated with *bleeding from the nose* · *headaches* · a *stroke* · kidney failure · *swelling of the ankles* · *obesity* · *blurred vision*. Sometimes it produces no symptoms at all, and is only found when the blood pressure is measured. Modern treatment has greatly improved the outlook in most common forms of raised blood pressure.

High pulse rate   See *fast heartbeat*.

Hirsutism   See *increased hair on the body*.

Hives   See *urticaria*

Hoarseness

Or alteration in the voice, is brought about by inability to move the vocal cords normally. This can result from shouting, singing or any over-use of the voice. Any generalized weakness can also result in voice changes. *Hypothyroidism* is a frequent cause of slight "gravelliness" in the voice.

Tonsillitis, laryngitis, *bronchitis* and other such respiratory infections are often accompanied by hoarseness because of in-infection of the vocal cords. Heavy smoking or the presence of foreign bodies in the larynx can cause hoarseness.

Ulcers of the larynx from *syphilis,* tuberculosis or *cancer* can also be responsible for hoarseness. Any interference with the nerves that supply the vocal cords can lead to altered movement of the cords. Virtually any disease of the nervous system or any pressure on the nerves in the neck from a *swelling in the neck* can cause hoarseness, *difficulty in speaking* or *loss of voice*.

For middle-aged or older people who suffer from hoarseness in the absence of obvious causes such as over-use of the voice or an obvious throat infection, and in whom hoarseness persists, there is the possibility of *cancer* in the larynx. An early visit to the doctor is therefore advisable.

Hodgkin's disease

Its common early symptoms are general tiredness, *itching of the skin,* and *swelling of lymph nodes*. The causes of the disease are not understood.

"Honeymoon cystitis"

Characterized by *frequency of urination* and by *pain on urination*. The urine and the bladder are not infected, and so the condition should not really be called "cystitis"—a term which should be reserved for infective and inflammatory disorders. The condition arises from *trauma* to the urethra during sexual intercourse. Sufferers from the condition should make sure the bladder is empty before intercourse, that lubrication is adequate to minimize trauma, and that the woman passes urine again immediately after intercourse.

Hormone sensitivity   See *cancer*.

Horner's syndrome

Due to pressure on the cervical sympathetic nerves on one side of the body resulting in *drooping of the eyelid,* with a small pupil

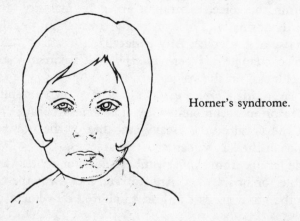

Horner's syndrome.

on the affected side (see *unequal pupils*). The causes of pressure on the cervical sympathetic nerves can include an *aneurysm of the aorta,* a bronchial *cancer* (lung cancer), any *swelling in the neck,* a *swelling in the thyroid* or pressure from a *cervical rib.*

Horny nail(s)

These develop in some people. The complaint is usually due to some disorder of the nail bed, but may follow an injury. If the nail cannot be cut and trimmed, it may have to be removed surgically together with the nail bed, so that it does not grow again.

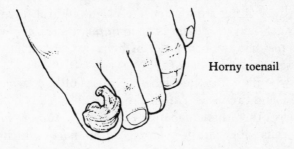

Horny toenail

Hot flashes   See *menopause.*

Hydatid cysts

Cysts formed by tapeworm larvae, and found in the intermediate host, usually sheep. Hydatid cysts occur in man mainly in the liver, lungs and muscles. The condition is spread by dogs harboring the tapeworm.

Hydrothorax   A clear *pleural effusion.*

Hypertension   See *high or raised blood pressure.*

Hyperthyroidism

The conditions in which too much thyroid hormone is secreted. This may be due to generalized disease of the thyroid gland (Graves' disease), or to a simple or malignant *tumour* of the gland which secretes too much of the hormone. Hyperthyroidism may therefore be associated with *a swelling in the neck* either in the midline or to one side of it and just above the top of the sternum (breastbone). There may also be *tremor, staring or protruding eyes* (exophthalmos) and a *fast heartbeat* associated with the hyperthyroidism.

Hypochondriasis

Could be defined as "enjoying bad health." The sufferer is determinedly ill, and always claims to suffer from the worst form of anything. Simple aches and pains are always taken to portend disaster. Reading this book may or may not help the condition.

Hypoglycemia

A low level of glucose in the blood, that is, a low blood sugar level. One cause is insulin overdose in a person suffering from *diabetes mellitus*. The individual may take too much insulin, or may miss a meal. The effect is the same—the blood glucose level falls, and the person may suffer from a sense of vague ill health, anxiety or panic, hunger and restlessness, *palpitations, excessive sweating, flushing of the face,* abnormalities of behavior, and finally loss of consciousness (*fainting*) or a *fit*.

In people who do not suffer diabetes, causes of hypoglycemia are lack of food, and tiredness. An uncommon cause is some disease of the pancreas other than diabetes, especially a tumor. Hypoglycemia can cause aberrant or even *violent behaviour* which may be mistaken for mental illness.

Hypothermia

A condition produced by chilling, which leads to a fall in the core temperature of the body. Fit adults can be affected by hypothermia when, for example, they are immersed in cold water, or in mountaineering when the weather is cold and inadequate clothing is worn. *Staggering, feeling cold,* confusion, disorientation and irrational actions may be the first signs of hypothermia. Babies and old people are easily affected by cold, and they may suffer from hypothermia if they are not in a warm environment. Loss of consciousness and death from chilling can occur. Hypothermia can cause a *slow heartbeat.*

Hypothyroidism (myxedema)

Due to lack of internal secretion from the thyroid gland in the neck. In infants this gives rise to cretinism. In adults the symptoms of hypothyroidism are lethargy · increasing tiredness · sensitivity to cold and *feeling cold · hoarseness · constipation ·* a general slowing of activity. *Depression, confusion,* impaired memory or *loss of memory,* slowness of comprehension, and puffiness or *swelling of the eyelids* and face may follow. The symptoms are usually slow and insidious in onset. Later, dry *scaly skin* and dull *brittle hair* are found. The condition responds well to treatment to replace the thyroid deficiency.

Hysteria

A form of mental illness in which emotional problems are converted into physical symptoms. It follows that in order to cure the disorder the underlying emotional problems must be examined, and the physical symptoms can be largely disregarded. The difficulty is to be sure of the diagnosis before discounting the symptoms. Expert help will be needed in every case of suspected hysteria because, without adequate assessment, mistakes can easily be made. For example, the early stages of *multiple sclerosis* may easily be mistaken for hysterical symptoms—and have been by doctors. Overbreathing in hysteria may cause *tetany*. *Loss of voice* is a common hysterical symptom.

Impetigo

An infectious disease of the skin which, in the early stages, produces a moist skin surface. The moist exudate dries into yellow crusts. The skin of the face is usually affected, but the condition can be found on other skin areas. It is very easily spread, but is usually simple to cure. It is common in children and young adults.

Impotence

The inability in a man to achieve an erection adequate for sexual intercourse. Impotence is thus usually accompanied by *inability to ejaculate*. Any severe disease, many drugs and some nervous diseases can lead to impotence.

The commonest reasons by far for impotence are, however, psychological. If a man can get an erection at such moments as first thing in the morning, or on masturbating, or at any other time, then physical disease is unlikely to be related to his difficulty. Shakespeare's porter in Macbeth knew about the effects of alcohol when he said "drink provides the desire, but it takes away the performance." Impotence often leads to anxiety and the anxiety to subsequent failure to get an erection. *Premature ejaculation* is sometimes a preliminary to impotence.

Inability to ejaculate

May be a part of *impotence*. Assuming that there is no impotence, that is, that sexual excitement can produce a normal erection, then the commonest reason for failure to ejaculate will be a psychological one. If ejaculation is normal with other partners, in dreams, and by masturbation, then there is no physical trouble. Some drugs, especially those used to treat high blood pressure, can lead to failure to ejaculate. *Diabetes,* some abdominal diseases which can affect the blood vessels and nerves, abdominal operations and operations for removal of the prostate in whole or in part, can all lead to ejaculatory failure. If none of these physical causes is present, the origins will probably be psychological.

Inability to urinate

This disorder is known in medical language as "acute retention of urine." It does not include the problem of the person who will not urinate because of *pain on urination*.

The inability to urinate is common in middle-aged and older men because of *enlargement of the prostate*. Other causes of inability to urinate include: injury to the urethra or bladder · diseases of or injury to the nervous system resulting in loss of the control mechanism of the act of urination (for example *multiple sclerosis*) · narrowing of the urethra by a stricture or blocking of the urethra by a *tumour* or by *gravel or stones in the urine*. See also *weak or poor stream when urinating*.

Increased hair on the body (hirsutism)

Some people and families tend to be hairier than others. Such a tendency is perfectly healthy and normal. An increase of body hair at puberty is also to be expected.

In women, any excess of hair is often regarded as undesirable and disfiguring. Many women will acquire some facial hair and a small mustache as they get older. In some parts of the world this is thought to be a desirable attribute. An excess of hair in women, especially in areas where hair normally grows in males, may be hormone-induced in such normal states as pregnancy, or may be the result of an abnormal condition such as imbalance of the glands producing the hormones or by *tumors* of these glands. Any woman who notices abnormal hairiness developing should consult her physician, so that any endocrine imbalance can be investigated. The causes may be found in the posterior part of the pituitary gland, in the thyroid, in the adrenal glands, and in the ovary. *Anorexia nervosa* is an occasional cause of hairiness.

Indigestion

A vague term for *pain in the abdomen* which may be associated with eating too much or eating unwisely. It can be caused by a *hernia through the diaphragm* · a *peptic ulcer* · *cholecystitis (infection of the gallbladder)* · *gas in the bowel or stomach* · and many of the other causes of pain in the abdomen. "Indigestion" may be *angina pectoris* from *ischemic heart disease.*

Infected gums (gingivitis)

Gums that are soft and bleed easily. A toothbrush may be found to have blood on it after brushing the teeth. Gentle pressure on the gums between the teeth may demonstrate the ease with which bleeding can occur. Some pus may also be seen. This condition can easily give rise to *bad breath* (halitosis). The condition will require treatment by the dentist.

Infected sputum

Usually results from recent or old (chronic) infection in the lungs. It may be associated with *spitting of blood.* Any acute throat or chest infection may give rise to it, but in these cases the reason for the condition will usually be obvious. Chronic chest infections as seen in *chronic bronchitis,* and especially *bronchiectasis,* can produce infected sputum. Other lung diseases, such as tuberculosis or bronchial *cancer* (lung cancer), can be associated with the complaint. Infected sputum will be a cause of *bad breath.*

Infection in the bladder

Can give rise to *pain on urination,* to *frequency of urination* and sometimes to *blood in the urine.* Infected urine will usually look turbid when passed into a clear glass.

Some urinary infections are accompanied by general upset and a *fever.* The patient feels generally unwell, and may have symptoms which arise from fever, such as shivering, feeling cold, aches all over and loss of appetite.

Infection in the middle ear

Causes pain and deafness, and often begins after a cold, sinusitis, tonsillitis or a *sore throat.* The infection travels up the eustachian tube, which connects the middle ear to the back of the throat.

When the eustachian tube is blocked, infection is trapped in the middle ear. The pressure rises, and if the eustachian tube does not open and drain the infection, it bursts through and perforates the eardrum. Before the eardrum perforates, the sufferer feels a dull, throbbing earache, which becomes increasingly painful. He may feel quite ill, and have *fever*. Moving the external ear up and down does not usually affect this middle ear pain, but will make an *infection in the outer ear,* such as a boil or an *abcess,* much more painful. The pain in the ear and side of the head continues for as long as the infection lasts. When the eardrum bursts, there is often some *bleeding from the ear passage* and bloodstained pus is found emerging. This *discharge from the ear* is usually accompanied by relief of the throbbing pain.

Occasionally the pus in the middle ear will spill over into the mastoid air cells before the drum perforates. This causes infection in the mastoid, which today is fortunately an unusual complication, for antibiotics can be given to children at the first sign of ear trouble. It is extremely important that any child who has an earache, especially a throbbing earache with deafness, general upset and a rise in body temperature, should see a doctor immediately.

Infection in the outer ear

A boil or *abscess* in the outer ear can cause considerable pain—often far out of proportion to the real severity of the condition. The reason is that all septic conditions usually result in swelling. In most situations, the swelling can occur outward without limit, but the skin of the ear passage lines the inside of a hard bony tube in the skull, and only limited swelling can take place without a considerable rise in pressure. This increase in pressure causes pain, usually of a dull throbbing character. If the external ear is pulled or tweaked, considerable pain will be felt. This is unlike *infection in the middle ear,* where moving the auricle seldom produces any increase or change in pain. Some ear passage infections are not localized like a boil, but are surface infections of the whole of the skin of the ear passage. Such infections usually cause *discharge from the ear* without pain.

Infection in the urethra

May be secondary to a *bladder infection* or be a *sexually transmitted disease* and associated with a *urethral discharge. Pain on urination* is a common symptom.

122

Infection of the gallbladder (cholecystitis)

Can cause *pain in the abdomen* in the right upper quarter. Infection in the gallbladder may be associated with a raised body temperature · *nausea* and/or *vomiting* · *indigestion* · *gallstones* · *biliary colic*. Fatty foods are particularly likely to cause symptoms of indigestion. *Pain in the shoulder* (right) may be felt. Th'is is *referred pain*. See also *biliary colic*.

Infectious hepatitis

A disease of the liver which can occur in epidemics. It ɾffects mainly children and young adults, and gives rise to *jaundice, fever* and general symptoms of being unwell. *Nausea, vomiting* and *diarrhea* may all appear in the early stage of the disease, about three to four days before the jaundice is seen. General lymph node enlargement may also be found in the early stages of the disease.

Many cases of infectious hepatitis occur in drug addicts who inject themselves. Alcohol should be avoided for a year after an attack of infectious hepatitis, so as not to damage the liver further.

Another form of infectious hepatitis may occur in persons receiving blood transfusions from donors who may have infectious hepatitis. Modern blood-bank techniques usually screen out "infected" blood, but persons who are recipients of multiple transfusions or who are undergoing hemodialysis are in some risk of acquiring hepatitis.

Infectious mononucleosis   See *mononucleosis.*

Infective arthritis   See *septic arthritis.*

Infertility

Failure to conceive. Normally fertile sexually active couples will, in the absence of contraception, usually conceive within six months. If conception is desired and does not occur by nine to twelve months, advice should be sought. Both partners should be examined. A common cause of infertility in a man is a low sperm count. In a woman, blockage of the fallopian tubes following infection may prevent the ovum and sperm meeting. Careful medical examination of both partners is always necessary if infertility is a problem. Sometimes no apparent reasons can be found for infertility, even after careful examination.

Ingrown toenail

Produces pain in the toe, and may cause an infected toe or a small *abscess* where the nail digs in. The nails should be allowed to grow to the tip of the toe, and should then be cut straight across, not on a curve like fingernails. This will prevent the nail from digging in. In cases where the nail is very troublesome, a small wedge of nail or the whole nail may have to be removed before the condition can be corrected.

Inguinal hernia   See *hernia*.

Insatiable appetite   See *excessive appetite*.

Insomnia   See *disorders of sleep*.

Intermittent claudication   See *pain in the leg*.

Intertrigo

The name given to a redness where two skin surfaces meet and rub. It is commonly found under the breasts and in the buttock and genital areas. Obesity increases the possibility of the condition, because in fat people greater areas of skin will tend to be in contact. Intertrigo may be associated with candidiasis or with epidermophytoisis (*fungus infections of the skin*).

Intestinal obstruction

Occurs when intestinal contents cannot pass freely from mouth through to the anus. Obstruction can be caused by *hernia* with strangulation of bowel · losses of blood supply to the bowel · rotation of bowel on itself (volvulus) · adhesions following operations · *cancers* or other *tumors* of the bowel · fecal or food bolus impaction · *diverticular disease* · intussusception (see *mucus in the stools*).

When the bowel is obstructed, the symptoms include: *vomiting* (often severe and resulting in dehydration) · *abdominal pain,* which is usually *colic* · abdominal distension because of *gas in the bowel*. If the cause of obstruction is solid, such as a *cancer* or other *tumor,* this may be felt in the abdomen.

Intestinal obstruction is a serious condition, which can easily result in dehydration, and which usually needs surgery to correct it.

Intolerance of light   See *photophobia.*

Inverted nipple

May be a normal condition in some women, and may possibly lead to difficulties with breast-feeding. A nipple which was previously normal and which becomes inverted may be a sign of breast *cancer,* so any *swelling or lump in the breast* or nipple, or *discharge from the nipple,* should be noted. An early visit to the doctor is therefore advisable.

Irregular hearbeat

In young people the heart rate normally speeds up on breathing in and slows on breathing out. This variation in heart rate occurs in all healthy young people, and does not indicate trouble of any kind.

Irregularities of heartbeat or pulse can be described in two main ways—regular irregularities and irregular irregularities.

Regular irregularities are usually associated with "dropped beats".

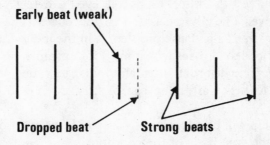

Dropped beats will occur at irregular intervals, but every second heartbeat will be regular, even if dropped beats occur after every normal beat.

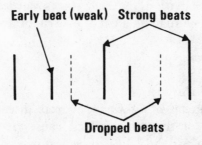

This condition can occur when the heart rate slows. If exercise is taken and the heart rate increases, the condition disappears.

An irregularly irregular heartbeat is usually associated with atrial flutter and atrial fibrillation, in which the rhythms of the atria (the receiving chambers) and the ventricles (the pumping chambers) are out of phase. This can occur commonly as a result of rheumatic heart disease, *coronary thrombosis* and *thyrotoxicosis*.

Irregular menstruation See *metrorrhagia*.

Irregular pulse See *irregular heartbeat*.

Irregular pupils See *unequal pupils · coloboma*.

Irritable bowel syndrome
A common cause of abdominal symptoms known in the past by a variety of titles: spastic colitis, spastic colon, mucus colitis, nervous diarrhea and irritable colon. The findings in this condition are always the same: the person suffers from stressful situations which affect the bowel, giving symptoms of *diarrhea, pain in the abdomen,* and sometimes *mucus in the stools.*
Medical investigation of the bowel, even if extensive, will always be negative. The disease is felt in the bowel, which is a target organ for *stress.* The basic problem is in the individual personality and reactions to stresses which may, for example, be social, family or sexual. The disorder is usually found in young women, and is unlikely to begin after the age of fifty. Men also can have the disorder.
Skilled help will be necessary to deal with the emotional problems that are the true basis of the condition.

Irritability
Can commonly arise from *tiredness, anxiety, hyperthyroidism* and mental stress. *Meningitis* in the early stages may lead to irritability. *Premenstrual tension* may be a cause of irritability in women.

Irritation See *itching*.

Irritation around the vulva
May arise from a *vaginal discharge,* or from diseases affecting the skin in the area of the vulva which cause *itching of the skin. Candidosis, pediculosis* and *diabetes mellitus* are common causes.
Irritation around the vulva may also be caused by wearing underwear that is too tight or made of nonabsorbent material. Cotton is generally the best and most comfortable material. Vaginal

deodorants and sprays can cause irritation. A daily shower or bath with soap and water is normally adequate for freshness and cleanliness.

Ischemia

The medical word for lack of blood supply to a part of the body. It may be due to narrowing of arteries in diseases like *arteriosclerosis* or *diabetes mellitus,* or may be due to *embolism* or *thrombosis.*

Ischemic heart disease

Occurs when the blood supply to the heart muscle is cut down or cut off as a result of a *coronary thrombosis.* Cutting down the blood supply slowly leads to *angina pectoris* or pain on exertion. Cigarette smoking causes an incidence of ischemic heart disease two or three times higher than normal.

Itching around the anus

Possible causes include: pinworms · fecal *soiling* for any reason · urinary incontinence · *intertrigo* · *sexually transmitted diseases* · *pediculosis* · *scabies.*

Itching of the skin around the anus is common in children, and is often due to infestation of the lower bowel with pinworms. Adults may also suffer from these tiny worms, and the whole family should be treated if pinworms are found in any member. Fecal soiling occurs in adults in association with any condition that may prevent the anal sphincter muscle from shutting securely and tightly. *Hemorrhoids* (piles) often prevent proper closure of the anal sphincter by hanging through the ring. In old people the muscle strength may be weak, and soiling can occur, especially on coughing, laughing or passing wind flatus (gas). Young children without control of their bowel and bladder will have fecal and urinary soiling. This causes the well known *diaper rash.* Illnesses associated with *diarrhea* can also give rise to fecal soiling, and thus to itching and discomfort around the anus.

Itching of the skin (puritus)

Can occur over all areas as generalized itching, or in limited areas, with or without other signs of skin disease.

The possible causes of generalized itching can include some systemic disorders, such as *leukemia* and *Hodgkin's disease* · *jaundice* · *cancer* (especially after secondary spread) · *uremia* ·

pregnancy · childhood infections (for example, chicken pox and German measles · parasitic infestation of the skin, such as *scabies* and *pediculosis* · *allergies, eczema* and *urticaria* · emotional disorders · dry *scaly skin* · *diabetes* · *lichen planus.*

Itching may also occur in certain locations, such as around the anus and around the vulva and vagina. *Irritation around the vulva* and *vaginal irritation* may be associated with other diseases in these areas, particularly with causes of *vaginal discharge* such as *vaginal candidosis* (thrush) and *trichomoniasis. Diabetes* and *pediculosis* may also give rise to itching of the skin or irritation in the genital area. (See also *itching around the anus.*) *Fungus infection of the skin* is a common cause of itching in the affected area(s), often between the toes. *Chilblains* can also cause itching.

Itchy eyes

Often associated with *allergic rhinitis,* are probably a part of the same allergy. *Conjunctivitis* may also lead to itchy eyes, usually with some discharge causing a "sticky eye" as well.

Itchy vulva

See *irritation around the vulva* · *itching of the skin* ·

Jaundice

A yellow coloring of the skin and eyes. It is associated with diseases of the liver, gallbladder, bile ducts, and certain blood diseases.

In the early stages of jaundice, the yellow color may be difficult to detect in the skin. However, a look at the eyes may show *yellowness of the eyes* in the part which is normally white. This yellow color is best seen in daylight, but may be very difficult or even impossible to detect in certain colors of artificial light, especially under fluorescent lighting. There is also usually alteration in the color of the urine, which becomes a darker, stronger yellow. The bowel movements may also alter in color in certain kinds of jaundice, becoming a dirty-white or clay color. The yellowness characteristic of jaundice is ultimately derived from the red pigment called hemoglobin present in red blood cells. Some of the yellow color from broken-down red blood cells is excreted by the kidneys, producing yellow urine; some of it is processed in the liver and excreted as green colored bile, which is ultimately responsible for the normal brown color of stools.

Accumulation of yellowness giving rise to jaundice can occur in a number of ways:

Blood cells may be broken down too quickly for the pigment to be disposed of—a case of over-production · an obstruction in the outflow of bile is present, and the normal amount of yellow pigment formed is retained in the body since it cannot go through the liver, gallbladder and bile ducts into the intestines · the liver is diseased, and cannot make bile. Diseases which may give rise to jaundice include infectious hepatitis and cancer · the liver is poisoned and cannot make bile. Alcohol is by far the commonest liver poison.

BLOOD DISEASES. Jaundice of the newborn is the form of jaundice occurring in four-day-old babies. The excess red cells which were necessary before birth are being destroyed, and the liver enzymes are not mature enough to dispose of the pigment. It is a hemolytic jaundice—the pigment is derived from breakdown of red blood cells. Small degrees of jaundice can occur in healthy babies; severe jaundice occurs where there is major blood group incompatibility between mother and baby. Certain kinds of *anemia* and blood diseases such as *leukemia* may also be associated with jaundice.

CONDITIONS STOPPING THE OUTFLOW OF BILE. *Gallstones* or liver parasites which block the bile ducts can stop bile outflow. Gallstones are a very common cause of jaundice in middle-aged people, especially women. Liver parasites are common in certain parts of the world. *Infection of the gallbladder* (cholecystitis) and bile ducts can lead to jaundice by giving rise to obstructed outflow of bile from the liver. *Fever* and a general feeling of being unwell will usually be symptoms of such infections. Cholecystitis can lead to pain in the right upper abdomen, and occasionally to right shoulder tip pain as well. Conditions which obstruct the outflow of bile by pressure from the outside of the bile ducts include *abscesses, cysts, tumours* and *cancers* in that area. A common cause of obstructed outflow in older people is cancer of the head of the pancreas.

DISEASES AFFECTING THE LIVER include: *infectious hepatitis* · Weil's disease (or leptospirosis) · *mononucleosis* · malaria, yellow fever and various tropical fevers. Weil's disease is a feverish illness usually found in people such as farmers and sewer workers who may come in contact with a rat-infested environment, because the disease is spread by the urine of infected rats. Tropical diseases associated with jaundice will be most readily recognized by their geographical distribution and other such features. Mononucleosis causes *swelling of the lymph nodes* and is associated with a *sore throat* and *fever*.

POISONS AFFECTING THE LIVER include many toxic substances found in certain industries and some drugs, for example Paracetamol. However, by far the commonest is alcohol.

Jaw, clicking See *clicking in joints.*

Jerks, involuntary See *fits · tremor.*

Keyhole-shaped pupil See *coloboma.*

Knee, cartilage injury of See *displaced or torn knee cartilage.*

Knee, clicking See *displaced or torn knee cartilage · clicking in joints.*

Knee, locking See *displaced or torn knee cartilage.*

Knee pain See *pain in the knee.*

Knee swelling See *swelling of the knee joint.*

Knock-out See *concussion.*

Kyphosis A backward *curvature of the spine.*

Lack of sensation See *loss of feeling.*

Large stools See *constipation.*

Lassitude See *tiredness.*

Leaking of urine See *urine leaking and stress incontinence.*

Leg, bowing See *bow legs.*

Leg ulcer See *ulcer of the leg.*

Leukemia

A disease in which blood is not formed properly and immature blood cells can appear in the circulating blood. The disease can be likened to a *cancer* of the blood-forming tissue in the bone marrow. The onset can be sudden or slow.

The symptoms of leukemia can be general ones such as *tiredness* and weakness, or *swelling of the lymph nodes*. Local symptoms arise from bleeding, often seen as *bleeding under the skin*. Bleeding from almost anywhere however can occur. This bleeding is due to lack of blood platelets, which are active in blood clotting. *Anemia* often accompanies leukemia.

See also *blood in the urine · bleeding from the vagina · bleeding from the mouth · bleeding from the nose · bleeding under the skin.*

Leukoplakia

A condition found in older people which causes *white patches on the tongue* or *white patches on the vulva and vagina*. It is often a precancerous (premalignant) condition.

Lichen planus

A skin disorder which may be accompanied by severe *itching of the skin*. The skin shows small lilac-colored spots, which may become silvery on top. The inside of the mouth is often affected before the skin. Inside the cheek will be seen white lines and patches, and there usually will be *white patches on the tongue*.

Limb pains

See *pain in the elbow · pain in the joints · pain in the leg · pain in the shoulder · pain in the wrist.*

Limited movement at a joint

May follow *trauma* which causes a *fracture, dislocation* or *swelling in joints*. The limited movement may be due to *pain in the joint*. (See also under the name of the joint.)

Limping

Can be due to any painful condition from the toe to the hip and lower back. The causes of the painful condition must be sought. These can include such diverse causes as a thorn in the foot with small *abscess ·* any disease of joints which causes *pain in joints · sciatica* and disk trouble · any of the conditions which cause *pain in the hip, pain in the leg* or *swelling in joints*.

Limping can also be associated with a *stroke, paralysis* or weakness of the muscles in the leg arising from disease.

Any person who has a limp that does not have an obvious cause, especially if the person is a child or young adult, should always be seen by a doctor within a few days. *Hysteria* is an occasional cause of limping.

In children limping may be due to a congenital dislocation of the hip, to Perthe's disease, which affects the cartilage in the hip, to traumatic synovitis or to infection in the hip joint in the form of a *septic arthritis*.

Lips, cracked   See *cracked lips.*

Lips, spots on   See *spots on the lips.*

Lips, ulcers on   See *ulcers on the lips.*

Locking of the knee   See *displaced or torn knee cartilage.*

Lockjaw   See *tetanus.*

Lordosis   A forward *curvature of the spine.*

Loss of appetite

Appetite usually diminishes with age. A healthy active fourteen-year-old boy will probably eat about a third to a half as much again as his father. At around thirty-five to forty-five years of age most people must cut back on the amount of energy-giving carbohydrate food which they eat in order not to become obese. True loss of appetite occurs as a temporary phenomenon in many illnesses such as a cold, influenza and *tonsillitis,* which are associated with *fever,* and in illnesses associated with *diarrhea* and vomiting. However, as these conditions improve, appetite is regained.

Many forms of "stomach trouble," such as gastric and duodenal ulcers (*peptic ulcers*), *hiatus hernias* and gastric *cancers,* will however lead to a genuine and often to a sustained loss of appetite. Tuberculosis may also be associated with appetite suppression. *Anorexia nervosa* is a condition of young women in which appetite suppression is very marked.

Loss of consciousness   See *fainting.*

Loss of eyebrows

Loss of the hair of the outer thirds of both eyebrows is found in *hypothyroidism* (myxedema). Hair loss is also found on the forehead and the back of the neck in many cases of hypothyroidism. The skin tends to be dry and rather rough. The condition is commonest in women after middle age. Loss of all the hair in the eyebrows may be associated with *loss of hair* over all the body in a condition called alopecia totalis.

Loss of eyelashes

Usually found in association with total *loss of hair,* or with scaliness and red eyelids accompanied by *scaly skin* and *seborrheic dermatitis.*

Loss of feeling (anesthesia)

May or may not be accompanied by loss of movement, or *paralysis.* Loss of feeling in any part of the body may be due to cold or to a lesion in the brain or in the spinal cord or nerve that goes to that area. Medical help will always be needed to diagnose the reason for any loss of feeling or paralysis.

Loss of hair

There are three main categories of hair loss.

HAIR FOLLICLES CEASING TO PRODUCE HAIR. Loss of hair all over the body, which can progress to total hair loss, is called alopecia totalis. Loss of head hair occurring with age is the commonest cause of baldness in men. The condition begins at the front of the head, with thinning and hair recession at each side. The crown area then thins and goes bald, and finally a rim of hair may be all that remains. Medical treatment or lotions have no effect on the condition, and are a waste of time and money. Loss of most or all hair in extreme old age can occur in both sexes.

SECONDARY TO SOME OTHER DISEASE OR INJURY. Hair loss can occur after slight burns, injuries or permanent-waving improperly carried out · as a result of hair pulling in children and in disturbed adults · in secondary *syphilis.*

These losses should be temporary. Permanent loss of hair may occur in any disease process or injury which destroys hair follicles. Examples of this are severe burns · *boils* or *carbuncles* · x-ray burns · late *syphilis.*

ALOPECIA AREATA. In this condition, normally only temporary, the hair falls out rapidly leaving circular patches which may coalesce. The pattern is characteristic and the edges are always circular, or formed by the meeting of several circles. The bald patches usually begin around the back of the neck and head. The patches will usually disappear and the hair regrow. White hair will usually appear first. In most cases this is eventually followed by hair of normal color. Sometimes the hair of the whole body may be lost permanently.

See also *loss of eyebrows · loss of eyelashes*.

Loss of memory

The remembering of any event depends, first, on attention which focuses the mind on the event, second, on the integrity of the brain itself in the areas in which memories are stored, and third, on the ability or will to recall the stored material to consciousness. *Tiredness, mental illness,* general illnesses such as *hypothyroidism,* drugs such as alcohol or tranquilizers, and head injuries can suppress all these three parts of memory.

In old people, the memory loss generally concerns recent events; events of childhood being recalled in great detail. This condition is usually related to the diminished blood supply resulting from *arteriosclerosis,* which reduces functioning of parts or all of the brain.

Certain brain diseases may attack or damage those regions of the brain concerned with memory. Examples in this category are: *meningitis · encephalitis · tetany · syphilis · cerebral malaria · tumors.* Head injury with brain damage may also lead to loss of memory. Any injury which causes *concussion* and loss of consciousness may cause impairment of memory. *Epilepsy*—even minor epilepsy with little obvious evidence of a fit—will usually result in some loss of memory both before and after the seizure. Loss of memory can also be a symptom of *anxiety* or other mental illness and emotional disturbance. The person found wandering about with a total loss of memory is usually suffering from some form of mental illness.

Loss of movement   See *paralysis*.

Loss of sensation   See *loss of feeling*.

Loss of sense of smell

Temporary loss of the sense of smell may be noted in conditions that cause blockage of the nose, such as colds, nasal polyps, a deflected nasal septum, hay fever or other *allergic rhinitis.* If the nose is very dry the sense of smell may not work properly. The olfactory nerve and the region of the brain that deals with the sensation of smell may be injured—for example after a fractured skull—or may suffer from a disease of the brain such as late *syphilis* or a *tumor,* or from a disease of the brain coverings such as *meningitis.* These may cause permanent loss of the sense of smell.

Loss of smell is an occasional possibility in *hysteria.*

When the sense of smell is lost, the complaint may be that there is *loss of sense of taste,* because a good deal of the taste of food in fact arises from its smell.

Loss of sense of taste

Much of what we consider the taste of food and drink is in fact due to aroma. In speaking of loss of sense of taste we should be quite sure that there is no *loss of sense of smell,* because, if this is lost, nothing will "taste" as much. Assuming that sense of smell is functioning normally, loss of sense of taste could be due, among other causes, to a coated tongue · glossitis · any mouth infection · conditions affecting the nerves that convey taste sensation to the brain · Bell's palsy, or facial paralysis · any affection of the brain areas that receive the messages about taste.

Hallucinations of taste may be found in association with causes of loss of taste in the brain.

Loss of taste is also an occasional possibility in *hysteria,* and similar mental disorders.

Loss of vision   See *blindness · detachment of the retina.*

Loss of voice

May be due to overuse of the voice · severe infections of the throat · paralysis of the nerves which lead to the vocal cords · tumors and cancers of the throat and larynx · severe swelling in the larynx following insect stings, burns, inhalation of noxious substances or *angio-neurotic edema.*

Loss of voice is common in *hysteria.* See also *hoarseness · difficulty in speaking.*

Loss of weight

Assuming that any loss of weight is not deliberately induced by dieting, the commonest reasons for unexplained weight loss in adults are pulmonary tuberculosis · *diabetes mellitus* · *cancers* or other *tumours* · *depression.*

Less common causes are *cirrhosis of the liver* from *alcoholism* or other causes · *hyperthyroidism* · prolonged *anxiety* · *anemia* · *anorexia nervosa* (a disease of young women). Any unexplained weight loss should always be a cause for concern.

In children the common causes of weight loss are insufficient dietary intake (malnutrition) · injudicious feeding · any illness with *diarrhea* and *vomiting* · gastroenteritis · tuberculosis.

Loud rumbling bowel sounds

Will be found in *intestinal obstruction,* when they will be accompanied by severe *colic* and by abdominal distension from gas. *Diarrhea* and colic may also be associated with them.

Low pulse rate See *slow heartbeat.*

Lumbago See *backache.*

Lump See *swelling,* and the parts of the body concerned.

Lump in the throat

See *difficulty in swallowing* · *swelling in the neck.*

Lying very still with abdomenal pain

Usually associated with a perforated *peptic ulcer.* See also *pain in the abdomen.*

Lymphangitis See *red lines in the skin.*

Malignant disease See *cancer.*

Malignant melanoma See *melanoma* · *cancer.*

Malignant tumor See *cancer.*

Mallet finger

The inability to straighten out the finger tip from the last joint. It is due to an injury to the tendon or to a fracture of one of the terminal phalanges. Treatment to restore the finger to the full straight position in most cases can only be carried out if the condition is diagnosed immediately.

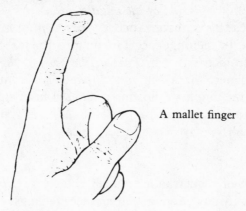

A mallet finger

Marfan's syndrome   See *aneurysm*.

Meatal ulcer
A small ulcer at the end of the penis found usually in baby boys. It gives rise to sharp *pain on urination* when the urine meets the ulcer may follow circumcision. A meatal stricture (narrowing of careful look at the end of the penis with slight gentle opening of the orifice will show whether or not an ulcer is present. A meatal ulcer may follow circumcision. A meatal stricture (narrowing of the meatus) may follow a meatal ulcer.

Melanoma
A melanotic (dark-brown pigmented) *tumor*. Many are highly malignant. Common sites for malignant melanomas are the skin of the leg, and the eye. Any brown spot which appears and grows should always be seen soon by a doctor. See *cancer*.

Memory, impaired or lost   See *loss of memory*.

Meniere's disease or syndrome
Characterized by *dizziness, tinnitus* (ringing in the ears) and progressive *deafness*. Medical help should always be sought within a few days if this condition is suspected.

Meningitis
Inflammation or infection of the meninges, the wrapping and

covering layers of the brain. Meningitis is serious, because it causes upset of brain function. It is usually an infectious illness, and the infection may spread locally from an *abscess* on the face or head or from a *infection of the middle ear*.

Systemic spread of infection occurs in mumps, in septicemia, and in *syphilis*. In meningococeal meningitis the infection spreads systemically from the throat. *Pain in the back of the neck, a stiff neck, fever,* general irritability and *photophobia* may be early symptoms of meningitis, following a *sore throat* or upper respiratory infection. A *rash* may be present. *Fits and convulsions* and *loss of consciousness* may occur in severe cases.

Menopause

The cessation of menstruation which usually occurs in middle-aged women. Many women experience feelings of emotional instability, and may suffer from many vague and general complaints such as *headache,* irritability, tension, frustration and *insomnia.* Hot flashes are a common symptom. These are brief periods of *flushing* when the skin, especially of the head and neck, becomes red. There may also be generalized sweating. Small doses of estrogens and mild tranquilizers will usually help to overcome the symptoms of the menopause. However, the value of long term estrogen replacement is not completely proven at present and is believed by some medical authorities to be cancer-producing.

Menorrhagia

Excessive menstrual periods. It is often associated with *metrorrhagia,* irregular menstruation. Menorrhagia may be accompanied by conditions of the uterus including *tumors,* and by general bleeding disorders. The commonest cause of excessive and/or irregular periods is, however, related to the hormone control of the menstrual cycle. Diagnostic curettage, taking a scraping from inside the uterus to examine microscopically, may be necessary.

Menstrual tension   See *premenstrual tension.*

Menstruation, absent   See *amenorrhea.*

Menstruation, excessive   See *menorrhagia.*

Menstruation, infrequent   See *metrorrhagia.*

Menstruation, irregular See *metrorrhagia*.

Menstruation, painful See *dysmenorrhea*.

Mental illness See *psychological illness*.

Metastases See *cancer*.

Metrorrhagia
Irregular menstruation. This is usually associated with *menorrhagia* (excessive menstruation). The subject is discussed more fully under *menorrhagia*.

Micturition The act of urination.

"Middle-age spread" See *obesity*.

Middle ear infection See *infection in the middle ear*.

Migraine
A particular type of headache which is usually one-sided, and is sometimes preceded by visual disturbances and by *numbness of the face* and tongue. Migraine may be accompanied by *photophobia, blurred vision, double vision* and *vomiting*. Between attacks the person is in good health. Migraine is commoner in women than in men. In some women the migraine is related to menstruation. The disorder is a familial one—about three quarters of those who suffer have a relative or relatives who suffer from migraine. Migraine may also be associated with *atopy* and *allergies*.

Miscarriage
An *abortion*. The term miscarriage is generally used to describe a spontaneous abortion. Most occur at about the end of the third month of intra-uterine life, counted from the first day of the last menstrual period.

Missed heartbeat See *irregular heartbeat*.

Missed menstrual period See *amenorrhea*.

Misty vision See *blurred vision · double vision*.

Mittelschmerz

(German for "middle pain," that is, pain in the middle of the menstrual cycle) is *pain in the abdomen* in the lower part and to one side or other of the midline which is associated with *ovulation*. It occurs about fourteen days before the predicted date of the next menstrual period, and is thought to be due to the very slight bleeding which occurs when the ovum frees itself from the ovary.

Moles   See *birthmarks · disorders of pigmentation.*

Mononucleosis

An infectious illness which usually begins with a *sore throat, fever* and *swelling of the lymph nodes* (it is also called glandular fever). It generally occurs in adolescence or early adult life. The throat may be red and in some cases is covered by a yellowish-white exudate. The lymph nodes are enlarged and usually tender. A skin *rash* is sometimes present. Mononucleosis can only be diagnosed with certainty by laboratory tests. The illness may last for up to about two months, and the person may feel very tired and lethargic during this period—occasionally for a longer time.

Morning sickness

Found in early pregnancy. The woman suffers from *nausea* and perhaps *vomiting* too. As the name suggests, the condition occurs in the morning, and gets better as the day progresses. The length of time since the last menstrual period should always be checked in morning sickness. If the menstrual period is overdue, then pregnancy is likely to be the reason.

Motion sickness

A condition characterized by *nausea* in the early stages. This is followed by *vomiting,* and later may even go on to general prostration from vomiting and *headache*. It is caused by disorder of the balance mechanism due to traveling by ship, automobile or airplane, or to fairground amusements and the like. *Nystagmus* may be noted in sufferers. The condition will usually disappear fairly rapidly when the cause is removed. Travel sickness remedies taken in advance will often help to prevent the condition. When symptoms are well established removal from the situation is the best course to follow if this can be done. Medical treatment may also help.

Mouth breathing

Usually due to a *blocked nose,* but may be a matter of habit after a blocked nose has cleared up. In children enlarged adenoids are the commonest cause of mouth breathing. The remedy is usually to deal with whatever is causing the blocked nose.

Movement, loss of   See *paralysis.*

Movement of the bowel   See *constipation · diarrhea.*

Mucus in the stools

Found alone or with blood staining. In young babies, a form of *intestinal obstruction* called intussusception is found in which the bowel slides into itself. This gives rise to blood and mucus in the stool.

Illnesses associated with *fever* and *diarrhea* such as dysentery and typhoid fever and various forms of enteritis may result in the passage of much blood and mucus. Polyps of the colon may give rise to bloodstained mucoid material being passed.

In adults, blood and mucus may be found in people who have *cancer* of the large bowel.

Mucus alone is found in some cases of constipation and in the *irritable bowel syndrome,* an illness associated with emotional problems rather than with physical disorders of the colon. *Diverticular disease* is also associated with mucus in the stool.

Multiple sclerosis

A disease of the nervous system which often begins in adults aged 20–40. It is common in women. As the name suggests, the symptoms are multiple and varied. *Double vision,* weakness in the limbs, difficulty in walking, *dizziness* and some *disorder of urinating* or *difficulty in urinating* are often among the first symptoms. The early stages of the disease can easily be mistaken for *hysteria,* because multiple sclerosis can cause many symptoms and is subject to remissions. The general course of the condition is, however, more towards relapses than remissions, with resultant worsening with time. The rate of progress is variable.

Myasthenia gravis

A disease of the muscles in which *weakness* is the most noticeable characteristic. The muscles are also readily fatigued and repeated movement of any part will quickly result in great difficulty in moving that part. Modern treatment has greatly improved the outlook in many cases. *Drooping of the eyelids* may be an early sign of muscle fatigue.

Myxedema   See *hypothyroidism*.

Nail biting
A habit (*tic*) which some people have. The reasons for nail biting are not understood, but the habit is relatively harmless and should not be dealt with by the use of punishment, ridicule or restraint, which can all lead to more harm than the habit itself. Colorless nail polish and bitter substances painted onto the nails have been recommended, but are seldom effective.

Nails, pitted   See *pitting of the nails*.

Nails, ridges and furrows on   See *ridges and furrows on the nails*.

Nails, splitting at the end   See *psoriasis*.

Nails, thickened
See *horny nails · ridges and furrows on the nails*.

Nails, unusually shaped
See *clubbing of the fingers · spoon shaped nails*.

Nails, white lines on   See *white lines on the nails*.

Narcolepsy
A *disorder of sleep* in which the person is seized by short irresistible attacks of sleepiness and sleeping. These attacks occur by day.

Nausea
The feeling which usually preceeds *vomiting*, which is often described as "feeling sick" and followed by vomiting, though nausea without vomiting can also occur. The sensation of nausea may be accompanied by a sinking feeling in the stomach, by a feeling of *weakness*, by *dizziness*, by perspiration and by excessive salivation. The person will often look pale and sweaty. Early

pregnancy is a cause of nausea, especially in the morning. See *morning sickness*. Nausea may also be part of *motion sickness*.

Neck, stiff   See *stiff neck · pain in the back of the neck*.

Neck swelling   See *swelling in the neck*.

Nervous breakdown

A euphemism for *mental illness* of one kind or another. See *anxiety · depression · schizophrenia* for details of these illnesses.

Nervous diarrhea   See *irritable bowel syndrome*.

"Nervousness"

Usually used to describe mild long-term *anxiety*. People who have been brought up in constant insecurity may have a lifelong habit of mild anxiety or nervousness as a result. *Stress* of any kind may precipitate an attack of anxiety. *Hyperthyroidism* also leads to nervousness.

Night blindness

May be congenital in origin. It is commonly associated with lack of vitamin A and with a disease of the retina called retinitis pigmentosa. Vitamin C deficiency (scurvy) is an occasional cause. In older people a developing cataract (lens opacity) may not be noticed in bright daylight but may cause the person to see badly at night, especially when driving. The headlights of oncoming vehicles may cause dazzle from the cataract. This however is not true night blindness.

Nightmares

Bad dreams. Almost everyone dreams but only some people remember their dreams or wake up from them terrified. In adults, nightmares are usually a part of a general condition of *anxiety* or unhappiness, which may be evident. Other *disorders of sleep* may be present. In children, occasional nightmares are of no importance, but persistent nightmares would suggest that the child should be seen by a doctor.

Night terrors   See *nightmares*.

Night urination   See *frequency of urination*.

Nipple, blood from See *blood from the nipple.*

Nipple, cracked See *cracked nipple.*

Nipple, discharge from See *discharge from the nipple.*

Nipple, inverted See *inverted nipple.*

Nipple, tender
See *cracked nipple · tightness in the breast and nipples.*

Nits
The eggs laid by female lice which are glued onto a hair. See also *pediculosis.*

Nocturia
Rising at night to urinate. See *frequency of urination.*

Nodules near joints
May be associated with *rheumatic fever, gout* or *osteoarthritis,* or they may be *swellings which can occur anywhere in the body* but which happen to be near joints.

Noise-induced hearing loss
May be temporary or permanent. Temporary deafness will follow any exposure to loud noise and, as the name implies, will disappear afterwards. However, repeated exposure to loud noise over about 90 decibels (dB) can lead to permanent damage to the organ of hearing and to *deafness.* The deafness will occur sooner with longer hours of noise exposure and with greater sound intensities. Sounds of about 120 dB or more can give rise to pain—the so-called "threshold of feeling." Explosive noises at close quarters, though very short in duration, are very high-energy noise which can result in permanent instantaneous deafness.
Hearing aids are unfortunately not much use in noise-induced hearing loss. The problem is one in which prevention is paramount—first, in not making loud noises, and second, in making sure that people who are exposed to loud noise have suitable hearing protection in the form of earmuffs or earplugs. Earplugs made from glass down (fine fibreglass wool) are nonirritating, and will provide suitable protection from noises up to about 100 dB. Above this volume muffs must be worn. A word of

144

warning should be given here about using absorbent cotton. This is USELESS for noise attenuation. Although it may look very like fiberglass, it does not act like it in attenuating noise.

Noises in the ear   See *tinnitus.*

Noisy bowels   See *loud rumbling bowel sounds.*

Noisy breathing
See *stridor · wheezing · asthma · bronchitis · difficulty in breathing.*

Nosebleeds   See *bleeding from the nose.*

Nose blocked   See *blocked nose · running nose.*

Nose crease
A crease across the nose at the junction of the soft tip with the bony part is found in children who suffer from *allergic rhinitis* and *hay fever*. It is produced by rubbing the nose upwards with the palm of the hand to relieve irritation and wipe away discharge. This gesture is known as the allergic salute.

Nose, running   See *running nose.*

No smell   See *loss of sense of smell.*

No taste   See *loss of sense of taste.*

Nucleotoxic drugs   See *cancer.*

Numbness   See *loss of feeling.*

Numbness of the face
May be found in *trigeminal neuralgia* and in *migraine.*

Numbness of the tongue
May occur as a temporary condition, usually lasting less than half an hour, as a preliminary feature of what is later found to be *migraine*. Transient *blurred vision* or *numbness of the face* or cheek may also be associated with the tongue numbness when it is a precursor of migraine. Persistant numbness of the tongue indicates interference with the nerve supply to the tongue. This will

require investigation by a physician. The causes can include diseases of the nerves—for example, *trigeminal neuralgia,* and diseases of the brain such as *cysts* or *tumors* which press on the nerves.

Nystagmus

A rapid and very small sideways movement of the eyes followed by a slower recovery movement. Nystagmus may be associated with the following:

ANY CAUSE OF DEFECTIVE VISION ARISING IN EARLY LIFE: congenital cataract · total color blindness · albinism. People with albinism will have white hair and pink eyes.

CERTAIN DISEASES OF THE BRAIN AND NERVOUS SYSTEM: *multiple sclerosis* · diseases affecting the cerebellum · *myasthenia gravis.*

DISTURBANCES OF THE BALANCE MECHANISM: diseases of the organ of balance · *motion sickness.*

Obesity

Fatness. Above-normal body weight will nearly always be because of fatness, except in athletes who have special muscular development. Many views about the origin of fatness seek to evade the basic physiological fact that fatness results from an excessive intake of food and/or drink in relation to the body's energy needs. When this happens, the body converts any excess into fat. The remedy is therefore to cut down sufficiently on food energy needs. When this happens, the body converts any excess and drink until weight is lost by using the stored fat for energy. When normal weight is reached the dietary intake can be adjusted to maintain weight.

There are few other reasons for obesity. Lesions of the brain in the region of the hypothalamus may cause a voracious appetite—but these lesions are rare. The lessons of starvation in any population are plain for all to see—no fat people are to be found. Obesity is therefore a self-induced condition associated with consumption of food and/or drink in amounts greater than the body requires. When fat people say that they "eat very little," it merely serves to illustrate that their notion of what is "a little" is, in fact, too much for them.

Obesity is often associated with *high or raised blood pressure* and there is general agreement that it tends to shorten life expectancy.

Obsessional states

An obsession is a feeling which, when experienced, cannot be got rid of, yet is recognized on reflection to be senseless. Many apparently normal healthy people have minor obsessions—for example about tidiness, money, cleanliness, punctuality and so on. It is only when these obsessions come to dominate the person that other people notice them. Three main characteristics show in obsessional personalities: orderliness, frugality and obstinacy. These are probably the outward manifestation of deeper seated insecurity, self-dissatisfaction and guilt feelings. These inward feelings are counterbalanced by scrupulous ordering of daily life so that errors can be eliminated. The exact causes of obsessional behavior and obsessional personalities are not understood, but many people who suffer from these problems can be helped by psychological counseling.

Odor, body   See *body odor.*

Odor, breath   See *bad breath.*

Onychogryphosus   See *horny nail.*

Orange urine   See *blood in the urine.*

Osteitis deformans   See *Paget's disease.*

Osteoarthritis

Related to a disorder of the cartilage in the joint. The exact cause is unknown. The disease does not usually appear before middle age unless there has been previous injury or damage to the joint. The onset is gradual with *pain in joints, limited movement at a joint*

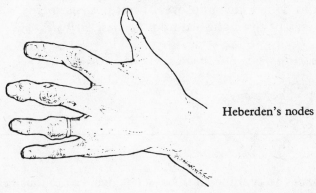

Heberden's nodes

and stiffness. Creaking and *grating in joints* may appear. The joints of the hands and feet and the knees are commonly affected. *Swelling in joints* may appear. Small swellings may appear in the joints of the fingers at the sides of each joint. These are called Heberden's nodes, and are associated with osteoarthritis.

Osteoarthrosis   See *osteoarthritis*.

Osteoporosis
A disorder in which the bones become rarified without loss of their basic structure. Like anemia, the disorder has many varieties. It is sometimes associated with old age, where it is not necessarily a sign of bad health but merely a cause of shrinking in height due to compression of vertebrae. This causes shrinkage of trunk length and *kyphosis,* which is an exaggerated backward curve of the spine, best seen in the middle of the back. Fractures may easily result from minor *trauma* in people who have osteoporosis. The *fracture* of the neck of the femur in elderly ladies is nearly always found in association with some degree of osteoporosis. Other causes of osteoporosis are uncommon, and are associated with prolonged inactivity, disease of the pituitary gland (Cushing's syndrome), severe malnutrition, chronic liver and kidney disease, and the use of corticosteroid drugs.

Otorrhea
The medical name for a *running ear*. See *infection in the ear passage* · *infection in the middle ear.*

Otosclerosis
A form of *deafness,* often hereditary, characterized by gradually progressive deafness beginning in middle life. In some people an operation can be done which improves or restores hearing. Otosclerosis must be distinguished from *familial early deafness.*

Outer ear infection   See *infection in the outer ear.*

Overbreathing   See *tetany*.

Overweight   See *obesity*.

Ovulation
The discharge of the ovum from the ovary which occurs fourteen

days before the date of onset of menstruation. Ovulation may give rise to a small sharp *pain in the abdomen,* which is felt to one side of the midline in the lower abdomen and is called *mittelschmerz.*

Paget's disease (osteitis deformans)
A disease of bone which occurs in older people. Only a minority of sufferers have symptoms, which may be an enlargement of the head, bowing of the legs and roundness of the back (*kyphosis*). The disease is associated with a raised level of bone *tumors* and *fractures* in the diseased bone.

Pain after drinking alcohol
May be due to local irritation in the stomach associated with a *peptic ulcer* or a *cancer* of the stomach. However, pain may be felt in places other than the abdomen after drinking alcohol, and this may occur in *Hodgkin's disease,* and occasionally with other *tumors.* The disease usually affects the part where the pain is felt. Sometimes the pain experienced may be *referred pain.*

Pain after eating
May be associated with: *peptic ulcer · reflux esophagitis · cancer* of the stomach · recent excessive drinking.

Pain around the umbilicus (navel)
Pain may arise from local lesion of the umbilicus or its immediate area—for example from an infection of the umbilicus or from an umbilical or para-umbilical *hernia.* Infection will show as a red, swollen, tender area, with the possibility of some pus being discharged. However, pain felt at the umbilicus may be *referred pain* from inside the abdomen. Early *appendicitis ·* abdominal *colic* associated with *diarrhea · gas in the bowel · intestinal obstruction* can all give rise to pain felt in the central area of the abdomen around the umbilicus. Any person who has pain around the umbilicus accompanied by *fever · nausea · vomiting* should be seen by a doctor soon. Cramplike colicky pain in the center of the abdomen, with no other symptoms, is found in lead poisoning.

Pain at the anus   See *pain on having a bowel movement.*

Painful gums

Will usually be associated with a generalized mouth infection involving locally *infected gums* (gingivitis), or with a condition of the teeth or jaws which may cause swelling under the gums. In this latter case the gums may be painful or the underlying painful condition may be mistaken for painful gums.
See also *toothache.*

Painful menstruation   See *dysmenorrhea.*

Pain in joints

Can be due to *trauma* or disease. It can affect many joints, a few, or only one. The onset of the pain may be sudden or slow.
PAIN OF SUDDEN ONSET IN JOINTS NOT ASSOCIATED WITH TRAUMA. This may be accompanied by *fever.* The joint pain may be only a symptom of fever, especially if the bones ache as well. If, however, there is *swelling of joints* in addition to pain in the joints and fever, *rheumatic fever* must be considered. Other forms of *septic arthritis* can occur in association with *pneumonia,* typhoid fever, scarlet fever and *gonorrhea.*
Rheumatoid arthritis may begin suddenly. In the early stages it affects mainly the joints of the hands and the feet. *Gout* can also cause the sudden onset of pain in a few joints or in a single joint which may be accompanied by fever and with redness and swelling around the joint. The red swollen area is usually extremely tender, and any movement gives rise to much pain. Characteristically gout affects the joint between the great toe and the foot, most often on the right.
Sudden pain in one joint associated with swelling of the joint and with redness, tenderness and pain on movement will probably be due to a septic (infective) arthritis. Any septic lesion near a joint such as an *abscess,* boil or *carbuncle,* may spread into the joint. The infection may also be spread systemically from a *sore throat* or from other infectious conditions.
PAIN IN JOINTS OF SLOW ONSET NOT ASSOCIATED WITH TRAUMA. The commonest cause of pain in joints of slow onset is *osteoarthritis.*
Rheumatoid arthritis may also appear slowly, as can gout. Psoriatic arthropathy is associated with *psoriasis,* and is a rather intractable form of joint disease.

150

Pain in the abdomen

May arise from pain in the abdominal wall or originating within the abdominal cavity. Pain in the abdominal wall can be caused by: *trauma* · twisting and pulling which damages muscle · *boils* and *abscesses* · *herpes zoster,* which can give rise to pain wherever the lesion is.

What follows is about pain in the abdomen. For simplicity, the abdomen can be divided into quarters by a vertical midline and by a horizontal line through the umbilicus. Some common causes of pain in the abdomen are shown in the illustration. More detailed listing of the possible causes of pain are given in the sections below.

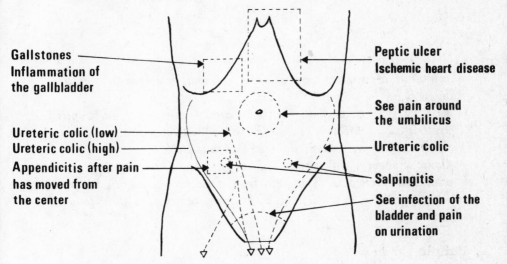

Gallstones
Inflammation of the gallbladder

Peptic ulcer
Ischemic heart disease

See pain around the umbilicus

Ureteric colic (low)
Ureteric colic (high)

Ureteric colic

Appendicitis after pain has moved from the center

Salpingitis

See infection of the bladder and pain on urination

Sites and distribution of some forms of abdominal pain

PAIN IN THE RIGHT UPPER ABDOMEN can be caused by: *inflammation of the gallbladder* · *stones in the gallbladder* · *biliary colic* · *colic* from *intestinal obstruction* and *diarrhea* · *peptic ulcer* · *pleurisy* (referred pain) · *pneumonia* (referred pain).

PAIN IN THE LEFT UPPER ABDOMEN can be caused by *peptic ulcer* · *ischemic heart disease* (referred pain) · *diarrhea* · *pleurisy* (referred pain) · *pneumonia* (referred pain).

PAIN IN THE CENTRAL UPPER ABDOMEN can be caused by: *peptic ulcer* · *diarrhea* · *ischemic heart disease* (referred pain).

PAIN IN THE CENTRAL AND MIDDLE AREAS OF THE ABDOMEN—See *pain around the umbilicus.*

PAIN IN THE LOWER RIGHT ABDOMEN can be caused by: *appendicitis* · *salpingitis* · *ureteric colic* · *infection of the bladder* · *colic* from

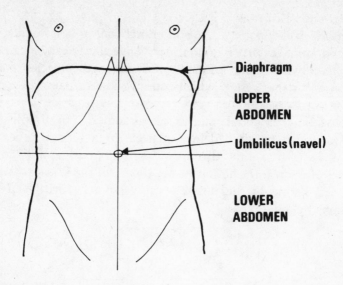

Diaphragm

UPPER ABDOMEN

Umbilicus (navel)

LOWER ABDOMEN

intestinal obstruction and *diarrhea · menstrual cramps · mittelschmerz.*

PAIN IN THE LOWER LEFT ABDOMEN can be caused by: *salpingitis · ureteric colic · infection of the bladder · colic from intestinal obstruction* and *diarrhea · menstrual cramps · mittelschmerz.*

Colic, if severe, will usually cause the person to be *rolling about with abdominal pain.* The pain from a perforated peptic ulcer, if severe, will cause the person to be *lying very still with abdominal pain.*

Pain in the ankle

Usually due to *trauma,* arises from a sprain of the ligaments around the ankle. Limping may occur. The ankle can be affected by any of the causes of *pain in joints* and *swelling in joints.*

Pain in the arm

See *pain in the elbow · pain in joints · pain in the shoulder · pain in the wrist.*

Pain in the back   See *backache.*

Pain in the back of the neck

May be found at the end of the day and may be accompanied by *headache.* This sort of pain is usually a *stress* or tension pain, and is a reaction to everyday problems and to mental strain and worry. Disk degeneration in the cervical spine which leads to narrowing of the disk spaces (spondylosis) can give rise to pain the back of the neck. This often spreads down to the middle of the back, and may be felt at the base of the neck and across the shoulders. In more severe cases the pain may be felt down the arms. *"Tennis elbow"* is often due to disk degeneration in the lower cervical region. The pain is felt in the elbow but the nerve root pressure is in the neck.

Trauma can also give rise to pain in the back of the neck because of strains, bleeding, injury to the disks or injury to the spine. A *stiff neck* will often be present with pain in the back of the neck. Occasionally causes of pain in the neck are diseases of the spine such as *ankylosing spondylitis* or other causes of *pain in the joints*. *Meningitis* is a cause of pain in the back of the neck with *fever* following a sore throat or upper respiratory infection.

Pain in the chest

Two kinds of chest pain can be present:

PAIN ARISING FROM THE CHEST WALL CAN BE FROM: *boils, abscess* or other infection · *herpes zoster* (shingles) · *pain in the (female) breast* · *Bornholm disease* · neuralgia · injury or fracture of ribs · "slipping rib" · *cervical rib* · any disease which can cause pressure on the nerves in the chest wall, including *cysts* · *tumors* · *aneurysm of the aorta.*

Pain arising from *boils, abscesses* and other infections of the chest wall should be easily recognized by the hot, red, tender swelling at the site of the pain. *Herpes zoster* (shingles) can give rise to considerable pain shortly after it develops, and for some time afterwards. The characteristic rash should indicate the reason for the pain. A "slipping" or "sticking" rib usually comes on with change of position, and can be clicked back with relief of pain.

PAIN ARISING FROM WITHIN THE CHEST AND ABDOMEN can derive from: *pleurisy* · *empyema* · *pneumothorax* · pneumonia · pulmonary *embolism* · *aneurysm of the aorta* · *ischemic heart disease* · *pericarditis* · obstruction of the esophagus by *cancer* or by *achalasia of the cardia* · *abscess* in the liver or under the diaphragm · *hernias* through the diaphragm into the chest (diaphragmatic hernia) · diseases of the gallbladder such as *cholecystitis* and *stones in the gallbladder* · ulcers of the stomach, which would be a *peptic ulcer* or an ulcer from *cancer.*

Infective and septic conditions such as cholecystitis or abscess of the liver or under the diaphragm will usually be accompanied by fever and general feelings of ill health.

Pain arising from within the chest and abdomen can to some extent be identified by things which make it better or worse. For example, pains due to pleurisy or lung disease will generally be made worse by deep breathing or coughing. Pains which arise from the heart will be made worse by anything which makes the heart rate faster such as exercise or excitement and other emotional states. The pain which arises from a deficient supply of blood to the heart muscle (*angina pectoris*) typically comes on with exertion such as walking uphill or climbing stairs. Pains connected with the digestive organs may be relieved or aggravated by eating and/or drinking.

See also *pain in the (female) breast*.

Pain in the ear See *earache*.

Pain in the elbow

May be due to *trauma* causing a *fracture* or a strain near the elbow. *Tennis elbow* is a common cause of pain on the outer side of the elbow. See also *pain in the joints · swelling in joints*.

Pain in the eye

Pain with *redness of the eye* may be due to: a foreign body · *conjunctivitis* · an ulcer of the cornea · iritis · iridocyclitis · *glaucoma · herpes zoster* (shingles).

Pain without redness of the eye may be due to retrobulbar neuritis which is an inflammation of the nerves behind the eye. A common cause of retrobulbar neuritis is *multiple sclerosis,* but there are many other diseases of the nervous system which can give rise to this complaint. *Sinusitis* may also produce pain felt in the eye.

Pain in the eye may be felt in the course of illness accompanied by *fever*, the commonest of which are probably common colds and influenza. Other causes of fever for feverish illness may also be accompanied by eye pains.

Pain in the face

See *herpes zoster · pain in the upper jaw · pain in the lower jaw · sinusitis · toothache · trigeminal neuralgia.*

Pain in the feet

Often due to *flat feet. Limping and pain in the heels* may also be present. Fractures of the metatarsal bones (the long bones in the feet) can give rise to pain. Pressure on the lower end of these bones can also cause pain. Such pressure is usually due in the first place to a fallen transverse arch (flat feet). This is a congenital condition which cannot be corrected anatomically but may be alleviated by special shoe fittings if the symptoms become troublesome in later life. *Gout, chilblains,* and a *bunion* are other common causes of painful feet. Many of the causes of *pain in joints* can cause pain in the feet. *Corns* and *plantar warts* can also cause pain in the feet.

Pain in the (female) breast
May be experienced normally from the slight increase in size and swelling which occurs at puberty, premenstrually, in pregnancy, and in breast feeing when the breasts are full of milk. These conditions usually affect both breasts.
Conditions of the nipple which can give rise to pain are cracking or inflammation. Painful swellings in the breast are often septic conditions such as a breast abscess. As a general rule it is the painless *swelling or lump in the breast* which is the most sinister. *Cancer* is usually painless, but not always. *Trauma* or its aftereffects can give rise to breast pain. Other more general causes of *pain in the chest* may be thought to give rise to breast pain.
If any breast pain is felt, it is always wise to search the breast for any swelling or lump. If a swelling or lump is found, always consult your physician as soon as possible.
See also *discharge from the nipple.*

Pain in the forehead
Possible causes include: neuritis in the nerves to the skin of the forehead, including *trigeminal neuralgia* · frontal *sinusitis* or other conditions of the sinus including *tumors* · *eyestrain* · *herpes zoster* or post herpetic neuralgia · *migraine* · mental strain and exhaustion · insufficient sleep · aftereffects of head injury or sunstroke · *headaches.*

Pain in the head   See *headache.*

Pain in the heart   See *pain in the chest.*

Pain in the heel
Can be a troublesome complaint in some children. Often little or nothing can be found to account for the complaint, even though

the child may be *limping*. A careful search should always be made in the thick skin of the heel for a thorn or other foreign body.

Chilblains may be found to cause pain in the heels. *Trauma* is a frequent cause. Infections in the heel region, such as bursitis, can also cause pain. A spur of bone on the heel bone can give rise to pain on walking or pain on pressure. X rays will be necessary to demonstrate these spurs. If found, surgical removal will usually be the best course to follow. *Gout* is an occasional cause of pain in the heel. Ligament trouble or injury in the heel region is sometimes the cause of the pain.

Pain in the hip

Often due to *osteoarthritis* of the hip, but may be due to any of the causes of *pain in joints*. *Limping* may be present. In children, pain in the hip should always be seen by a doctor, especially if it is accompanied by limping.

Adults who have osteoarthritis of the hip may find that when they are sitting on the floor or on a hard bed with the legs stretched out the foot cannot be rotated outwards on the affected side. The test must be performed with the knee straight. This rotation test is nearly always an accurate indication of whether osteoarthritis of the hip is present.

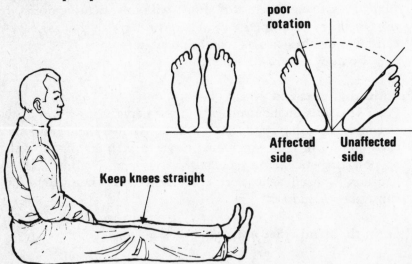

poor rotation

Affected side   Unaffected side

Keep knees straight

Pain in the knee

Often follows trauma when the causes may be a torn ligament, a *displaced or torn knee cartilage* or an effusion into the knee ("fluid

156

in the joint"). Effusions can be recognized by *swelling of the knee joint*. Some effusions are caused by bleeding into the knee joint, while others are caused by an excess of joint fluid. Any septic condition near the knee can cause the knee to swell, and may result in a *septic arthritis*. An *abscess* or boil will usually be accompanied by redness, swelling, *fever* and *swelling of the lymph nodes*. The knee may be affected by diseases which cause *pain in joints* and *swelling in joints*. In older people the knee is often affected by *osteoarthritis*. It is particularly important in this disease to minimize the strain on the joint by making sure that no *obesity* is present or, if it is, by reducing to normal body weight. Pain in the knee may also be *referred pain* from the hip.

Pain in the leg

Can be caused by *trauma, sciatica* and *deep vein thrombosis,* in addition to the more obvious causes related to an *abscess* or boil or to infection in the deeper tissues, bones or joints. See also *limping, pain in the knee* and *pain in the heel*. Muscle cramps following unaccustomed exercise may cause severe pain in the leg. A condition called intermittent claudication causes pain in the leg after walking a certain distance. The pain disappears on rest and reappears on exercise. It is due to insufficient blood reaching the muscles, and is made worse by cigarette smoking. Investigation by a doctor of the arteries which supply blood to the legs is necessary.

Pain in the lower eyelid

May occur as a part of *trigeminal neuralgia · pain in the upper jaw ·* local diseases of the eyelid, such as a sty · *abscess · cyst · ulcer of the skin*.

Pain in the lower jaw

Usually due to dental caries (*toothache*). Unerupted wisdom teeth may also cause the pain. *Trigeminal neuralgia* may also be a cause of severe one-sided pain in the lower jaw. The pain of trigeminal neuralgia usually comes on in bouts, and often is accompanied by *flushing* of the face on the same side. *Herpes zoster* (shingles) may also cause pain in the lower jaw. The pain may come on with the skin rash, or it may appear when the rash is gone as post-herpetic neuralgia.

Occasionally *ischemic heart disease* may cause pain in the lower jaw.

Pain in the shoulder

May be due to injury to the joint, or to the muscles, tendons and ligaments around the joint. The pain may be from any cause of *pain in joints,* or may be pain referred to the shoulder region— for example from a cervical disk lesion which causes *pain in the back of the neck* and pain in the shoulder and arm. Shoulder tip pain may also be felt in any condition which affects the region of the diaphragm, because visceral pain from these areas is referred to the shoulder. *Pleurisy · pneumonia · pneumothorax · peptic ulcer · cholecystitis* and other conditions can all lead to *referred pain* in the shoulder. *Angina pectoris* can also spread to the shoulder region. See also *frozen shoulder.*

Pain in the teeth   See *toothache.*

Pain in the testicle

May easily follow a blow to the area. Infections from *sexually transmitted diseases* or mumps also commonly give rise to pain. Most of the causes of *swellings in the scrotum* can give rise to a feeling of pain in the testicle, and of these torsion of the testicle and an inguinal hernia sliding into the scrotum are the commonest causes of pain felt in the organ.

Ureteric colic can give rise to referred pain in the testicle, but in this case the other symptoms are usually very obvious.

Pain in the throat   See *sore throat.*

Pain in the toe   See *abscess · gout · pain in joints · ingrown toenail.*

Pain in the upper jaw

The causes include: *toothache · trigeminal neuralgia · herpes zoster · sinusitis.* The commonest is toothache.

Trigeminal neuralgia can give rise to very severe pain in the upper jaw which is characteristically one-sided, and may be stabbing like a red hot needle and accompanied by *flushing* of the skin of that side of the face.

Sinusitis often follows a cold or other upper respiratory infection, and may be of rapid or slow onset. Sometimes an infected tooth may cause a sinusitis, and the two conditions may thus occur together.

Pain in the wrist

May be due to *trauma* causing a sprain or strain or a *fracture*. Pain associated with *tingling in the hands* is probably from the carpal tunnel syndrome. An ununited fracture of the scaphoid bone in the wrist can give rise to pain. See also *pain in joints · swelling in joints. Rheumatoid arthritis* and *osteoarthritis* are probably the most common of the conditions listed there that affect the wrist.

Pain on having a bowel movement

Usually associated with *constipation,* hard stools, or a painful condition around the anus.

Common conditions which can give rise to pain around the anus are: a *boil* or *abscess · hemorrhoids* (piles).

A small clot associated with a hemorrhoid (a thrombosed external pile) can give rise to a small pea sized *swelling at the anus* which can be very tender. The condition is self-correcting but if pain is severe, the clot can be removed surgically. Piles may be associated with *bleeding from the anus ·* an anal fissure (a small split in the skin and mucous surface at the anal sphincter). When the fissure is stretched or touched, as happens when the bowels move, very sharp pain can result.

Some men suffer from a sharp fleeting pain which can give rise to stabs of pain felt in the region of the anus, forward of it, and sometimes deep into the rectum. The cause is not known, but the condition is not serious and is not associated with anything, nor does it give rise to any other trouble. It may occur at times other than when having a bowel movement.

Pain on swallowing   See *sore throat.*

Pain on urination

The causes of pain on urination include *infection in the urethra · infection in the bladder ·* kidney infection *· enlargement of the prostate ·* stone in the bladder or urethra *· gravel in the urine · "honeymoon cystitis."*

Pain can be felt as urine is passed, or at the end of urination, or both. It is important to note the kind of pain—whether it is scalding and burning, or sharp and stabbing. Scalding and burn-pain is usually associated with inflammation of the bladder and urethra. Stabbing pain is most often associated with stones or gravel.

In boys a small ulcer may be found at the end of the penis (*meatal ulcer*). This can give rise to very sharp pain as the urine meets the ulcer.

In every case of pain on urination it is worth looking at a specimen sample of urine in a clear glass. Normal urine is nearly always clear, the color will vary from very pale yellow to yellow. Occasionally concentrated urines are found when a person has been perspiring a lot or has not taken fluid. Concentrated urine is clear and dark yellow in color. Abnormal urines can sometimes be recognized because they are misty, cloudy or faintly muddy in appearance. Small amounts of blood in urine make it orange and slightly turbid looking—the crystal clarity is lost. Larger amounts of blood turn the urine red. This redness is easily recognized as blood.

Phosphates are found in the urine of healthy people, and may occasionally make a urine turbid. However, it is probably a useful presumption that *cloudy urines* are abnormal until proven otherwise. Phosphates are soluble in acetic acid, so it may be worth adding some vinegar to the urine. If this clears the turbidity with the effervescence of a few bubbles, then the urine was probably cloudy from phosphates.

Pain, referred   See *referred pain*.

Pale stools   Associated with *jaundice,* and often with *dark urine*.

Pale urine

Pale urine is diluted urine, found when a person drinks a lot and the weather is cold, so the excess fluid is gotten rid of in the urine. If the weather is warm, much fluid will be lost through the skin, so a *dark urine,* which is a normal concentrated urine, may result.

Pallor

Paleness of color. Extreme paleness will probably be due to *anemia* from blood loss—for example, from a bleeding *peptic ulcer* or from *menorrhagia.* Acute and chronic illness may also cause anemia by suppressing normal red blood cell formation. Lesser degrees of pallor may be a general symptom of being unwell. People who are cold or *feeling cold* will look pale. So pallor may be found in the early stages of a *fever. Fainting* or *fits* may cause pallor. Some people with very white skin who are not exposed to sunlight may look pale even when in good health.

160

Palpitations

Thumping or fluttering sensations felt in the chest when we become conscious of the heart beating. Strenuous exercise can produce normal palpitations. The rhythm of the heart may be normal—it is beating regularly and evenly. But sometimes the rhythm may be abnormal, and the heart is beating irregularly and unevenly. *Fast heartbeat* and *irregular heartbeat* are often the cause of the sensation.

Another frequent cause of palpitation is one irregular beat in a heart which is beating quietly and strongly. This is typically noticed in bed just before going to sleep when there is a *slow heartbeat*. Palpitations by no means always, or even frequently, indicate heart disease, contrary to many popular impressions on this subject.

Fast heart rates can be produced by: *hyperthyroidism · hypoglycemia · paroxysmal tachycardia. Anemia · aneurysm · coronary thrombosis* and recent or old valvular diseases of the heart can all lead to palpitations. An overfull stomach pressing upwards on the heart can also cause palpitations.

Last, any strong emotion, such as *anxiety,* can accelerate the heart rate and give rise to palpitations.

Panic attacks   See *phobic anxiety*.

Paralysis

In limbs or on the face, of sudden onset, is commonly the result of a *stroke*. Paralysis of one side of the face of sudden onset may be due to a Bell's palsy, which is a paralysis of the facial (seventh cranial) nerve. This results in inability to close the eye on the affected side.

Paralysis may occur in the course of an illness with *fever,* and may be associated with poliomyelitis or *meningitis*.

When paralysis comes on slowly in one part of the body there may be a disease or *tumor* in the brain, in the spinal cord or in or near the nerves which go to the affected area. Paralysis may occur without any *loss of feeling,* or it may be accompanied by loss of feeling. Medical help will always be needed to diagnose the reason for any paralysis and/or loss of feeling.

Paralysis agitans   See *Parkinson's disease*.

Paranoid schizophrenia   See *schizophrenia*.

Para-umbilical hernia   See *hernia*.

Parkinson's disease (paralysis agitans)
A degenerative disease usually seen after the age of fifty, in which a characteristic coarse *tremor* appears affecting the limbs, the head and the neck. In the early stages the tremor ceases when the affected part is moved. Sooner or later it progresses to muscular rigidity, to a shuffling gait, and to an inexpressive mask-like face. *Excessive salivation* may also be noted.

Paroxysmal tachycardia   See *fast heartbeat*.

Pediculosis
Means infestation by lice. There are three kinds of lice: head, body and pubic (crab) lice. All can cause intense *itching of the skin*. Lice are small creatures about the size of a large pinhead and can be seen easily with the aid of a magnifying glass. They are transmitted by close body contact. *Nits* (the eggs of the female) are glued onto hair, and can usually be seen only with good magnification.

Peeling of the skin
Can follow sunburn, burns or streptococcal infections. Streptococcal sore throats which cause scarlet fever may be followed by large "snakeskin" casts of shed skin. A *scaly skin* at times will look like peeling skin.

Peptic ulcer
An ulcer of the stomach or duodenum associated with decreasing ability of the organ to withstand the digestive secretions of hydrochloric acid and pepsin. When ulcers develop, they give rise to *pain in the abdomen*—usually in the upper abdomen and most often where the ribs divide in the upper central abdomen. The pain is burning or boring and comes on usually about half an hour after eating or when the stomach is empty, so the person may be wakened in the middle of the night by the pain. The pain is relieved by alkaline "stomach tablets" or mixtures. Fried foods, spiced foods and sauces often bring on the pain.
Peptic ulcers may cause bleeding from the stomach and duodenum, and can thus give rise to *vomiting blood* and to *black stools* (melena). A well known complication of a peptic ulcer is perforation, which allows acid stomach or duodenal contents to

leak inside the abdomen. Perforation is accompanied by sudden intense pain, and usually by some general collapse. Unless the perforation is tiny, it is obvious that medical assistance is urgently required. The sufferer from a perforation is usually *lying very still with pain in the abdomen,* because any movement greatly increases his pain. He may even refuse to be moved to a hospital because of the increase of his pain on movement. In this way, he is quite different from the person who has severe pain from *biliary* or *ureteric colic,* because these people will be *rolling about with abdominal pain* and will lie first on one side and then on the other, in an endeavor to find a comfortable position.

Pericarditis
Inflammation of the pericardium, the membrane around the heart. Disease of the pericardium will often result in *pain in the chest* and/or *difficulty in breathing.*

Period pain
See *dysmenorrhea · premenstrual tension · mittelschmerz.*

Periods   See *menstruation.*

Peritonsillar abscess   See *quinsy.*

Perniosis   See *chilblains.*

Perspiring   See *fever · excessive sweating.*

Petit mal   See *epilepsy.*

Peyronie's disease   See *chordee · Dupuytren's contracture.*

Phlegm
Stringy mucus from the upper respiratory tract. Phlegm is only noticed when it is found in excess and is expectorated. *Infected sputum* may be found. Phlegm is associated with cigarette smoking, chronic *bronchitis, bronchiectasis* and chest infections.

Phobias   See *phobic anxiety.*

Phobic anxiety
Any form of *anxiety* that could be described as "fear of something."

Common forms are agoraphobia (fear of open places) and claustrophobia (fear of being shut in). Many people have phobic anxieties, and are afraid of things which reason tells them they needn't fear but which still bother them. This illogical fear is a characteristic feature of phobic anxiety. Animals of all kinds, spiders, toads, frogs, birds, snakes and many other creatures can give rise to phobic anxiety. Fear of vomiting or of seeing other people vomit, fear of eating in public, and fear of traveling in airplanes, trains or automobiles are other common phobic anxieties. Some phobic anxiety can be helped by treatment, but cure is not always possible.

Photophobia
A special form of pain in which the person feels that light, especially bright light, hurts his eyes. It is found in *meningitis* · measles · *herpes zoster* of the eye · during an attack of *migraine* · *snow blindness* due to an ultraviolet burn of the cornea · *trigeminal neuralgia* (see *pain in the upper jaw* · *pain in the lower jaw*). Hysteria sometimes is found as a cause of photophobia. Photophobia should be distinguished from spasm of the eyelids due to a painful eye condition.

Pigment abnormalities See *disorders of pigmentation of the skin*.

Piles See *hemorrhoids*.

Pink eye See *redness of the eye* · *conjunctivitis*.

Pink urine See *blood in the urine*.

"Pins and needles" See *tingling in the hands and/or feet*.

Pitting of the nails
Found in *psoriasis*. The nails look as if a pin had produced small downward indentations.

Pitting on pressure See *edema*.

Plantar warts See *warts on the feet*.

Pleural effusion
The accumulation of fluid in the pleural space between the lungs

and the chest wall. The fluid can be clear (a hydrothorax), or can contain pus (an empyema) or blood (a hemothorax).

The symptoms of a pleural effusion may be *difficulty in breathing* or a *pain in the chest*. Clear fluid is found in heart failure and in a tuberculous pleural effusion, secondary to tuberculous infection in the lung. Pus is usually secondary to a lung infection such as pneumonia, or may follow a chest injury. A hemothorax is usually associated with injury to the ribs or lung or with malignant disease in the chest, which may arise in the lung or may be a secondary growth from elsewhere.

Occasionally, serious abdominal disease which causes infection under the diaphragm, such as a perforated *peptic ulcer, appendicitis, cholecystitis* (gallbladder infection) or an *abscess* in the liver may result in a pleural effusion.

Pleurisy

A general term used to describe diseases of the pleura, the membranes covering the outside of the lungs and the inside of the chest wall. The function of the pleura is to provide a smooth glide between the chest walls and the lungs. Pleurisy can give rise to tearing, sharp or stabbing *pain in the chest,* and to *difficulty in breathing*. Dry pleurisy is usually more painful than the pain of a *pleural effusion* which may follow dry pleurisy.

Pneumoconiosis

Lung disease related to the inhalation of dust. The dust inhalation usually occurs at work. Silicosis, "black lung," asbestosis and many other pneumoconioses have been described. They often result in shortness of breath and *difficulty in breathing*.

Pneumothorax

A condition in which air escapes from the lung into the pleural space, and the lung collapses. This may result from rupture of a blister or weak area in the lung, or it may follow *trauma* to the chest and ribs. If this occurs suddenly as in an acute pneumothorax, the person may feel a sharp and often severe *chest pain.* This may be accompanied by *fainting. Difficulty in breathing* may also be experienced. As a rough guide, the more the lung is collapsed the greater the difficulty in breathing.

Poor appetite

Can occur both during and following any serious illness. Sometimes the habit of not eating persists, but "the appetite comes with eating," so people who have this problem must be tempted, persuaded and cajoled to eat. Loss of appetite which is unexplained may be an early symptom of *cancer* of the stomach. *Depression* may lead a person to eat less. In young women, *anorexia nervosa* is a dangerous form of voluntary starvation.

Port wine stain   See *birthmarks.*

Post-herpetic neuralgia   The pain which follows *herpes zoster.*

Postnasal drip
The sensation of something coming down the back of the throat caused by nasal secretion or by material from the nasal sinuses going down the back of the throat. It is found in association with *catarrh* · a *running nose* · *allergic rhinitis* · *hay fever* · *sinusitis.* It may be associated with *bad breath.*

Potato nose   See *rhinophyma.*

Pregnancy
See *missed menstrual period* · *morning sickness* · *nausea* · *swelling of the breasts* · *tubal pregnancy.*

Premature ejaculation
A male suffering from this disorder will ejaculate as soon as he is in contact with the female or after a few thrusts only. The effects of this on the female can lead to no satisfaction from intercourse and to *frigidity.* Techniques are available to alter the habit of premature ejaculation. The condition may later be associated with *impotence.* Medical help should be sought.

Premenstrual tension
Many women experience premenstrual tension for a few days before the period begins, and a small number suffer from mild *depression* during this time. They feel bloated, swollen and miserable before the period starts. *Headaches,* pain, and/or tenderness, *tightness in the breasts,* and *irritability* are common. Premenstrual tension may or may not be associated with *dysmenorrhea* (painful periods) or *menorrhagia* (excessive periods).

Priapism
Persistent erection of the penis, not associated with sexual excitement. The erection may be painful. The condition is associated with blood diseases such as *leukemia* or sickle-cell anemia and with injury to or diseases of the spinal cord related to *syphilis,* venous *thrombosis* and *tumors.*

Prickly heat See *excessive sweating.*

Problem drinking See *alcoholism.*

Prolapse of the vagina and uterus
Means falling forwards or downwards of these parts. This leads to a sensation of something coming down which is usually felt at first only after a long and tiring day or after standing for a long time. The later stages of prolapse will have symptoms of *urine leaking or dribbling* and of *stress incontinence.* Occasionally pelvic congestion and ulceration of the cervix can cause *bleeding from the vagina* or a *vaginal discharge* which is bloodstained.

Prostatic enlargement See *enlargement of the prostate.*

Protruding ears
Sometimes a source of embarrassment to their owner. Plastic surgery can remedy the condition if this course of action is felt to be appropriate or necessary.

Protuberent abdomen See *abdominal distension.*

Pruritus
The medical word for itching. For a discussion of the causes of itching, see *itching of the skin.*

Psoriasis
A disease of the skin which is characterized by redness, usually first appearing as red spots covered by a scaly top. These spots may join together to form larger red areas and the tops may form scaly patches. The disease often appears on the scalp, on the points of the elbows and the fronts of the knees, in the midline between the buttocks and in the sacral region (lower back) where it causes *scaly skin.* The nails too are often involved with characteristic pinhead pitting of the nails and later thickening of the nail

with fraying and splitting at the end. The disease may cause discomfort and embarrassment on account of the scaling which can occur. It is, however, usually a relatively benign condition on the skin, where it seldom gives rise to serious illness or complications, although it can cause a rather intractable joint disease (psoriatic arthropathy) which produces *pain in joints* and can be disabling.

Psoriatic arthropathy See *psoriasis.*

Psychological illness or problems
These are conditions which require expert assessment and skilled treatment. Amateur psychologists should be avoided. A few common psychological illnesses or problems mentioned in this book are: *anxiety · phobic anxiety · depression · hysteria · obsessional states · schizophrenia · sex problems. Stress* may be a precipitating factor in psychological illness. *Hypoglycemia* may be mistaken for mental illness.

Psychosis
Describes serious mental illness, in which the sufferer usually lacks insight into what is happening to him or her, and may be out of touch with reality. In these disorders, the thought processes are disturbed and the normal train of thought is disrupted. *Schizophrenia* is the commonest psychosis. Drug-induced psychoses can occur, for example, from alcohol, amphetamines and LSD. Brain infections from *syphilis, meningitis* and *encephalitis* may give rise to psychoses. Degenerative disease (for example, *arteriosclerosis*) and brain tumors can also cause psychoses.

Puffiness of the eyelids and face See *hypothyroidism · edema.*

Pulse, fast See *fast heartbeat.*

Pulse, irregular See *irregular heartbeat.*

Pulse, slow See *slow heartbeat.*

Pupils, unequal See *unequal pupils.*

Pupils, uneven See *unequal pupils · coloboma.*

Purple color of face, lips and skin See *blueness of the skin.*

Purpura
A group of diseases which are characterized by *bleeding under the skin* and elsewhere. These small hemorrhages give rise to purple or bluish marks under the skin—hence the name purpura. The bleeding areas under the skin are easily seen, but it should be remembered that bleeding in purpura can occur anywhere in the body.

Purpura is due to disorders affecting the platelets in the blood, which are necessary for normal clotting. As a result there is a tendency to bleeding.

Various kinds of purpura occur: the platelets may not be formed in sufficient numbers, as in *leukemia* or in poisoning of bone marrow by chemicals or drugs; or the platelets may be destroyed by chemicals and drugs. Purpura can also result from allergic disorders of small arteries which allow bleeding to occur (anaphylactoid purpura or Henoch-Schönlein syndrome). Many infections such as measles, *meningitis* and *tonsillitis,* from beta hemolytic streptococci, can cause purpura.

See also *black stools* (melena), *blood in the urine* and all the entries under *bleeding from . . ..*

Pus from the ear
The causes include *infection in the ear passage · infection in the middle ear.*

Pyloric stenosis   See *stenosis.*

Pyorrhea   See *infected gums.*

Pyrexia   The medical word for *fever.*

Quick heartbeat   See *fast heartbeat.*

Quinsy (peritonsillar abscess)
An *abscess* around the tonsil, usually following *tonsillitis.* The condition gives rise to *difficulty in swallowing* on account of pain. Surgical treatment is sometimes necessary to drain the abscess.

Radiomimetic drugs   See *cancer*.

Radiotherapy   See *cancer*.

Rainbows around lights
May be seen by a person suffering from *glaucoma*.

Raised body temperature   See *fever*.

Rapid breathing   See *breathlessness*.

Rapid heartbeat   See *fast heartbeat*

Rash
Any skin eruption. In children, rashes are commonly found in association with childhood fevers such as measles, German measles, and chicken pox. They may also be associated with *allergies* and may appear as *urticaria* (hives). Allergic rashes will not be accompanied by *sore throats, fever, headaches* and other symptoms of illness. The word rash can also be used to describe any undiagnosed skin disease.

Raynaud's syndrome or disease
A condition characterized by *white cold fingers* which appear to be dead. The coldness appears in attacks which last anything from five minutes to a few hours, and are usually brought on by cold. Occasionally the attacks appear to be precipitated by emotion. The condition is due to spasm of the blood vessels in the fingers. The exact cause of the spasm is not understood but sometimes the sufferer is found to have an extra rib—a cervical rib which can cause pressure in the neck. Excessive smoking and arteriosclerosis may also be related to the condition. The toes may also be affected.

Receding gums   See *infected gums*.

Receding hair   See *loss of hair*.

Red birthmarks
Of two main kinds—"stork marks" which are pink flat areas usually seen on the head and on the back of the neck, and angiomas which are usually slightly raised and are very red or

even reddish purple in color and can appear anywhere. "Stork marks" will usually disappear in time. However, angiomas will require expert advice because some tend to get larger as the baby grows, though some disappear after several years.

All birthmarks should be seen by a doctor, and a small number of angiomas may need surgical treatment, especially those which are constantly irritated or bleeding.

Red eye   See *redness of the eye · conjunctivitis.*

Red eyelids
Found in blepharitis, where the redness is confined to the margins of the lids. The margins tend to be dry and scaly, and the condition is usually associated with *loss of eyelashes.* A *stye* can also cause redness, swelling and pain.

Red face   See *redness of the face.*

Red lines in the skin
May be found associated with an infectious condition such as an *abscess* or *boil.* The red line shows the spread of the infection through the lymphatic system to the lymph nodes. This is called lymphangitis. It is usually accompanied by heat and swelling. This condition should be seen by a doctor immediately. Another cause of red lines in the skin is recent *stretch marks.*

Red marks in the skin   See *disorders of pigmentation of the skin.*

Redness and soreness at the corners of the mouth (angular stomatitis)
Said to be due to a deficiency of riboflavin (vitamin B), nicotinic acid (niacin), or iron. It may also be related to badly fitting dentures, debilitating diseases and to *candidosis* (thrush). In elderly people the condition may be related to a number of these possible causes rather than to any particular one.

Redness of the eye
Two main kinds of redness have to be distinguished:
CONJUNCTIVAL REDNESS is dull in color. Careful examination will show that the redness is greatest at the edges of the white of the eye, and that the blood vessels which make the eye red appear to come from the corners of the eye and from around the outside.

The vessels are thicker at the edges of the eyeball and thinner towards the middle. Conjunctival redness also affects the inner surfaces of the eyelids which are lined by the conjunctiva.

Conjunctival redness is associated with infection or injury of the conjunctiva, the clear "skin" which lines the inner surfaces of the eyelids and the front of the eye over the white, but not over the cornea. *Conjunctivitis* is the name given to infection of the conjunctiva. *Allergies* may also make the conjunctiva red, as in *hay fever*.

CILIARY REDNESS is brighter than conjunctival redness, and is produced by a number of very fine blood vessels which radiate outwards from the edge of the cornea—the clear window in the middle of the eye. The vessels are thickest at the middle and thin out after a short distance. Ciliary redness does not affect the inner surface of the eyelids.

Ciliary redness indicates that there is trouble affecting the cornea, the iris or deeper structures in the eye. It may be all around the cornea, or confined to one area.

Corneal ulcers · iritis · iridocyclitis · uveitis · *glaucoma* and other serious conditions are accompanied by ciliary redness. If the eye is painful, if the pupil is different in size from the other, or if the cornea does not look absolutely transparent but slightly steamy or cloudy, then it would be wise to have expert advice quickly.

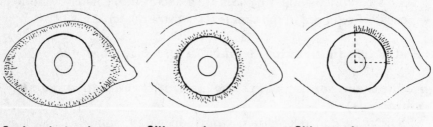

Conjunctival redness   **Ciliary redness**   **Ciliary redness**
Redness of the eye

Redness of the face

Due to *flushing*, which comes and goes, is dealt with under that heading. Other redness of the face may be related to the following: High or raised blood pressure. This will produce a generalized redness of the face.

Polycythemia is the opposite of *anemia*. It arises from an excess of red blood cells, and redness in the face is part of the general redness associated with the increased number of red blood cells in circulation.

Mitral valve heart disease produces a characteristic flushing of the upper part of the cheeks in many, but not in all, people who have the condition.

Pneumonia can produce a very red coloring of the cheeks, usually associated with the other signs and symptoms of pneumonia such as fever, chest pain and general feelings of being unwell.

Any cause of *fever* may give rise to redness of the face. A check with a clinical thermometer will soon show whether or not this cause should be considered.

See also *rosacea*.

Red nose   See *rosacea · rhinophyma*.

Red spots on the skin
See *cherry spots on the skin · rash · red birthmarks*.

Red stool   See *bleeding from the rectum*.

Red urine   See *blood in the urine*.

Referred pain
Pain generated in one structure but felt in another. For example, pleurisy affecting the diaphragm may cause pain to be felt in the

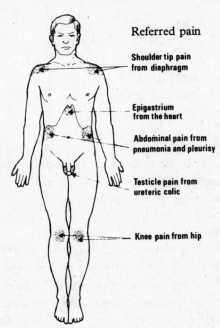

Referred pain

Shoulder tip pain
from diaphragm

Epigastrium
from the heart

Abdominal pain from
pneumonia and pleurisy

Testicle pain from
ureteric colic

Knee pain from hip

shoulder, and the pain of an acute appendicitis is felt first as referred pain in the center of the abdomen around the umbilicus and later in the right lower quarter of the abdomen.

Common sites of referred pain are shown in the illustration.

Reflux esophagitis

Produced when the valve at the lower end of the esophagus leaks and allows acid stomach contents to get into the esophagus. The pain is felt as a burning sensation under the lower half of the sternum (breastbone). Commonly there is a *hernia through the diaphragm* (a hiatus hernia) which causes the leak. Not all reflux esophagitis is associated with a hernia, but all will show the effect of gravity—lying down or reaching forwards will bring on the pain. The squirt effect can also produce pain when a full stomach under pressure pumps acid into the lower end of the esophagus. This often occurs when a person sits in an easy chair after a large meal.

Regurgitation of food   See *vomiting*.

Renal colic   See *ureteric colic*.

Restlessness   See *anxiety · hyperthyroidism*.

Restlessness at night

See *disorders of sleep · anxiety · peptic ulcer · depression*.

Restricted movement at a joint

See *limited movement at a joint*.

Retching

The muscular contraction which takes place to produce *vomiting*. The word is used to describe both the heaving which takes place before and during vomiting and also to indicate "dry vomiting." It is often associated with *nausea*.

Rheumatic fever

A disease following throat infection by a type of streptococcus bacterium. It is characterized by: *fever · swelling in joints · pain in joints · redness of the joints · skin rash · nodules* under the skin, particularly at the back of elbows and wrists and at the back of the head and down the spine · heart involvement, which can sometimes lead to rheumatic heart disease affecting the heart valves—for example, mitral stenosis.

Rheumatism
See *pain in joints · swelling in joints, osteoarthritis · rheumatic fever.*

Rheumatoid arthritis
A long-term disease affecting joints which can lead to destruction, deformity and loss of function in the joints. The cause is unknown. The disease usually shows first as *pain in joints* and later as *swelling in joints* with loss of joint movement. Early in the disease the joints of the hands and wrists are commonly affected, but later many joints can be involved. As the disease progresses, joint movement diminishes. Movement is often particularly difficult after a period of rest.
A juvenile form of rheumatoid arthritis occurs (Still's disease). It begins most often in the 1–3 age group, but may come on at any time before puberty.

Rhinophyma
A condition of the nose in which the end of the nose becomes red, and enlarges to give a "strawberry" or "potato" nose. It is associated with *rosacea*. Contrary to popular ideas, rhinophyma is not linked to excessive drinking.

Ridges and furrows on the nails
Those across the nail are found in *eczema,* and may also often be found in association with *white lines on the nails,* and for the same reasons.
Those along the line of the nail and finger may be healthy and normal in some people. However, ridges and furrows which appear where a smooth nail was found previously may be associated with *trauma* to the nail bed, or with diseases caused by infection—for example *candidosis*—or fungus infections of the nail bed.

Ringing in the ears See *tinnitus.*

Ringworm See *fungus infection of the skin.*

Rising at night to urinate (nocturia) See *frequency of urination.*

Rolling about with abdominal pain
Usually seen in severe *colic*. The colic may arise from the bowel, and may be associated with *diarrhea · intestinal obstruction · biliary colic · ureteric colic* (renal colic). See also *pain in the abdomen*.

Rosacea
Affects the areas of the face which can flush or blush. *Flushing* often occurs after meals, but in time may become permanent. A complication of rosacea is *rhinophyma* ("strawberry nose").
A condition of the cornea called interstitial keratitis is associated with rosacea. The eye and skin conditions are unrelated in severity, and sometimes serious eye problems can be associated with minor degrees of skin involvement.

Round shoulders   See *curvature of the spine · kyphosis*.

Roundworms   See *worms*.

Rumbling bowels   See *loud rumbling bowel sounds*.

Run-down   See *tiredness*.

Running ear
See *infection in the ear passage · infection in the middle ear*.

Running nose
The common causes of a running nose are colds, influenza and other upper respiratory infections. *Hay fever* and *allergic rhinitis* are also fairly common.
Chronic infection in the nasal sinuses—*sinusitis,* may also lead to a running nose.
A rare cause after a head injury is a small leak of cerebrospinal fluid into the nose.

Rupture   See *hernia*.

Salivation, excessive   See *nausea Parkinson's disease*.

Salpingitis

Inflammation and infection in the fallopian tubes commonly associated with *gonorrhea*. Salpingitis can give rise to *pain in the abdomen* which is generally accompanied by *fever*. If the right side only is affected, the condition can easily be mistaken for *appendicitis*. Some women who have gonorrhea have no symptoms of *sexually transmitted disease* as such, and are therefore unaware that investigation and treatment is needed until some secondary symptom such as pain in the abdomen occurs.

Sarcoidosis

A generalized disease which is found usually in the age group 30–50 years. Shortness of breath or *difficulty in breathing* is a common symptom, but the disease may present a variety of symptoms including general *tiredness, swelling of lymph nodes*, skin changes, and many other complaints.

Sarcoma See *cancer*.

Scabies

A skin disorder accompanied by intense *itching of the skin* especially at night. It is caused by infestation of the skin by a mite. The female burrows in the skin to lay her eggs. In the early stages, the disease is distributed in skin folds and creases such as the folds of the elbows, under the arms, in and around the navel and groin, and in the finger webs. General irritation may follow if the disease is not recognized and treated. In men the penis is often affected early in the disease. Scabies may be a *sexually transmitted disease*, or spread by any close body contact.

Scalding pain on urination See *pain on urination*.

Scaly skin

May be a disease that runs in families and produces fish-skin scaliness (icthyosis) of the skin. Scaliness in patches with a very white top may be due to *psoriasis*. After scarlet fever or streptococcal *sore throat*, the skin may peel in scaly patches, and may be shed. Late *syphilis* of the skin may also give rise to scaly patches or to scaly areas, especially on the soles of the feet. *Fungus infections of the skin* will give rise to scaliness and to peeling skin, either in circular patches (ringworm) or between the toes. Peeling between the toes usually begins in the 4/5 space, and spreads inwards first to the 3/4 space and then perhaps to the rest of the foot.

Scaliness of the scalp skin is called dandruff. A certain amount of shedding of surface skin is normal, and dandruff is not necessarily abnormal or unhealthy.

It is only when the condition becomes excessive that it can be considered abnormal. *Seborrheic dermatitis* of the scalp, psoriasis and occasionally ringworm of the scalp will cause scaliness.

Pityriasis rosea, a generalized transitory but non-serious skin disease which is accompanied by a rash of red scaly patches, is an occasional cause of scaly skin.

Generalized slight scaliness of the skin may be associated with *hypothyroidism*. See also *peeling of the skin*.

Scanty menstrual period   See *metrorrhagia*.

Schizophrenia (literally, "splitting of the mind")

The name given to a mental disorder of unknown origin which affects about one per cent of people everywhere. Some recover from schizophrenia, but it is often a serious long-term disorder which shows in a variety of ways, from coldness of response through disorders of thinking to easily recognizable madness. No short description of this illness is possible, on account of the complexity of the behavior and symptoms found. However, disordered thinking in clear consciousness is a central feature of the condition, the personality is not split into halves as is often supposed, but is fragmented into many small pieces.

Delusions and *hallucinations* may be found. Feelings of persecution may dominate the thoughts of a person suffering from paranoid schizophrenia. In adolescents and young adults who have a schizophrenic-type illness, the possibility of drug abuse should always be considered. In the 20–30 age group unusually disturbed behavior of any kind without obvious cause may be due to schizophrenia. Expert psychiatric assessment is always necessary if schizophrenia is suspected.

Sciatica

A particular kind of *pain in the leg* associated with disease or injury of the intervertebral disk. It is usually felt as a pain which runs down the leg, beginning in the buttock and traveling down the back of the thigh and the outside of the leg below the knee. It may even reach as far as the ankle and foot. Some *loss of feeling* and numbness may be found also. The pain and loss of feeling can be traced to the nerves trapped by the collapse of the disk at the point where they exit from the spinal cord. *Backache* is often present at the same time as sciatica—and for the same reason. When sciatica is present, the area of nerve root pressure will be in the lumbar region at the bottom of the spine.

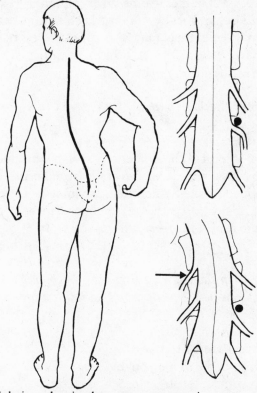

Lumbar disk lesions showing how nerve compression causes pain on either side. The person will tilt the spine to get relief. The pain is a referred pain down the leg.

Scoliosis   A sideways *curvature of the spine.*

Scratching   See *itching.*

Scurvy
The disease caused by deficiency of Vitamin C. The symptoms of scurvy are those of bleeding, usually into and around bones and joints, but also in the mouth and gums. *Bleeding under the skin* occurs too.
See also *black stools · blood in the urine · bleeding from . . . .*

Seasickness See *motion sickness*.

Seborrheic dermatitis (seborrheic eczema)
A disease associated with a skin that is particularly easily infected. The sufferer may have *red eyelids* (blepharitis) and infected fissures behind and above the ears. A very early manifestation is the "cradle cap" of babies. Some forms of dandruff are associated with this disease, and *scaly skin* on the chest and behind the ears is often seen. These areas may also appear to be red and glazed, and may have yellow crusts or greasy scales. Occasionally a moist lesion of the skin may be found.

Sensitive tooth See *toothache*.

Septic arthritis
Infection in a joint. The infection may be produced by local *trauma* or by local spread of infection from an *abscess, carbuncle* or other septic lesion. Sometimes the joint is infected through blood-borne systemic spread of infection. *Pain in the joint* and *swelling in the joint* with *fever* will often result.

Sex problems
See *bleeding from the vagina · frigidity · impotence · masturbation · premature ejaculation · priapism · sexually transmitted diseases · vaginismus.*

Sexually transmitted diseases
Spread from person to person by heterosexual intercourse, by homosexual contact or by close body contact. They include: *syphilis · gonorrhea ·* non-specific urethritis (NSU), or non-gonococcal urethritis (NGU) · *trichomoniasis ·* genital *herpesvirus infection ·* infestation with acarus (mite causing *scabies*), crab lice (*pediculosis* pubis) · *genital warts,* and other less common diseases. In any case where sexually transmitted disease is suspected or likely, all sexual partners should be examined by a physician, preferably by one who specializes in these problems.
Syphilis first gives rise to an ulcer which heals by itself. This ulcer is nearly always on the genitals, but may also be found in other parts of the body such as the lips, mouth, tongue, and tonsil and on the finger.
In the secondary or middle stage of the disease (three months to about two years), the infection is characterized by generalized

skin rashes which are seldom irritable, by ulcers in the mouth, and by genital and anal syphilitic warts called condylomata lata. Gonorrhea usually gives rise to a *urethral discharge* in males. In females, more than 80 per cent of the patients have no symptoms, and do not know that they are infected. Any woman who suspects that she may have been infected with gonorrhea can only find out in two ways: she passes on the infection to a man who then suggests to her that she may have the disease, or she can go to a doctor who will make special examinations and tests to look for the gonococcus causing the disease. Some women with gonorrhea have a *vaginal discharge* and/or *pain on urinating* or pain after urinating. They are probably the lucky ones, because they know that something is wrong and can seek help.

Non-specific urethritis (NSU), sometimes called non-gonococcal urethritis (NGU), is a disease of males in which the symptom is a urethral discharge.

Shaking

For shaking in one part of the body, see *tremor*. For shaking all over, see also *chill · fits*.

Shingles   See *herpes zoster*.

Shivering

The sensation that occurs when a person feels cold and the muscles contract involuntarily to produce heat and thus raise the body temperature. Teeth chattering may be noticed as a part of shivering.

Shivering will occur under two main conditions—first when a person is in a cold environment or is insufficiently clothed and his body temperature is tending to fall. Second, when the body temperature is rising in *fever* there will be an initial stage of *feeling cold* before the stage of *feeling hot* and flushed is reached. A *chill* may occur.

Shoulder pain   See *pain in the shoulder*.

Shortness of breath   See *difficulty in breathing*.

Sick, "being sick"   See *vomiting*.

Sighing   See *uremia · depression*.

181

Sinking feeling in the stomach See *nausea · anxiety.*

Sinusitis
Inflamation in the nasal sinuses, the bony spaces inside the skull communicating with the inside of the nose. When they become infected they can give rise to symptoms of *pain in the forehead* and *pain in the upper jaw* and face. Infected sinuses can also lead to a *postnasal drip* and to *bad breath.*

Skin blisters See *blisters in the skin.*

Skin itching See *itching of the skin.*

Skin pigmentation See *disorders of pigmentation of the skin.*

Skin, scaly See *scaly skin.*

Sleep difficulties See *disorders of sleep.*

Sleepiness, excessive See *narcolepsy · disorders of sleep.*

Sleepwalking
Usually associated with *nightmares* and *anxiety.* Expert help will be needed if the sleepwalking occurs more than rarely, so that the basic problems can be discovered and dealt with.

Slimy stools See *mucus in the stools.*

Slow heartbeat (bradycardia)
Occurs in some normal, healthy people, and can even be as low as 40–50 beats per minute. Slow heart rates are commoner in athletes. They also occur in *heart block,* and may result in *fainting.* A pacemaker will control the heart rate in this condition. *Hypothyroidism* and *hypothermia* may be associated with a slow heartbeat.

Slurred speech
Will usually be found in people who have had a *stroke.* Abuse of alcohol and drugs may also cause slurred speech. See also *difficulty in speaking.*

Smell, loss of See *loss of sense of smell.*

Smooth tongue   See *anemia · sore tongue.*

Sneezing

A reflex triggered off usually by irritation of the nasal mucous membrane lining the nose. The commonest cause is a cold. Irritation by dust or by other substances such as pepper, snuff and "sneezing powder" can produce sneezing. *Hay fever* and other causes of *allergic rhinitis* may lead to bouts of sneezing associated with a *running nose.*

Other occasional causes of sneezing are bright sunlight on the eye and sexual excitement.

Sternutation is the medical term for sneezing.

Sniffling   Due to a *stuffy nose,* a *running nose* or a blocked nose.

Snoring

The noise of snoring is made by vibration of the soft palate in people who breathe through their mouth when sleeping. It usually occurs when lying on the back. Any cause of nose blockage or preferred mouth breathing will tend to produce snoring.

A list of possible causes include: smallness of the nasal passages · common cold · deflection of the nasal septum · sinusitus · *hay fever* or other *allergic rhinitis* · nasal polyps · nasal *catarrh* · enlarged tonsils and adenoids · pharyngitis · other causes such as a *cyst* or *tumor.*

Hypothyroidism (myxedema) may also make people prone to snore. Fat people also seem to snore more freely than thin ones.

"Snow blindness"

Not a dangerous or serious condition and does not lead to loss of vision, so it is badly named. It is a form of sunburn caused by the ultraviolet rays of the sun reflected from the snow. Dark glasses—or even clear ones—will prevent the condition. The eyes feel red, gritty and painful. Staying indoors for twenty-four hours will usually result in sufficient improvement to resume activities wearing glasses.

Soiling

Relates to the incontinence of stools which may be associated with *diarrhea* and with illnesses which cause that complaint. Disorders affecting the anal sphincter, including *hemorrhoids* (piles), and muscle laxity due to old age may also cause soiling. Any condition which causes pain at the anus or *pain on having a bowel movement* may lead to incomplete closure of the anal sphincter, and so to soiling. *Itching around the anus* may be caused by soiling. Children under the age of about 2½ normally will soil, because they are not old enough to have gained voluntary control of their anal sphincter.

Sore eye   See *pain in the eye.*

Sore throat
Commonly associated with an upper respiratory infection such as a cold or influenza, and with *tonsillitis* and *pharyngitis.* These illnesses are often accompanied by *fever.* Severe pain on swallowing may be due to a *quinsy* (peritonsillar abscess) or to a foreign body such as a fishbone in the pharynx.

Sore tongue
Local causes such as injury, small *ulcers in the mouth,* or abrasion from sharp edges of teeth or dentures will be readily apparent. Streptococcal glossitis—an infection of the tongue—produces a painful tongue with redness of the tip and the margins in the front half.
In other cases of streptococcal glossitis, tongue fissures are found. These may be discovered by putting out the tongue and spreading it by a slight pull with the fingers on each side.
Pernicious and some other types of *anemia* are associated with a painful tongue. In these cases the soreness is usually felt most acutely along the sides of the tongue, which will look smooth and shiny.

Soreness in the mouth
May be due to a *sore tongue,* to *painful gums* or *infected gums,* or to *ulcers in the mouth.* In babies *spots in the mouth* may be sore, and in elderly people especially there may be *redness and soreness at the corners of the mouth.*

Specks before the eyes
See *black specks before the eyes · spots before the eyes.*

Speech difficulty   See *difficulty in speaking.*

Spitting blood See *blood from the mouth · coughing or spitting blood.*

184

Spondylitis, ankylosing See *ankylosing spondylitis.*

Spondylosis See *backache · pain in the back of the neck · sciatica.*

Spoon-shaped nails (koilonychia)

Found in people who have *anemia.* The curvature across the nails is flattened, resulting in a slight hollow in the center of the nail.

Spots before the eyes

Can be described as fixed spots or moving spots. If a spot cannot be seen after several rapid blinks, it was probably due to mucus or dirt on the surface of the eye. Fixed spots are usually associated with areas of loss of vision due to disease of the retina or diseases which affect the retina. *Glaucoma* may cause a fixed blind spot. Moving or floating spots are usually due to opacities in the vitreous humor, the jelly-like fluid in the back of the eyeball. *Redness of the eye* may be present in some cases. See also *black specks before the eyes.*

Spots in the mouth

In babies spots are often due to infection with the yeast-like organism candida albicans. The infection—sometimes called *candidosis*—is usually easy to treat. In children who have measles tiny bluish white spots may appear inside the mouth and on the inside of the cheeks and lips. The spots are abouttpin-head size (Koplik's spots). At this stage of measles the temperature is usually slightly raised, the eyes may be red, and the child feels unwell.

Spots in the mouth may be associated with bleeding disorders such as *purpura, Vitamin C deficiency, leukemia* and *hemophilia.* Such spots will be red or reddish purple, and are local areas of bleeding into the tissues of the mouth. Yellowish or brownish spots may be found in the mouth associated with *Addison's disease,* a disease related to the adrenal glands. Spots in the mouth should be distinguished from *ulcers in the mouth,* from *white patches on the tongue,* and from the grayish patches seen in *Vincent's infection.*

Spots on the lips

A single yellow-colored "cold spot" which appears at the height of a common cold or just after is probably due to *herpesvirus* infection. Multiple yellow spots on the lips may also be seen due to herpesvirus infection. The spots usually break down at the surface and discharge their yellowish contents. This discharge is highly infectious. Spots on the lips should be distinguished from *ulcers on the lips.*

Sputum See *phlegm · infected sputum.*

Squinting eyes (strabismus)
May be seen in young babies and children. If the condition is not recognized and treated early in life, it is unlikely that binocular vision can be restored. Even a very mild squint can give rise to *amblyopia.* If later the eyes are straightened by operation, with good cosmetic effect, monocular vision will result. Squints coming on in later life will usually be due to paralysis or weakness of the muscles which move the eyes. This may cause *double vision.* Diseases of the brain and of the nerves to the eye muscles are possible causes. *Cysts* and *tumors* which affect the brain or press on nerves may be the cause of the symptoms. Expert diagnosis is always necessary, and help should be sought soon by anyone who has these symptoms later in life.

Staggering
May be due to extreme tiredness, but if persistent, it is probably related to diseases of the nervous system which affect the control of muscular coordination. There are a great number of possible reasons for lack of coordination, and expert medical help will be necessary to sort them out. Some reasons are comparatively trivial but others are serious, so help should always be sought if even slight staggering is found. *Hypothermia* may be a cause of staggering in cold conditions.

Staring or protruding eyes (exophthalmos)
Usually associated with *hyperthyroidism.* If you have this symptom you should look also at the front of the neck in the midline around the notch above the top of the breastbone (sternum) to see if there is any evidence of *swelling in the neck* which may arise from the thyroid gland.
Some people have mildly protruding eyes as a family characteristic. Protrusion of one eye only is probably due to a tumor behind the eye which is pushing the eyeball forwards. Occasionally bleeding behind the eye may do this—sometimes after *trauma.*

Status epilepticus
Severe *epilepsy,* in which one fit runs into the next before the sufferer has recovered from the previous attack.

Stenosis
The term used to describe failure of a sphincter, or valve, to open. Failure to open the valve at the lower end of the stomach (the pylorus) is pyloric stenosis. This disease in babies causes projectile vomiting, in which the contents of the stomach are shot out, often for a distance of three feet or more. Pyloric stenosis can also be due to cancer of the stomach. See also *achalasia.*

Sterility   Inability to have children. See *infertility.*

Sternutation   See *sneezing.*

Sticky eyes   Usually due to *conjunctivitis.*

Stiff neck
A stiff neck of sudden onset without apparent injury is most often related to a cervical disk lesion or narrowing. Commonly this narrowing is in the 5/6 or 6/7 cervical disk spaces. Any injury or cause of arthritis or degeneration in the joints of the spine also may produce a stiff neck. Disease may cause collapse of a vertebra or vertebrae leading to a stiff neck. Tuberculosis in the bone, late *syphilis,* and *tumors* may be involved. X rays will often help to indicate the cause or causes.
Tetanus and *meningitis* can cause neck stiffness. There will usually be fever and other signs of general illness in these cases. See also *pain in the back of the neck.*

Stiff shoulder   See *frozen shoulder · pain in joints.*

Stiffness in joints
See *limited movement at a joint · pain in joints · swelling in joints.*

Still's disease   See *rheumatoid arthritis.*

Stomachache   See *pain in the abdomen.*

Stomach pain   See *pain in the abdomen.*

Stomatitis

Inflammation in the mouth. It is often associated with *infected gums* (gingivitis). *Vincent's infection* is a common form of stomatitis. Stomatitis may also be related to *tonsillitis*.

Stones in the gallbladder

Can cause *pain in the abdomen* and *indigestion,* particularly after eating fatty food. Gallstones may give rise to *biliary colic,* and may be associated with *infection of the gallbladder*. If the gallstones obstruct the outflow of bile, *jaundice* can result.

Stones in the urine   See *gravel or stones in the urine*.

Stools, bloody or streaked with blood

See *bleeding from the rectum · constipation*.

Stools, bulky   See *constipation*.

Stools, dry   See *constipation*.

Stools, hard   See *constipation*.

Stools, large   See *constipation*.

Stools, pale   See *pale stools*.

Stools, slimy   See *mucus in the stools*.

Stoop   See *curvature of the spine · kyphosis*.

Stopped-up bowel   See *constipation · intestinal obstruction*.

"Stork marks"   See *disorders of pigmentation of the skin*.

Strabismus

The medical word for *squinting eyes* due to weakness or imbalance of the extraocular eye muscles. The squint is said to be an external strabismus if the affected eye looks outwards when the normal eye is looking straight ahead, and an internal strabismus if the affected eye looks inwards. Often squints can be corrected by operations on the eye muscles. However it may not be possible to restore binocular vision, and *amblyopia* may persist in the affected eye. In this condition the eye sees, but the brain does not perceive the visual signals from the eye, or *double vision* would result.

Strain, feeling of   See *stress*.

Strain of   See *pain in . . . · swellings of . . .*

Strawberry nose   See *rhinophyma*.

Strawberry tongue
A red mottled tongue resembling the pattern of a strawberry which appears in the early stages of scarlet fever. It usually lasts until after the rash has appeared.

Stress
A condition brought about by pressure, tension, overwork or strain of any kind. The particular symptoms experienced by individuals can vary widely, but are often related mainly to one *target organ* or system of the body.
The following may be brought on or made worse by stress: *asthma · allergy · migraine ·* the *irritable bowel syndrome · atopy · palpitation · peptic ulcers ·* some skin diseases.
If a person feels that he or she is under stress, then he or she probably is. *Irritability, anxiety, depression* and various other *psychological illnesses* or problems can all be associated with stress.

Stress incontinence
A problem suffered by women, usually due to *prolapse of the vagina and uterus.* Prolapse follows difficulties in childbirth which causes damage to the control mechanism. When the sufferer coughs, laughs or strains, she suffers from *urine leaking or dribbling.* Operative treatment is usually necessary to deal with the condition if it is other than slight.

Stretch marks
As their name implies, are caused by stretching of the skin. These marks are commonly found over the lower abdomen of pregnant women, but they can also occur on the thighs and breasts. In *obesity* stretch marks may be found all over the body. Recent stretch marks tend to be red or pink. Old ones become white.

Stridor

A high-pitched *wheezing* heard when the larynx or trachea is partially obstructed. Stridor is usually associated with *difficulty in breathing*. See under that heading for the causes of stridor. Whooping cough may also be a cause. The most common cause of stridor in children is infection, either viral or bacterial. Stridor can occur in some healthy children under two years of age, who will also usually have noisy breathing. See also *croup*.

Stroke

A destruction of brain brought about by interruption of its blood supply. This may be the result of bleeding into the brain substance (cerebral hemorrhage), or cessation of blood flow due to a cerebral *thrombosis,* or a cerebral *embolism.* The symptoms of a stroke are usually of sudden onset, and include *paralysis* and inability to use the muscles on one side of the body. The amount of disability will depend on the amount of brain damage. The inability to use muscles will be shown by lack of movement, by dragging of a leg, or by difficulty in making certain movements, especially fine movements. *Difficulty in speaking* can often occur —sometimes inability to speak, in other cases thick *slurred speech. Loss of memory* may also result.

Stroke, heat   See *heatstroke*.

Stuffy nose   See *blocked nose · running nose*.

Stye

A small *abscess* in the hair root of an eyelash. It can give rise to pain, swelling and *redness of the eyelids*.

Suicidal thoughts   See *depression*.

Sweating   See *excessive sweating*.

Swelling at the anus

May be due to *hemorrhoids,* an *abscess,* or to one of the causes listed under *swellings which can occur anywhere in the body. Pain on having a bowel movement* may also be felt.

Occasionally a *cancer* of the rectum may appear as a swelling at the anus. This may be accompanied by *bleeding from the rectum.*

Swelling behind the knee

Can often be caused by *bursitis* in which an excess of fluid is found in one of the small bursae which are around the knee. *Swellings which can occur anywhere in the body* may be found behind the knee. *Varicose veins* are commonly found behind the knee. An *aneurysm* may also be found. Less common causes are *tumors* and *cysts* arising from the bones. See also *swelling on a bone*.

Swelling in joints

Can occur as a result of *trauma* or disease. *Rheumatic fever* will cause swelling of joints associated with general upset, *fever* and *pain in joints*. *Gout* and *rheumatoid arthritis* can cause joint swellings of sudden or slow onset. *Osteoarthritis* will generally begin slowly, but occasionally sudden swelling may occur due to an excess of fluid in the joint (a joint effusion). An occasional cause of joint swellings is *psoriatic arthritis,* which is associated with *psoriasis*.

Some infectious diseases can be associated with an infective arthritis, and these include pneumonia, typhoid fever, scarlet fever and gonorrhea.

Swelling in the abdomen

Can be due to enlargement of any of the abdominal organs, to tumors or cysts arising from any of these organs or to fluid (ascites) distending and filling the abdominal cavity.

Normal swellings in the abdomen, which are so obvious they are sometimes overlooked, can result from overeating · *obesity* · *gas in the bowel* · a full bladder · pregnancy. Any swelling in the abdomen needs prompt medical examination.

Swelling in the ear cartilage   See *gout* · *cauliflower ear*.

Swelling in the neck

Swellings in the neck can be divided into three groups.

MIDLINE SWELLINGS include thyroglossal cysts, that is, cysts arising from a congenital defect. They can appear at any time, but are commonest in childhood and at and after puberty. A pharyngeal pouch may also be a cause of a midline swelling. This is a pouch formed from the pharynx which fills with food and swells. Some pouches can be emptied by pressure from the outside. Large pouches result in *difficulty in swallowing*. *Swelling of the thyroid* can also cause a midline swelling in the neck.

SWELLINGS NOT IN THE MIDLINE may be one-sided or occur on both sides. The commonest swelling in the neck is from *swelling of the lymph nodes,* and this is most frequently secondary to teeth, throat, pharynx and tonsil infections. There are, however, many other possible causes of swelling of lymph nodes which are listed under that heading. Swelling of the thyroid is another common neck swelling. Rare causes of neck swellings include swellings in the sterno-mastoid muscle, cervical ribs, bronchial cysts, actinomycosis, and infections deep in the neck or cervical spine which track outwards.

The third group of neck swelling are among *swellings which can occur anywhere in the body.*

Swelling in the scrotum

Described according to where the swelling arises.

SWELLING IN THE SKIN may arise from *boil* or *abscess* · sebaceous *cyst(s)* or other *swelling which can occur anywhere in the body* · *warts* · primary *syphilis* · skin *cancer.* The latter is common in people who are exposed to soot, pitch, tar or oil in the course of their work.

SWELLING UNDER THE TUNICA VAGINALIS may arise from a hydrocele, an accumulation of clear fluid which appears between the testicle and the tunica vaginalis, the interior covering of the testicles. It is the commonest scrotal swelling in elderly men and young male infants. Other swellings under the tunica vaginalis can be of blood or pus, and are uncommon.

SWELLING OF THE TESTICLE may arise from torsion of the testicle, when it rotates and cuts off its blood supply. Urgent surgery is usually necessary. Other causes of swelling are mumps or other infection in the testicle with epididymitis. Swellings of the testicle are sometimes secondary to a *sexually transmitted disease,* for example *gonorrhea* or *syphilis* of the testicle. Tumors of the testicle, especially seminoma and teratoma, can cause swelling. Any firm swelling of the testicle in younger men, especially if it is painless, should always be viewed with great suspicion, and should be seen by a doctor with minimal delay.

SWELLING OF THE EPIDIDYMUS may be secondary to urinary infections or *sexually transmitted diseases.*

SWELLING OF THE CORD may be due to a varicocele, which is *varicose veins* in the scrotum. Varicocele is commoner on the left side, but can occur on either or both sides. The contents of the scrotum are said to feel like a bag of worms in those who have a varicocele. Cysts of the cord may cause swelling of the cord. SWELLING IN THE SCROTUM can also be caused by an inguinal *hernia* sliding down into the scrotum.

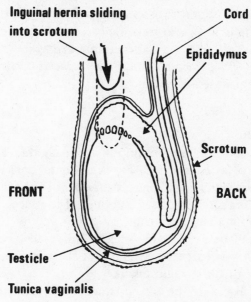

Inguinal hernia sliding into scrotum

Cord

Epididymus

Scrotum

FRONT

BACK

Testicle

Tunica vaginalis

Possible causes of a swelling in the scrotum

Swelling of the ankle(s)

When not due to *trauma* is usually worse at night, and is associated with fluid retention and *edema* in *heart failure* and kidney failure. Local circulatory failure in *deep vein thrombosis* and *varicose veins in the legs* will also lead to swelling of the affected ankle(s) or leg(s).

Local *trauma* may also cause an ankle to swell, but this will usually be associated with *pain in the ankle.*

Swelling of the eyelid(s)

Swelling of the lids of both eyes may be due to *conjunctivitis*, with grittiness and sandiness being felt in the eye, or may be part of a general condition. For example *hypothyroidism* (myxedema) may cause baggy puffy, or thick eyelids. Kidney disease and heart failure may result in fluid accumulation, *edema* and puffiness of the eyelids. *Allergies* and *angio-neurotic edema* may cause much swelling of one or both eyelids.

Localized conditions which cause swelling of one eyelid are styes, an infection of a hair follicle, a condition which affects the glands in the eyelid · a virus disease called molluscum contagiosum · nevi · moles · simple and malignant tumors.

Xanthelasma palpebrarum is the name given to two little yellowish swellings which appear on the upper lids on the nasal sides of each. The condition is associated with hyperlipidemia (excess of lipid in the blood), and in some cases with *high blood pressure*. For cosmetic reasons the xanthelasmata may be removed. See also *swelling of the face* and *swelling of the lips. Drooping of the eyelids* can be caused by swelling.

Swelling of the face

The causes may include: mumps · stone in the salivary duct · infections such as *boils* and *carbuncles* · dental *abscess* (gumboil) · *swelling of the lymph nodes* · *cysts* or *tumors* of the salivary glands · cysts or tumors of the sinuses or bones of the face.

A stone blocking the duct can lead to a swelling of the salivary gland that can be seen in the cheek. This will come up rapidly when anything is eaten or drunk, and then may subside slowly until food or drink is again taken.

Infections will usually be accompanied by pain, especially throbbing pain, and by fever and general feelings of being unwell.

Swelling of the lymph nodes may be secondary to infectious illnesses locally, or may be part of a condition causing generalized swelling of all the lymph nodes, such as *Hodgkin's disease, leukemia* or secondary *syphilis*.

Cysts or tumors will usually give rise to swellings of slowly increasing size which may be painful or painless.

See also *swelling of the lips · swelling of the eyelids*.

Swelling of the knee

May be a swelling in the joint itself caused by an excess of joint fluid or by bleeding into the joint associated with *trauma. Bursitis,* in which an excess of fluid is found in one of the small bursae around the knee is common. "Housemaids knee" is a popular name for this form of bursitis.

Other swellings can be due to varicose veins, to an *abscess* or to one of the *swellings which can occur anywhere in the body. A cyst* of the knee cartilages or a *displaced or torn knee cartilage* may cause a swelling of the knee. Swelling may be associated with the conditions listed under *pain in joints.*

Swelling of the lymph nodes

Can occur all over the body as a result of systemic disease or locally as a result of disease in that area.

Swelling of lymph glands all over the body can, among other causes, be due to: *Hodgkin's disease* · *leukemia* · German measles (rubella) · *syphilis* · *mononucleosis* (glandular fever) · *sarcoidosis* · *tumors* of lymph glands · generalized skin infections.

Glandular fever and German measles will usually be accompanied by *fever*, a *sore throat*, a feeling of being unwell and a skin *rash*. Generalized skin infections are usually fairly obvious.

The local swelling of lymph nodes will commonly be associated with infectious lesions in the area drained by the lymph glands— for example, a *boil* or *abscess* on the thumb may cause enlargement of the lymph node at the inner side of the elbow and enlargement of the nodes in the armpit.

Cancers and malignant disease can also cause swellings of lymph nodes in the areas affected.

Sometimes enlargement of a lymph node in any one area examined can be mistakenly thought to be due to something in that area when in fact it is the only discovered part of generalized enlargement of lymph nodes all over the body.

Swelling of the throat or larynx

Sudden onset may be the result of *allergies* or insect stings. Swellings that may suddenly appear anywhere in the body in *angio-neurotic edema* can be dangerous in the throat area because of obstruction to breathing. Treatment should aim to combat the allergy and to keep the victim breathing. (See first aid section). Swellings of the throat may cause *difficulty in swallowing,* and may be related to infections—for example *tonsillitis, quinsy* and upper respiratory infections.

See also *swellings in the neck* · *stridor* · *difficulty in breathing.*

Swelling of the thyroid gland

The thyroid gland is situated in the lower part of the neck, above the top of the breastbone. It moves upwards on swallowing. So any swelling in the lower part of the neck which moves on swallowing is probably of or in the thyroid. Swelling of the thyroid may be uniform, or may affect only one part of the gland. Thyroid swellings therefore can appear in the neck on one side or both or in the midline. Swellings may be associated with *hyperthyroidism* or *hypothyroidism,* or with a normal state of secretion from the gland. Swellings of the thyroid may compress the trachea, giving *stridor* or *difficulty in breathing,* or may press on the esophagus giving *difficulty in swallowing.*

Pressure on the nerves to the larynx may result in *hoarseness* or alteration of the voice, or in paralysis of one or both vocal cords. The thyroid may also enlarge downwards into the chest giving rise to chest symptoms.

A simple swelling of the whole of the thyroid is often called a goiter. See also *swelling in the neck.*

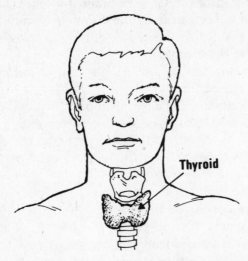

The position of the thyroid gland in the neck

Swelling on a bone

May be due to a recent or old fracture · disease of the bone, such as osteomyelitis · rickets · Vitamin C deficiency (scurvy) · systemic diseases affecting bones, such as *acromegaly* or *Paget's disease* · bone *cyst* or *tumor.*

A swelling on a bone may easily be mistaken for a *swelling of a joint,* or vice versa, if the swelling is near the joint. Any swelling of the bone, with or without any other systemic symptoms such as pain or fever, should be evaluated by a doctor.

Swelling or lump in the breast

Can be divided into several categories:

SWELLING OF THE WHOLE OF BOTH BREASTS can be related to

puberty · the premenstrual phase of the menstrual cycle · pregnancy · lactation (breast feeding).

SWELLING OF ONE BREAST may be due to uneven development at puberty. This is common and unimportant in the long term, because it usually comes right. It can, however, lead to emotional problems in young girls. Explanation by the right person may be all that is necessary. Rarely, where there is marked asymmetry, plastic surgery may correct the problem.

LOCALIZED SWELLING IN ONE BREAST. This is the danger category. The causes of localized swelling in one breast include acute mastitis (breast *abscess*). This condition is commonest when breast feeding, and may be associated with a painful or *cracked nipple* · other breast abscess, such as a tuberculous abscess. This is uncommon · fat necrosis, an uncommon condition in which local areas of fat in the breast are deprived of blood supply and "die" · cysts of the breast or skin and fat layer · non-malignant *tumors* · *cancers* and other malignant tumors.

Breast cancers are common. It may not be possible to know the exact nature of a breast swelling without removal and subsequent examination of the lump under a microscope. So waste no time. Any woman who notices a lump or swelling in one breast should consult a physician immediately so that she can have the condition expertly diagnosed and treated. The outlook in early breast cancer is favorable and can be improved by early diagnosis and treatment.

MULTIPLE SWELLINGS IN BOTH BREASTS are usually due to fibroadenomata or multiple cysts. However, it is wise to take advice soon from your physician about any breast swelling or lump, in case it is a cancer. Multiple swellings are usually not cancer.

SWELLINGS THAT ARE NOT IN OR OF THE BREAST. For example from other diseases of the ribs and chest wall · from an *abscess* of the chest wall · *empyema*.

See also *pain in the chest*.

Swellings in the groin and crotch area

Commonly due to *swelling of the lymph nodes* in that area, or to a *hernia*. Other causes, such as an *abscess* or *swellings which can occur anywhere in the body*, should also be considered. The lymph nodes in the groin are related to the legs and to the genital, buttock and anal areas. *Sexually transmitted diseases* and cancers of the genital areas and rectum can cause enlarged lymph nodes in the groin. See also *swelling in the scrotum*.

Swellings near joints

May be from *bursitis,* or may be the nodules of *rheumatic fever,* the tophi of *gout,* or Heberden's nodes found in *osteoarthritis.* They may also be *swellings which can occur anywhere on the body* which just happen to be near joints.

Swellings of the lips

Sudden onset will be seen in *allergies · angio-neurotic edema ·* insect stings and bites · infections or *ulcers of the lips.* See also *swelling of the face · swelling of the eyelids.*

Swellings which can occur anywhere in the body

On, in or under the skin may be caused by: sebaceous *cyst ·* bleeding (bruise) · lipomas · *allergies · urticaria · angio-neurotic edema · boils · abscesses · carbuncles ·* infections of all kinds · insect bites and stings · neurofibromas · gummas from late *syphilis · cancers,* or other *tumors.*

Sebaceous cysts are usually oval or round-shaped smooth swellings due to a blocked sweat gland. They will be felt just under the skin.

Bleeding will usually be easy to recognize because of the bluish discoloration that it causes.

Lipomas are simple local overgrowths of fat, and so occur in the fat layer under the skin. They feel like fat.

Insect bites and stings can usually be recognized by the mark of the bite or sting and the recollection of having been bitten or stung.

Neurofibromas appear under the skin anywhere on the body. They are usually slightly irregular knotty swellings. In some people they can be very numerous, and the whole body may be affected with them.

A safe rule for swellings of any kind is to assume that they may be related to a serious condition until you are assured by your physician that they are not serious.

Swelling under the arm

Probably due to a *swelling of the lymph nodes* or an *abscess.* Other causes listed under *swellings which can occur anywhere in the body* should also be considered. The lymph nodes under the arm are related to the breast, so any *swelling or lump in the breast* or *discharge from the nipple* should be looked for.

198

Swelling under the nail (paronychia)

Usually due to infection around the growing edge of the nail. This may result in a red, raised horseshoe-shaped swelling around the nail. A small *abscess* may form.

Syphilis

A *sexually transmitted disease* caused by infection with a spirochete called treponema pallidum. The first sign of the disease is an ulcer or sore, which is usually in the genital area but may be on the lip, mouth or tongue, and can also be found on the finger or elsewhere. The primary ulcer or sore usually appears from six to eight weeks after contact with the previously infected person, but can appear from nine days after contact up to about three months. This so-called primary ulcer heals without treatment. The ulcer is highly infectious.

If the disease is not diagnosed and treated in the primary stage when the ulcer is present, it goes on to the secondary (middle) and tertiary (late) stages of the disease. In these stages the infection is generalized and the treponemata are present throughout the body.

The secondary stage of the disease begins when the primary ulcer has healed. A generalized skin rash may be present. Lymph nodes all over the body will be enlarged, and ulcers may appear in the mouth. Warty growths called condylomata lata may appear in the genital area and around the anus. These and the ulcers in the mouth are highly infectious. This secondary stage of syphilis appears any time from four to twenty-four months after the primary ulcer. Again, if the disease is not diagnosed and treated, it goes on to the tertiary or late stage of the disease.

In the late stage the disease can be very destructive of many body structures. It causes narrowing and obliteration of small arteries. In the brain this leads to serious effects of many kinds. Ulcerative destructive lesions called gummas appear, capable of eroding and destroying tissues. *Aneurysm* of the aorta is a disease caused by late syphilis.

Syphilis can be diagnosed in the primary stage by looking under a special microscope for the causative organism in serum from the surface of the primary sore. Around the time that the primary sore heals, blood tests become positive. So syphilis can be diagnosed if present, even though there are no general effects of the disease. Because syphilis can be so destructive in the later stages it is always wise to try to diagnose and treat it at as early a stage as possible.

Tachycardia See *fast heartbeat*.

Tapeworms See *hydatid cysts*.

Target lesions on the skin See *blisters on the skin*.

Target organ
The name given to the organ or part of the body which reacts in cases of *allergies* or *stress*. For example, allergy to grass pollens may cause the nose to become congested and the eyes to become itchy (from hay fever). Worry and tension may bring on an attack of *migraine* affecting the brain, or may cause the *irritable bowel syndrome* affecting the *colon*.

Taste, loss of See *loss of sense of taste*.

Teeth chattering See *shivering · rigor · feeling cold · fever*.

Teeth, cracked See *cracked teeth*.

Temperature, raised See *fever*.

Tenderness in the breast See *pain in the (female) breast*.

Tenderness in the breasts and nipples
See *tightness in the breast and nipples*.

"Tennis elbow"
A form of dull nagging pain felt at the outer side of the elbow, often by gripping things in the hand. In some cases the pain may be so sudden and sharp as to cause the person to let go. Even lifting a cup full of coffee can give rise to pain. If the palm of the hand is used in support, no pain is felt.
Medical opinion is divided about the exact causes of "tennis elbow." However, there is no doubt that many cases are con-

nected with pain in the back of the neck and shoulders which is associated with narrowing of the cervical disks. This narrowing leads to entrapment of the nerves as they leave the spiral cord. Pain is then felt in the areas served by these nerves. So an X ray of the neck may be required in cases of "tennis elbow" rather than attention to the elbow.

Tenosynovitis See *creaking under the skin.*

Tension See *anxiety · stress.*

Tension, premenstrual See *premenstrual tension.*

Tetanus (lockjaw)
An infectious disease caused by clostridium tetani. It can arise following any cut or wound, particularly if deep and sustained outdoors. The infection results in very intense spasms and contraction of all the muscles of the body, which may be mistaken for a *fit.* At the height of the disease, however, there may be severe convulsions. An early sign of the disease is spasm in the jaw muscles (trismus)—hence the name lockjaw. Today the disease is prevented by inoculation with tetanus toxoid which most people will probably have received in childhood. They should have it again in case of a deep or dirty wound or an extensive burn.

Tetany
A condition which shows as muscle twitching and *cramps · difficulty in speaking · difficulty in breathing · convulsions* or *fits.* The condition may resemble *epilepsy.* It may arise from a lowering of the blood calcium content as a result of deficiency of the secretion from the parathyroid glands—hypoparathyroidism.
Another cause of tetany is overbreathing. This can occur because of injury, burns, excitement, *hysteria* and other causes. Overbreathing washes out the carbon dioxide from the blood. Carbon dioxide in solution is a weak acid, and when this is lost the blood becomes more alkaline resulting in a condition of metabolic alkalosis. This alkaline condition of the blood gives rise to the symptoms known as tetany because there is less blood calcium available in an alkaline environment.

Thinness See *loss of weight.*

Thirst

If excessive, this may be a symptom of *diabetes mellitus* or *diabetes insipidus*. In these cases it will usually be associated with *frequency of urination,* and perhaps also with *loss of weight*. Other causes are hot weather · *fever* · loss of fl·id associated with *diarrhea* and *vomiting* · fluid retention associated with kidney and heart failure.

Thought disorders

See *anxiety* · *confusion* · *depression* · *loss of memory* · *psychosis.*

Thrombosis

Means the formation of blood clots within the heart or a blood vessel. Clotting can occur in an artery, a vein or the blood spaces in the skull, for example the cavernous sinus.

CORONARY THROMBOSIS means clotting of blood in the coronary arteries which supply blood to the heart muscle. As a result of this clotting, the blood supply to the heart muscle is cut off or reduced, and therefore the heart muscle cannot function properly or at all, for lack of the oxygen supplied by the blood. This results in *ischemic heart disease* or death.

Clotting is usually due to one or all of the following: slackening of circulation · changes in the composition of the blood · changes in the internal lining of the blood vessels.

Thrombus

A clot of blood in a blood vessel, either an artery or a vein, which can give rise to a vascular occlusion such as a venous *thrombosis*. A piece of clot which detaches and circulates is an *embolus.*

Throwing up See *vomiting.*

Thrush

See *vaginal candidosis* · *spots in the mouth* in babies · *redness and soreness at the corners of the mouth.*

Thumping of the heart See *palpitations.*

Thyroid swelling See *swelling of the thyroid.*

Thyrotoxicosis See *hyperthyroidism.*

Tic

A nervous twitch found in some people. It usually consists of some movement which is repeated, for example eye-blinking or twitching of the face. Nose-picking, nail-biting, head-banging and bed-wetting are often found in children with tics.

The tic may persist into adult life. A tic should not be confused with *tremor*. Tic douloureux is found with *trigeminal neuralgia*.

Tickle in the throat   See *cough*.

Tightness in the breasts and nipples

A feeling of tightness, fullness, swelling and tenderness in the breasts and nipples is common in the premenstrual period, when it may be a part of *premenstrual tension*. This is due to the normal hormone changes which occur at that part of the menstrual cycle. Early pregnancy is another cause of the same feeling, for the same reason.

If the tightness is in both breasts, then the condition is of systemic origin and is probably hormone induced. Tightness in one breast or nipple only should always suggest that a search should be carried out for any *swelling in the breast, discharge from the nipple,* or *swelling of the lymph nodes* in the armpit on that side.

Tightness in the chest   See *angina pectoris · pain in the chest.*

Tinea cruris   See *fungus infection of the skin.*

Tingling in the hands and/or feet

This sensation, commonly referred to as "pins and needles", is usually due to compression of the nerve going to the parts where tingling is felt. A blow on the "funny bone" at the elbow gives rise to transient tingling.

More prolonged tingling is usually due to more prolonged pressure on the nerve or nerves. A *cervical rib,* or fibrous band in the neck, may be the cause of tingling in the hands. The median nerve can be compressed at the wrist in the carpal tunnel syndrome. The tingling will be felt in this case in the thumb, index and long fingers and possibly also in one side of the ring finger. The carpal tunnel syndrome is usually due to generalized fluid accumulation and retention, which produces entrapment in the tight carpal tunnel through which the median nerve passes. The sufferer is usually a woman who is menopausal. Typically, she wakes up with the condition. It usually improves during the day, but returns again after sleeping. A small operation enlarges the tunnel and cures the condition. Tingling in medical language is acroparasthesia.

Diabetes is an occasional cause of "pins and needles."

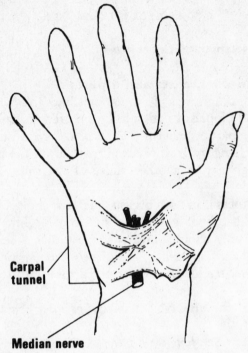

Carpal tunnel

Median nerve

The median nerve is trapped in the carpal tunnel

Tinnitus

A high-pitched ringing sound in the ears. It is usually experienced when nerve cells in the ear are wearing out or giving out, or after exposure to loud noise. The ringing may be temporary after noise exposure, or may be of long duration in certain cases. *Menière's disease* is associated with tinnitus. Large doses of aspirin and moderate ones of streptomycin can cause tinnitus.

Tiredness

Unexplained tiredness, weakness or lassitude should always suggest that a visit to your physician is necessary. There are many causes of these symptoms—some serious, others trivial. Tiredness may be the earliest symptom of a serious disease.

It would not be possible to list here all the causes of tiredness, but some of the serious causes are *anemia · leukemia ·* kidney failure and *uremia ·* heart failure · serious systemic infections · *cancers* or other tumors.

The sorting out of the reasons for tiredness, particularly when unexplained, is a matter which will require medical help. Delay in seeking help could make a difference to the future outlook in many cases. So if you are tired without obvious reason, you would be wise to consult your doctor soon.

See also *disorders of sleep.*

Toenail, horny   See *horny toenail.*

Toenail, ingrown   See *ingrown toenail.*

Tongue, black   See *black tongue.*

Tongue, numb   See *numbness of the tongue.*

Tongue, sore   See *sore tongue.*

Tonsillitis
Infection of the tonsil, which may become red and inflamed as part of a generalized upper respiratory infection. Occasionally the tonsil may be seen to have gray-white spots all over it (follicular tonsillitis). An *abscess* may be found around the tonsil and this is known as *quinsy* (peritonsillar abscess). Tonsillitis can cause *bad breath* and *difficulty in swallowing.*

Toothache
Two main kinds of pain are felt in teeth. One arises from hot and cold or eating very sweet things. This is usually sudden, and goes away with removal of the heat or cold or after having finished eating. This pain is felt in a sensitive layer which is found in the tooth just under the outside enamel. In a perfect looking tooth it probably indicates a small cavity which a dentist can easily identify, as it will be soft to his probe. A small filling will usually be required. Similarly, this condition can occur around the edge of existing repair work or at points of friction with dentures or dental braces.

The second kind of pain commonly felt in a tooth is due to an infection or abscess of the pulp or nerve cavity. It results from the increased pressure in the pulp induced by the swelling. This pain will usually be dull or throbbing, and may radiate along the jaw.

If the pain is not clearly felt in one tooth, a simple test will usually establish which one is at fault. A blunt tap on the top or side of the affected tooth, or even clenching the teeth, will increase the pain in the affected tooth. This may be dramatic with even a light tap—so begin very gently.

If you have the second type of pain from an infection in the pulp cavity of the tooth, you would be well advised to seek help quickly —it may already be too late to save the tooth, but some can be saved by very skilled treatment. In any case, you will undoubtedly save yourself a good deal of pain by not waiting, even if it does have to come out. If a pulp infection is left to follow its natural course a gumboil or root abscess will develop. The abscess destroys the nerve to the tooth. Even if the infection clears up the result will be a dead tooth.

Torticollis (wryneck)

This condition may be caused by a sudden spasm of muscles or by *swelling of the lymph nodes* in the neck. It is normally a self-limiting condition. Occasionally a disk lesion in the neck may be the cause.

In young infants congenital torticollis is caused byt-n olive-sized tumor of the neck muscles. This is usually "stretched out" with a passive range of motion exercises. Surgical treatment is rarely needed.

Trauma

An injury or wound. The word is used to describe any condition resulting from violence or injury.

Travel sickness   See *motion sickness*.

Tremor

Can be defined as involuntary shaking or quivering. Tremor may be fine or coarse, depending on the amplitude of the movement. It may be present all the time, or only occasionally. It may affect one part of the body only, or may occur in all the limbs.

Tremors which could be regarded as normal will be found in people who are cold and tired, and in very old people. In some people and families, tremor appears to be congenital and familial but unrelated to disease.

The infirmity can be deomonstrated by holding the hands out from the body, palms down, with arms straight and fingers spread out. A sheet of paper placed on the back of the hand will magnify any tremor. Tongue tremor can best be demonstrated with the tongue half out.

Some tremors cease when the person uses the part or moves it, but others are unaffected. Hand tremors often show in handwriting.

Tremors can be associated with diseases of the nervous system and with other diseases.

TREMOR ASSOCIATED WITH OTHER DISEASE will include *hyperthyroidism*. In diseases of the thyroid gland which secrete too much thyroid hormone, a fine rapid regular tremor will be found · *hypoglycemia* may also cause tremor, often associated with weakness and sweating.

TREMOR ASSOCIATED WITH DISEASES OF THE NERVOUS SYSTEM will include *Parkinson's disease* (paralysis agitans) · *alcoholism*. "The shakes" are a well known symptom of withdrawal from alcohol, and delirium tremens ("the DT's") are easily recognized in those who drink to excess. This tremor is rather coarse and uneven · head injuries. During the recovery phase, tremors may appear. If certain areas of brain are damaged, tremors may persist. Many other diseases of the brain can produce tremor, including Wilson's disease, late *syphilis* and *epilepsy* · *anxiety* and *hysteria*.

Trichomoniasis

An infection with a small ciliated protozoan, trichomonas vaginalis. Females suffering from trichomoniasis will usually complain of an unpleasant smelling *vaginal discharge* which can be profuse. Males may get a *urethral discharge,* or may not complain of any symptom. The condition is usually easy to diagnose and treat.

Trigeminal neuralgia

Causes *pain in the upper and lower jaws,* face and forehead region. The cause is unknown. The condition affects people who are generally over the age of fifty, and is uncommon under forty. Severe and sometimes excruciating pain can be experienced. It is usually sharp and stabbing, and may be brought on by touching or toweling the face, by chewing or by cold. There may be spasm of the muscles of the face, and this is the origin of the alternative name for the condition, tic douloureux. *Flushing of the face,* numbness of the face and *numbness of the tongue* on one side may be associated with trigeminal neuralgia.

Trigger finger

A condition in which the finger will bend to make a fist but will not straighten out unaided. In less severe cases it has to be forced past a point where it clicks. The condition is due to a swelling on the tendon or to a tightness in the tendon sheath which causes obstruction to the free passage of the tendon. Cure is by surgery.

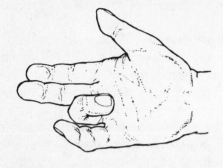

A trigger finger

Trismus

Spasm in the jaw muscles which may be seen in any painful conditions of the jaw, such as an impacted wisdom tooth, a dental *abscess* or gumboil, a facial neuralgia, or in *tetanus* and *tetany.*

Tubal pregnancy   See *ectopic pregnancy.*

Tumor

A *swelling* or lump. The word is not generally used to describe the the swelling associated with an enlarged organ or part of the body, or an *abscess* or cyst, though these do give rise to swellings. Tumor is more commonly used to describe solid swellings. These may be simple nonmalignant tumors, or may be malignant, such as a *cancer.*

Twitching   See *tic · tremor.*

Ulcerative colitis

The commonest cause in temperate climates of *diarrhea* associated with *blood in the stools. Poor appetite,* slight *fever* and *loss of weight* may follow. *Mucus in the stool* is common. Urgency, *soiling* or even fecal incontinence may be found in severe cases.

Ulcer, duodenal   See *peptic ulcers.*

Ulcer of the foot
Usually found in people who have a disorder either of blood supply or of nerve supply to the foot. Occasionally both are found. These causes include among others: *diabetes mellitus* · late *syphilis* · cerebral hemorrhage or *thrombosis* · *Raynaud's disease* and sickle-cell anemia. Other causes of foot ulcer can be associated with plantar warts · fungus infections · severe *chilblains* · frostbite · immersion foot · burns and trauma · skin *cancer.*

Ulcer of the leg
The commonest leg ulcer is a *varicose ulcer* associated with *varicose veins.* The ulcer is usually preceded by a patch of *varicose eczema* which is itchy and pigmented, and found usually just above the inner side of the ankle bone and over the lower inner part of the skin. The areas of varicose eczema and varicose ulceration may extend upwards as the condition progresses.
Other leg ulcers can be due to · alteration of blood supply to the leg or part of it · *trauma* · burns or excessive cold · *diabetes mellitus* · skin *cancer* · late *syphilis* · *malignant melanoma.*

Ulcer, peptic   See *peptic ulcer.*

Ulcers in the mouth
Small white mouth ulcers are very common. They may be found in association with a sharp tooth or with sharpness or roughness or pressure from dentures, although some have no obvious cause. They are, however, easily recognized and distinguished from other mouth ulcers, because they are white, shallow, painful, and heal completely within seven to ten days, provided, in the case of those which are induced by sharp edges or by pressure, that these causes are removed.
Other causes of mouth ulcers include *syphilis* and *cancer.* These ulcers are generally painless. Some infections in the mouth may cause superficial ulceration, but in these cases the cause of the ulceration is usually seen to be associated with the infection.

Ulcers on the lips

A single ulcer may be due to *herpesvirus, syphilis* or cancer of the lip. Multiple small ulcers are probably due to *herpesvirus*. Herpesvirus ulcers will generally be associated with a common cold. See also *spots on the lips*.

Ulcer, stomach See *peptic ulcer*.

Ulcer, varicose See *varicose ulcer*.

Umbilical hernia See *hernia*.

Unequal pupils (anisocoria)

Small differences in the size of the pupils of the eyes can occur normally in healthy people. However, any marked difference in size is likely to indicate some abnormality. Certain drugs used in the eye can cause variation of pupil size, and the following possible causes may also occur: iritis · *glaucoma* · *Horner's syndrome* resulting from an *aneurysm* · *cervical rib* · *tumor* pressing on the cervical sympathetic nerves.

Unpleasant breath See *bad breath*.

Uremia

A condition which arises from kidney failure. It was thought to be due to a rise in the concentration of blood urea—hence the name—but this substance together with many others, such as creatinine, are found in increased concentration in the blood when the kidneys fail to act as purifiers.

The symptoms of uremia are increased *irritability* · *tiredness* · *drowsiness* · *headache* · *dizziness* · inability to think straight and to perform customary tasks. Deep sighing, breathing, general *weakness* and passing very small amounts of urine occur later. These symptoms can go on to unconsciousness, *convulsions* and death.

Uremia is usually associated with other signs of kidney failure such as *edema,* that is, *swelling of the ankles* and legs and bottom of the back due to fluid retention. In some people uremia may also give symptoms of *diarrhea* and *vomiting* and of *pains in the chest* due to *pericarditis*.

Ureteric colic

Usually found as a severe *pain in the abdomen* of sudden onset. The pain has the distribution characteristic of colic, as shown in the illustration. Ureteric colic is usually due to a stone in the ureter, but it may also be caused by blood clots or by fragments of other tissue, for example, tissue detached from a *tumor* that lodges in the ureter.

The sufferer from ureteric colic will usually be *rolling about with abdominal pain,* and may cry out when a sharp stab of pain occurs. The sufferer may appear pale and may perspire, due to the severity of the pain. Occasionally turning upside down or lying over the edge of the bed may disimpact a stone in the upper part of the ureter and thus produce temporary relief. It is certainly worth trying until medical help is obtained. Strong pain-relieving drugs only can help to reduce the pain of ureteric colic. The stone may eventually be passed by itself, or surgery may be necessary. In either case, medical help is needed to investigate the reason for stone formation and to prevent recurrence.

Ureteric colic may be associated with or followed by *blood in the urine* and *gravel or stones in the urine.*

Urethra, infection of

See *urethral discharge · pain on urination · sexually transmitted disease.*

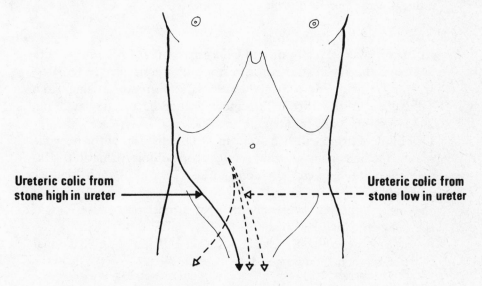

Ureteric colic from stone high in ureter

Ureteric colic from stone low in ureter

Sites and paths of pain in ureteric colic

Urethral discharge

Seen in males as pus or sticky material coming from the end of the penis. It is usually due to a *sexually transmitted disease*. The causes may include: *gonorrhea* · non-specific *urethritis* · *trichomoniasis* · *candidosis*.

Women can suffer from a urethral discharge in a similar way, but the discharge is usually throught by the woman to arise as a *vaginal discharge*.

Urethritis   See *infection in the urethra*.

Urgency of urination

Found when there is irritation in the region of the neck of the bladder. When the person feels the need to urinate, this need is urgent and delay means great discomfort and sometimes leaking. The causes of urgency include: *infection of the bladder* · warts or ulcers at the neck of the bladder · stones or gravel at the neck of the bladder · *cancer* of the bladder.

Always check the urine in cases of urgency by looking at it in a clear glass. *Pain on urination* is often associated with urgency. See also *cloudy urine* · *blood in the urine* · *gravel or stones in the urine* · *frequency of urination*.

Urine, cloudy   See *cloudy urine*.

Urine, dark   See *dark urine*.

Urine leaking or dribbling

In males this is usually due to *enlargement of the prostate*. There is often difficulty in starting or in stopping the stream. In females, leaking or dribbling is usually a *stress incontinence* arising from difficulties in childbirth. The incontinence occurs on laughing, coughing or on any sudden strain.

Dribbling of urine will also occur in certain diseases of the nervous system which damage the nerves controlling urination. Extremely old people can also tend to lose control of their bladder and bowel.

In young children, overexcitement or fright may cause loss of control of the bladder.

A *fistula* between the bladder and the vagina may be an occasional cause in women following a difficult childbirth.

Urine, pale   See *pale urine*.

Urine, red   See *blood in the urine.*

Urticaria ("hives")

A skin disorder characterized by raised white itchy welts with a red margin. The welts may last for a few minutes and disappear, or they may take hours to disappear without trace. Sometimes the welts can be produced by pressure on the skin. Blunt pressure along a line can produce a linear welt, or even a handwritten message on the skin. Occasionally severe urticaria in children may lead to blistering.

Urticaria is a form of *allergy.* It may follow eating many foods, including seafood and shellfish, eggs, chocolate and strawberries. Other cases arise from drugs such as penicillin, and stings by bees or wasps may produce the condition. Very severe urticaria may be associated with *angioneurotic edema,* a condition which is a medical emergency because swellings may suddenly appear almost anywhere. If a *swelling of the throat or larynx* appears suddenly, the sufferer may suffocate. Swellings are commonly found in the head and neck, and may cause closure of the eye from *swelling of the eyelids* or gross deformity of the lips from *swelling of the lips.* Other parts of the body may also be affected.

Vaginal candidosis (thrush)

Due to a yeast-like organism which can live and multiply in the vagina. It causes white spots resembling blobs of cream on the walls of the vagina which are usually accompanied by a good deal of *itching of the vulva and vaginal entrance.* The organism also lives in the bowel, and sometimes in the mouth of babies.

Vaginal discharge

A certain amount of white vaginal secretion is normal and may be mistaken for a vaginal discharge. Normal vaginal secretion increases before menstruation and is stimulated by sexual activity, and so more secretion would normally be found at these times.

Many vaginal discharges are associated with *sexually transmitted diseases* such as *gonorrhea. Pain on urination* may be associated with any vaginal discharge. Sometimes vaginal discharges are accompanied by irritation. The common reasonstfor these irritant discharges are *vaginal candidosis* and *trichomoniasis.*

Lesions, infections, inflammation and erosions of the cervix may cause a vaginal discharge. Benign or malignant *tumors* can also be associated with a discharge, but in many cases this will be a bloodstained discharge.

Any such bloodstained discharge, apart from normal menstruation, should be viewed with concern. See *bleeding from the vagina*.

Vaginal irritation

May be due to a *vaginal discharge* or to *irritation around the vulva*.

Vaginismus

Spasm of the vagina. This is a response which may be conscious or unconscious, and consists not only of spasm of the vagina, but usually includes arching of the back and closing of the thighs, thus making penetration difficult or impossible. Vaginismus may be due to some painful condition at the entrance of the vagina, for example *herpesvirus* infection or a *sexually transmitted disease*. Most vaginismus, however, is due to a psychological response which expresses distaste, reluctance or avoidance of sexual intercourse. Medical help is necessary in all cases to diagnose and treat the condition. The longer nothing is done to help, the worse will be the consequence for the partnership.

Varices   See *varicose veins*.

Varicose eczema

A form of eczema associated with varicose veins. It should be distinguished from *eczema,* which is associated with *atopy*.

Varicose ulcer

Found in association with *varicose veins* and often follows *varicose eczema.* The varicose ulcer appears as an *ulcer of the leg* usually on the inner or front-to-inner surface of the leg just above the ankle.

Varicose veins

Thick, prominent and tortuous veins usually seen in the legs, where they can give rise to *swelling of the ankles,* to skin ulcers and to pigmented patches of *varicose eczema* around the ankles. A varicocele is varicose veins in the scrotum. Esophageal varicose veins (varices) can lead to *vomiting blood* and may be associated with *cirrhosis of the liver* and with *jaundice*.

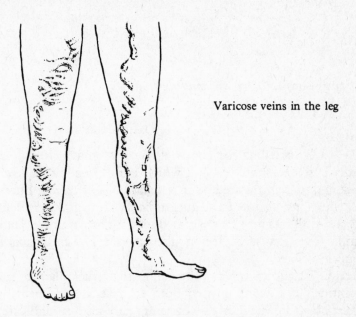

Varicose veins in the leg

Venereal disease   See *sexually transmitted disease*.

Vertigo   See *dizziness*.

Vincent's infection
A form of *stomatitis* (inflammation of the mouth). The condition gives rise to a painful mouth, with swollen tender *infected gums* (gingivitis) which bleed easily. Grayish patches and *spots in the mouth* and throat may be seen. *Bad breath* may be very obvious in this condition.

Violent behavior
See *psychological illness · alcoholism · diabetes · hypoglycemia*.

Vision, defective
See *amblyopia · defective color vision · blindness in one eye · blurred vision*.

Vitiligo   See *disorders of pigmentation of the skin*.

Vomit, black

Black "coffee grounds" vomit is due to the presence of digested blood in the vomit. For the causes of this, see *vomiting blood · vomiting. Black stools* may also occur.

Vomit, bloodstained   See *vomiting blood.*

Vomit, green   See *green vomit · vomiting.*

Vomiting

The act of expelling the contents of the stomach. *Vomiting blood* is discussed separately. Food which is not swallowed down may stick and be regurgitated, as in *achalasia of the cardia.* Pharyngeal pouches may also cause regurgitation. Regurgitation of food in these conditions may be described in error as vomiting. In babies, simple overflow after feeing also should not be mistaken for vomiting.

Retching is the muscular contraction that takes place to produce vomiting. The word is used both to describe the heaving that takes place in the act of vomiting and also to indicate "dry vomiting." *Nausea* often precedes vomiting.

CAUSES OUTSIDE THE STOMACH AND ABDOMEN include: infectious *fevers* in childhood, in which vomiting will usually occur in the early stage of the disease, often as the temperature is rising, and frequently before the disease can be diagnosed from general signs and symptoms and from the *rash* · early pregnancy causing *"morning sickness"* (vomiting in late pregnancy may be a serious sign of toxemia of pregnancy and of high blood pressure) · *high blood pressure · motion sickness* · head injury, *concussion,* cerebral hemorrhage, cerebral *thrombosis* · brain *tumor* (the location of the tumor in the brain may affect the vomiting reflex) · *meningitis* · disorders of balance, such as *dizziness, Menière's disease* and motion sickness · *migraine* · bad smells, unpleasant tastes and disturbing sights · emotional disturbances of many kinds · radiation sickness (and radiotherapy, especially to the abdomen with resultant irradiation of the bowel) · trauma to some locations, such as a blow on the knee or the testicle).

CAUSES WITHIN THE STOMACH AND ABDOMEN include: eating or drinking unsuitable, tainted or poisoned things · diseases of the stomach—for example, a *peptic ulcer* (causing pain after food and when the stomach is empty) · *cancer* of the stomach (often accompanied by loss of weight) · pyloric *stenosis* · *intestinal obstruction* (accompanied by colic) · acute pancreatitis (usually a disease of older people or those who drink to excess) · cholecystitis (*infection of the kidney*) · *appendicitis* · *cirrhosis of the liver* (which can lead to *vomiting blood*) · *biliary colic* · *ureteric colic* · *ectopic pregnancy* (which can produce symptoms at about two and a half to three months after the date of the *missed menstrual period*) · *trauma* to the abdomen · any kicks, punches or other injuries to the abdomen.

Vomiting blood

It is always important to differentiate between actual vomiting and *coughing or spitting blood*. The differences are referred to in detail at the beginning of that entry. Blood swallowed following *bleeding from the nose* or *bleeding from the mouth* may be vomited, but will not be considered here. The common causes of vomiting blood in any quantity other than teaspoonful amounts are the ones listed here. The causes of vomiting blood include:

DISEASES OF THE ESOPHAGUS.

Cancer or ulcers (*difficulty in swallowing* or food sticking after swallowing will usually be the first symptoms) · foreign bodies in the esophagus (for example fish bones) · *varicose veins* in the esophagus (as a result of *cirrhosis of the liver*).

DISEASES OF THE STOMACH

Gastric ulcer · *cancer* of the stomach.

SYSTEMIC DISEASES CAUSING BLEEDING.

Leukemia · *purpura* · *hemophilia* · *scurvy*.

Taking aspirin may cause bleeding from the stomach. It is thus important in every case of vomiting blood or *black stools* to determine if the person takes aspirin regularly or occasionally. Many medicines and tablets containing aspirin are not actually called aspirin.

Vulva, itchy   See *irritation around the vulva*.

Waterbrash See *acid regurgitation*.

Water on the knee See *swelling of the knee*.

Watery eyes
Can be produced by an increase in tear production from crying, by a foreign body irritating the eye, or by inefficient disposal of the normal amount of tears. The latter case usually produces the medical problems. The tear drains or ducts may be blocked as a result of infection or tiny stones, or may narrow from injury or burns or from unknown causes. When the entrance to the tear ducts is too narrow, a small rod can be inserted to enlarge the opening. The tear ducts may also be blocked either near the corner of the eye at the tear sac or where they drain into the nose. A very cold atmosphere, in which evaporation of tears becomes difficult, may give normal people watery eyes. Lesser degrees of cold will show up those who have drainage difficulty. Epiphora is the medical term for a watery eye.

Warts on the feet (plantar warts)
These are infectious, and transmitted in public showers and swimming pools. They do not grow outward into the typical cauliflower shape because of the pressure of the individual's weight when standing. Instead, the wart is pressed into the skin to form a small, hard piece of "skin" which is tender on pressure. The warts are commonly seen in children and teenagers.

Warts on the genitals See *sexually transmitted diseases*.

Warts on the hands
The light-brown cauliflower-shaped warts that are commonly found on the fingers and hands are due to a virus infection. In most people, natural immunity develops, and usually, after about two years from their first appearance, the warts go. If these warts are many or are causing distress, they can be treated by freezing with liquid nitrogen. This is painless, but must be done by an expert, otherwise damage can easily result.

Warts on the penis   See *sexually transmitted diseases.*

Warts on the vulva   See *sexually transmitted diseases.*

Wax in the ear
Normal and healthy. It is only if it forms a hard plug and causes *pain in the ear* or *deafness* that any action needs to be taken. Before an ear is syringed to remove wax, the wax should be softened by putting a few drops of vegetable oil or hydrogen peroxide solution into the ear for two to three days. This will make the job of syringing the ear easy.

Weakness
Of an arm, leg, hand or foot is usually due to a disorder of the nervous system or the muscles, as is found in a *stroke, multiple sclerosis, myasthemia gravis,* or *sciatica.* Weakness can also be a part of a general debilitating illness which causes *tiredness.*

Weak or poor stream when urinating
The common reasons will be either obstruction of the outflow of urine, or loss of control of the mechanism of urination due to disease or injury of the nervous system. Obstruction of outflow is commonly seen in middle-aged or elderly men due to *enlargement of the prostate.* Both sexes can suffer from injury, from *gravel or stones* or from *tumors* that may block the urethra. Men sometimes suffer from narrowing of the urethra due to a stricture. This may be the consequence of gonorrhea in the past. See *inability to urinate.*

Wheezing
The noise heard of air going through a narrow tube, heard in association with *asthma* and *bronchitis. Stridor* and *difficulty in breathing* may be associated with wheezing.

White cold fingers
May be due to cold or to *Raynaud's syndrome or disease.* Another

occasional cause is the use of vibrating tools such as power saws, pneumatic chisels and drills, when the condition may be known as "dead hand" or "dead fingers." See also *chilblains · blueness of the skin.*

White lines in the skin   See *stretch marks.*

White lines on the nails
Lines across the nail may be a sign of past illness or injury, or of present systemic disease. They may be associated with furrows across the nail. See *ridges and furrows on the nails.*

White patches in the skin   See *disorders of pigmentation of the skin.*

White patches on the tongue
Usually seen in older people, appearing as areas of rather shiny smooth whiteness on the tongue. The condition is often precancerous—that is, it may be followed later by a cancer. Therefore anyone having this should be examined by a physician. These shiny smooth patches of whiteness should not be confused with a *furred tongue,* in which the normal roughness of the tongue is preserved.
Another cause of small white patches on the tongue is *lichen planus.*

White patches on the vulva and vagina (leukoplakia)
Found in older women. The patches are white or grayish-white in color. The condition is often precancerous, that is, it may be followed by cancer. Anyone having this should be examined by a physician.

"Wind"   See *flatulence.*

Worms
May be pinworms, tapeworms or roundworms. All will require

treatment. Any worm or part of a tapeworm should be kept to show the doctor. Pinworms will cause *itching around the anus*. Tapeworms may also be found in the form of *hydatid cysts* in the body.

Worry   See *anxiety · stress*.

Wryneck   See *torticollis*.

Xanthelasmata

Yellow patches on the skin, usually seen as yellow patches or spots on the upper eyelids. The patches appear in the inner third of each upper eyelid. See also *swelling of the eyelids*.

Yellow crusts on the skin

Often due to *impetigo* or may be related to *seborrheic dermatitis*.

Yellow eyes   See *jaundice*.

Yellowness of the eyes

If the whites of the eyes look yellow, then *jaundice* may be present. The color of the urine and stool should be noted carefully. Commonly in jaundice the urine is dark and the stool is pale.

Yellowness of the skin   See *jaundice · anemia*.

Yellow patches on the eyeballs

Seen in certain people and are due to small amounts of fat under the conjunctiva. The condition is of no medical importance.

Yellow patches or spots on the upper eyelids
    See *swelling of the eyelids.*

Yellow serous discharge from the nipple
    See *blood from the nipple.*

Yellow skin
    See *jaundice · anemia.*

Systematic approach to illness and diagnosis

Nursing at home

First aid

The systematic approach to illness and diagnosis

Complaint and Duration

Use the book to investigate the symptoms. Ask the person what he/she feels to be wrong and for how long he/she has suffered. *Write down* the complaint, or main symptom(s).

History

Use the book to investigate symptoms and to list possible or likely diagnoses.

The history of the present illness

Try to find out more about this illness. Begin at the beginning and go over the whole story of the present illness in detail and in chronological order. List the main symptoms.

The past history

List and review all past illnesses which are not trivial.
List the main symptoms.

The family history

List and review any illnesses which run in the family and list the main symptoms.

The social history

List all problems and relate these to the history of the present illness and to past and family history.
List all main symptoms.

The occupational history

Review work and hobbies. Relate these to the rest of the history.
List all main symptoms.

Examine the person

Record the TPR: Temperature · Pulse rate · Respiratory rate. Normal readings are given in the **Nursing at home** chapter.

Look

Look at the whole person   look at the parts he/she complains of   compare "good" and "bad" sides   look at all the rest of the person.

Feel

Describe and note what you feel.

Make notes of anything abnormal noticed by looking and feeling.

Use the book to check any new symptoms.

List the possible diagnoses

Write down a list of likely diseases which fit the person's story and what you found when you examined him or her by checking TPR, by looking and feeling.

Use the book to recheck if necessary the symptoms and diseases which you have found. Try to discover the diseases which best fit the complaint and duration, the history, the symptoms, and what you found when you examined the person.

Recheck with the book if necessary.

Make a diagnosis

Try to select out of the above list of possibilities the illness which you think is the most likely.

If you cannot make a diagnosis, what is the worst possibility?

Possible Actions

Send the person to a hospital · telephone the doctor · go to the doctor now · go to the doctor later · treat the condition at home · observe and await developments · decide that no action is required.

Nursing at home

There are a number of simple things which can be done to help anyone who is ill at home. Some of the advice given below may seem obvious, but experience shows that it is not always followed. As a result, some people are less comfortable or less well treated than they might be for their symptoms or illness.

When should a mildly ill person go to bed?

If the person who is ill is a child, the first question to ask is does he or she look ill. Children who look and act ill probably are. Malingering in young children is very unlikely. Next, check the temperature, the pulse rate and the rate of respiration to help to ascertain the degree of illness. If the child is only slightly ill then he or she is probably best kept indoors, but not in bed. The child will want to see what is going on and likes to be in contact with mother across the room. It may be a good idea to have a large chair or a couch with cushions and a blanket or rug that can act as a makeshift bed in the room where everyone is. However unless the child is distinctly unwell, he or she will probably want to move about and will be much happier in contact with other members of the family. If the illness becomes worse, the child may become irritable and will then wish either to be left alone or to sleep. In these circumstances going to bed in his or her own room is probably best. Sometimes children are banished to bed in their room when they feel slightly ill. They may then become bored from isolation and inaction and will thus be more difficult to manage. Even new toys and games can fail to appease an irritable child, though it is probably a good idea to keep some small things in reserve for such a situation. The basic rule for deciding whether to put a child to bed on account of illness is similar to that for adults—the patient should usually decide. Parents will, of course, have the last word, but it is best to give the child as much say as possible in matters which affect him or her. Adults will decide for themselves whether or not to go to bed. This decision will be made better if all the information available is used including how the person feels, and also the TPR (temperature, pulse rate and respiratory rate). Often the TPR are not measured. Occasionally some "brave" (foolish?) people try to keep going when they have a temperature of 101 °F (38·3 °C). While this may be necessary in some emergency or crisis conditions, there are many times when the person could and should have gone to bed. Rest is important in nearly all illnesses and will frequently speed recovery. Fatigue and chilling may only make matters worse. So, use all the information which is available about what the illness is, what the symptoms are and what basic examination of the person such as TPR, color and looking ill or not, can reveal. Most simple infectious illnesses like colds, sore throats and flu will cause some rise in body temperature at the height of the illness. If the temperature reaches over 100 °F (37·8 °C) in the morning the person should consider staying off school or work as the evening temperature will probably be about 1 °F higher—around 101 °F (38·3 °C). With this amount of fever, bed rest or staying quietly at home would be the most sensible course to follow under normal circumstances. In the case of children, deviations from normal behavior patterns, irritability, unaccustomed lethargy and lack of appetite are often early signs of illness. Any or all of these could indicate the need to be watchful and if the child looks ill, to keep him or her at home.

Choosing the room

If any member of the family looks like being ill in bed for a few days, consideration should be given to which room in the house is most suitable to make the task of caring for the person easy and, if the illness may disturb or infect others, to give the person a room to himself or herself. The person's own room is not always or necessarily the best for this purpose. Ease of access, absence of stairs, nearness to the bathroom or convenience for those who look after the patient can all influence decisions about the most suitable room.

Easy access to both sides of the bed can greatly ease some nursing problems—so this should be considered. A single bed is easier to manage for access than a large double bed. Bed coverings should be suitable for the season, the room temperature, and the condition of the patient. Warmer rooms with light coverings for the patient are generally preferable to colder rooms and more blankets.

Room temperature is therefore important—the room should

be neither too hot nor too cold. A temperature of around 70°F (21°C) will usually be best. Babies and old people must have a room with at least this temperature for they can easily suffer from hypothermia if bed coverings slip off.

Plenty of pillows will be required so that the patient can sit up in comfort. About four pillows stacked up with a spare for an arm rest will be required.

By the bedside

Alongside the bed should be a table so that the person can keep a drinking glass at hand, lay a book down and keep any pills or medicines (adults only). The bed should not face directly onto bright light since this can be tiring.

Some means of summoning other people should be available if calling out is not easily heard.

Caring for people in bed

In simple illnesses it is assumed that the person can get up and go totthe bathroom normally—so he or she is not *confined* to bed. Normal use can thus be made of the bathroom for washing and for other purposes. This greatly simplifies some of the tasks of nursing.

The bed should be tidied up often. It is uncomfortable to lie on a creased or folded sheet and unpleasant to have the coverings slipping half off. Excessive or obsessive tidiness can however be almost as uncomfortable, with the toes bound down by tightly tucked in sheets and covers, and the patient feeling like an Egyptian mummy. So, be sensible. If the patient is perspiring much, sheets and bedding should be changed frequently, as also should the patients pajamas or other clothing. Daily showering or bathing is very important too for comfort and freshness.

Patients who are breathless for any reason will generally be more comfortable in a half sitting up position either leaning back on many pillows piled high or leaning forward onto a bed table or onto a pillow on the knees.

Drinking and fluids

In many illnesses treated at home the patient will have a fever and may not want to eat. Not eating for a few days is of little importance in well-nourished people. It is, however, *very important* that fluid intake is maintained because the body cannot do without fluid for long. Children may not feel the need to drink as adults do, and so require positive encouragement. The best way to accomplish this is to have a supply at the bed table of something which the child enjoys drinking so that he or she can drink at any time. Cool citrus fruit juice is often very well accepted because it feels clean in the mouth when the patient feels hot and sticky. The 1 to 5 age group are the ones who will generally need most encouragement to drink. Anyone, child or adult, who has diarrhea and/or vomiting will be losing a considerable amount of fluid. So, one of the nursing aims must be to encourage drinking. If in addition to diarrhea and vomiting the person has a raised body temperature and is perspiring freely, body fluids will become depleted rapidly. In these circumstances, urgent fluid replacement is vital. When fluids cannot be replaced by mouth because of vomiting the person should not be nursed at home for intravenous fluid may become necessary. Infants who are bottle fed, and who suffer from gastroenteritis (a rare condition in breast fed babies), can quickly become moribund from dehydration caused by the fluid loss in vomit and diarrhea. These infants are especially at risk as a result of fluid loss and are too young to be asked tc drink plenty. So call your doctor at once in these circumstances.

In summary, in any simple illness it is a good idea to ensure that plenty to drink is at hand. When anyone is losing fluid rapidly, it is of the utmost importance to replace the fluid quickly. Should replacement by mouth not be possible, you should call your doctor.

Eating and diet
Anyone suffering from diarrhea and vomiting must be given fluids in plenty, but fluids *only* for at least the first 24 hours of the illness. Solid food will be rejected and will merely serve to make matters worse by increasing vomiting and diarrhea, and thus fluid loss. Then, when and if the patient feels that he or she would like some food in the following 24 hours, only small amounts of baby-type food should be given. If, however, diarrhea persists it is much wiser to give fluids only, in plenty, and to avoid food.

In other illnesses, the best general policy is to give the patient what he or she wants. This is particularly so with children. For example a child who has a sore throat with some fever may find ice cream both satisfying and easy to swallow. The child may want to eat nothing else for about 3 days. This does not matter, nor does it set a precedent in diet. A balanced diet is one which, *over a reasonable period of time*—say a month—gives the person all that is needed. So, there will be plenty of other days to eat other foods. Experience also shows that when children are offered an unrestricted range of foods that they will select for themselves over a period a balanced diet.

When anyone is getting over a slight illness and has not been eating, appetite may return quickly and the person can feel ravenously hungry. With the exception of diarrhea, food should be given as required. In the case of diarrhea, a return to normal diet should be *slow* over days 3–5 of the illness and not until about day 6 should a normal diet be taken. Even using this suggested proceedure, if diarrhea begins again the diet should be cut back or fluids only should be taken. Make haste slowly is a good motto in diarrhea.

Bowel movements in illness

This often worries people. There is no need for the bowels to move every day, nor is it in any way unhealthy if the bowels do not move for a week and the person feels well. In illness, food intake is often restricted and, on the basis of less in, less out, bowel motions will not be expected to follow their normal pattern and will probably become more infrequent. (For a fuller discussion, see *constipation*.)

When to resume normal activity after slight illness

There are a number of guides which can be used. First and most important is how the patient feels. Adults and older children will have no difficulty in this respect. Younger children however may find difficulty in saying how they feel. However, behavior is a sure guide. Any child who acts normally is probably well and any child who behaves as if he or she is unwell probably is.

Other information such as TPR should also be used. With temperature a good guide is that the temperature should be normal in the evening (around 6 p.m.) before a return to ordinary activities. If the illness has lasted longer than 48 hours, it is probably wise to have one day of convalescence before returning to school or work so that normal "bounce" can be regained. There is little point in convalescing at school or work, or in appearing to be carrying out normal activities when tiredness makes this an exercise in deception for all concerned. It is far better to wait an extra day and return with vitality and zest.

Notes about TPR (temperature, pulse and respiration)

TEMPERATURE

The normal body temperature is 98·4° Fahrenheit (36·9° Celcius or centigrade) and lies in the range 97·4–99·0°F (36·3–37·2°C). Body temperature is lower in the morning and higher at the end of the day. In good health, variations in temperature are slight.

Body temperature is *low* in conditions which cause fluid loss (dehydration) such as diarrhea, vomiting, severe bleeding and severe illnesses of a non-infectious kind.

Body temperature is *raised*, and fever is said to be present, in infectious conditions and in a few disorders which affect the heat regulating mechanism in the brain.

Body temperature in degrees		
FAHRENHEIT	CENTIGRADE	
105·5	40·8	
105	40·6	
104·5	40·3	Very high
104	40	
103·5	39·7	
103	39·4	High
102·5	39·2	
102	38·9	
101·5	38·6	Moderately raised
101	38·3	
100·5	38·1	
100	37·8	Slightly raised
99·5	37·5	
99	37·2	
98·4	36·9	NORMAL RANGE
97·8	36·6	

When body temperature rises and falls again to normal, three stages can be described. In the *first* or *cold stage,* the person feels cold and shivery and may look pale or even slightly blue. The skin feels cold. At this point, the body temperature may be considerably up even though the person feels cold. When the temperature has risen, the *second* or *hot stage* follows in which the person looks and feels hot. The skin is red, dry and warm and the person feels hot and thirsty. He or she may suffer from headache and may be very restless at this stage. The temperature may still continue to rise.

In the *third* or *sweating stage,* the temperature falls and the person may sweat profusely, becoming wet through. As this happens, he may need a change of clothing and may feel cold if left in the wet clothing or bedding. During the *cold stage,* the person should have warm blankets put around him to keep him warm. As he reaches the *hot stage,* he should be given cool drinks. If the temperature rises above 104°F (40°C) cool sponging or even a cool bath may be required to prevent further rise of temperature. In the *sweating stage* the clothing and bedding should be changed. If the body temperature rises rapidly, the person will shiver uncontrollably in the first or cold stage. This is often described as *"a chill."*

PULSE

The pulse may conveniently be felt at the wrist, elbow or in the neck, or the heart rate may be counted by listening to heartbeat over the left side of the chest. The pulse rate varies with age, sex and activity. It is more rapid when a person is standing than when sitting or lying.

The pulse rate is increased normally by exercise and excitement including fear and anxiety and anger, and is decreased by sleep and to a lesser extent by relaxation.

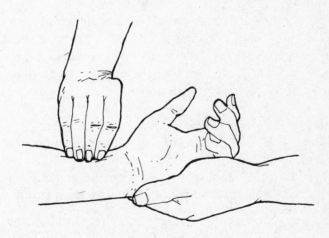

Feeling the pulse at the wrist

pulse rate (number of heartbeats per minute)	
newborn infant	120–140
age 1	110–120
age 2–5	about 100
age 5–10	about 90
adults, male	65–80
adults, female	70–85

RESPIRATION

The respiratory rate varies with age, sex and activity. It is increased normally by exercise, excitement and emotion and is decreased by sleep and rest.

respiratory rate (number of breaths per minute)	
newborn infant	40
age 1	30
age 2–5	24–28
adult, male	16–18
adult, female	18–20

THE RATIO OF THE PULSE RATE TO TEMPERATURE

The pulse rate will usually rise about 10 beats per minute for every degree Fahrenheit over 100 °F. In heart disease, a high pulse rate may be found with a normal temperature.

THE RATIO OF PULSE RATE TO RESPIRATORY RATE

The pulse rate will usually rise about 4 beats per minute for every rise of 1 respiration per minute. This 4:1 ratio will be altered in chest diseases such as pneumonia which cause a great rise in respiratory rate. In these cases the ratio may even be 2:1, for example pulse rate 100, respiratory rate 50.

An alphabet of simple treatment

BACKACHE Use heat on the affected area from a hot water bottle or an infra-red lamp. Give soluble aspirin or aspirin substitutes to provide relief from pain. If fever accompanies backache, think of urinary infection, check for *cloudy urine* and if necessary call your doctor.

BLEEDING—see the section on first aid p. 242.

BRUISES If pain is troublesome take soluble aspirin or aspirin substitutes. Ice packs will give relief in the early stages. Firm bandaging will prevent further bleeding under the skin if applied early and may limit swelling in the first 48 hours. A crepe bandage is best.

BURNS—see the section on first aid p. 245. *Caution:* Only minor burns should be treated at home.

COLDS If you have fever with a cold, check TPR (see p. 232), and go to bed. Take plenty of hot drinks and use soluble aspirin or aspirin substitutes to relieve pain. If you become breathless or wheezy, call your doctor. Smoking will only make matters worse. Nasal decongestant sprays or "cold" tablets may give initial symptomatic relief but can make matters worse in the longer term. They should be used sparingly.

COUGHS Any tickly coughs are often relieved by breathing warm air, so make sure that the room is heated sufficiently (p 228). Hot drinks are also of value. Coughs with much sputum or phlegm may be associated with bronchitis or other lung disease and your doctor may be needed. Remember that people who are breathless will breathe more easily sitting up (p. 229).

DIARRHEA Stop eating. Give copious fluids. If the patient is a child *make sure* that he or she drinks plenty (p. 229). Diarrhea and vomiting under the age of 6 months especially in bottle fed babies can be a serious illness, so call your doctor. Any diarrhea which lasts for more than 2 days will need to be further diagnosed and treated by your doctor.

FEVER Always measure TPR (the temperature, the pulse rate and the respiratory rate, see p. 232). If the fever is 101 °F (38·3 °C) or more, consult your doctor especially if the person looks ill. Fever is associated with infections. Go to bed, take plenty to drink, and if the reason for the illness is not obvious—for example a cold or flu—call your doctor if the fever does not settle within two days.

HEADACHE Simple pain relieving drugs such as soluble aspirin or paracetamol will usually provide relief of pain. If headaches are other than occasional, consult your doctor. Never go on taking pain relievers for persistant headache—see your doctor to find out the reason for the headache not going away.

INDIGESTION Antacid tablets or mixtures may give relief. Always try to find out why indigestion is present. If no reason is obvious and the indigestion recurs, consult your doctor.

INFLUENZA—see colds.

SORE THROAT If there is much pain on swallowing simple pain relievers such as soluble aspirin or a substitute will help. If fever reaches 101 °F (38.3 °C) and the person looks or feels ill, consult your doctor. Some degree of enlargement of the lymph nodes ("glands") in the neck is usually found with a sore throat. This can give a tender swelling on both sides of the neck. If the tonsils look very red with white or yellow spots on them, consult your doctor.

SPRAINS and STRAINS—see the section on first aid. Remember that an X ray may be necessary. Rest, firm bandaging and soluble aspirin or a substitute can be used immediately.

STOMACHACHE—see indigestion. If pain is severe, if the pain moves, if the temperature is raised and there is vomiting, call your doctor and give fluids only till then. (See *abdominal pain*.)

TRAVEL SICKNESS Preventive treatment can be given. Remember that no travel sickness remedies should be given to pregnant women. Be careful when giving travel sickness preventers to children that you give the correct dose. Sleepiness or drowsiness can result if too much is given. These preventers are useless when a person has nausea or is vomiting. (See *travel sickness*.)

VOMITING Always try to determine the reason for vomiting. Give plenty to drink to replace the fluid lost in vomiting and nothing whatever to eat. If vomiting is associated with diarrhea and/or the person looks ill, call the doctor. See also the remarks about children and babies under diarrhea above.

First aid

What is first aid?

The words first aid are used to describe two quite different courses of action. In the first meaning of first aid it is used to describe what to do for a person who has sustained an injury, often serious, which will subsequently require treatment in a hospital. First aid in this sense describes the emergency aid to be given to that person before passing him on to a hospital for further treatment. This is the proper and true meaning of *first* aid. What is done subsequently in the hospital is *second* aid. It could therefore be said that true *first* aid is always followed by *second* aid. There is no attempt to do everything or to provide definitive treatment. The victim is *always* passed on to a hospital or to a doctor for second aid. The other common meaning of first aid is a misuse of the term, when the term first aid is used to describe the definitive treatment of minor or trivial injuries. Here, the person who gives the treatment hopes to do all that is necessary and does not intend to pass the victim on to a hospital or to a doctor for further treatment. This could be described as *only*-aid.

The importance of self-help in first aid

Another traditional view of first aid suggests that everything is done by the first-aider and that the situation is always that of an active first-aider and a passive victim. Many victims of accidents and injuries are not unconscious. If they know what to do, they can, could and should do many things to help themselves including sending for help or attracting attention in order to get help, and dealing with their injuries if no one else is around. The notion of the active first-aider and the passive victim should be forgotten. If you are ill or injured there may be a great deal that you can do to help yourself provided that you stay calm, that you have learned what to do, and that you do the correct things. Many people find it strange to think that they should be expected to do things for themselves when they are ill or injured. However, there may easily be circumstances when a person is alone and something happens. Self help is an important part of good first aid.

What follows below is mainly about true *first* aid. A small section appears at the end dealing with the definitive treatment of minor injuries.

What are the real emergencies in first aid?

For the untrained or casual first-aider there are three conditions which have to be dealt with rapidly and correctly in order to save lives. They are what to do for someone who is unconscious, bleeding or not breathing. Many people think that not breathing is the most important of these three conditions. It is important, but it is relatively uncommon beside the other conditions. Many more lives could be saved by the correct first aid being given for someone who is unconscious or bleeding, because these emergencies are common. If only one of these emergencies could be covered in this book the choice is unconsciousness, because this is the commonest emergency in which good first aid will save the life of the victim and is the commonest reason for death which could be avoided by good first aid. In the minds of many people the importance of a first aid measure is in proportion to its dramatic content—the "kiss of life" or the heart massage being administered while seconds count. This is, statistically speaking, not true. We should concentrate on learning the simple lifesaving procedures which will save the most lives. This means learning what to do for common emergencies. Unconsciousness and bleeding are common emergencies. Not breathing, while important, is relatively uncommon.

The need to train and practice now

If you wish to be useful in emergency conditions it is essential that you learn, think about, and practice first aid NOW. Failure to do this will probably mean that you will be unable to remember what to do, or that you will be much less effective than you could be. Skilled first aid to save lives is not difficult. The essential things to do for someone who is unconscious, bleeding or not breathing can be taught to children and carried out very effectively by 10-year-olds. But what to do must be known about and practiced *before* any emergency situation appears so that in the emergency the correct actions will be carried out smoothly and without panic and with the knowledge that what is being done is correct. A moment's thought will suggest that you do not know whose life you may be saving—perhaps a stranger, perhaps a member of your own family. If you succeed, the rewards are obvious. If you fail through lack of knowledge or not bothering to learn, you may regret it for a long time. So, try to learn the emergency treatment for someone who is unconscious, bleeding or not breathing. In this way you will be able to save lives. This surely is the minimal amount of first aid that should be expected of any responsible person.

Priorities

Before going on to the detail of what to do in an emergency for the victim or victims of an incident it is first necessary to look at the incident and at the total situation. There is, for example, little point in rushing into a burning house to become the next victim yourself just because you think that there is a vague possibility that someone may still be in the house. Similarly, in an automobile pileup on a highway there is little point in trying to rescue the victims until you are sure that the next vehicles are not going to add to the pileup. The idea of priorities is to carry out the *correct actions in the correct order*. In the examples given above the first priority is to look after yourself. Nothing useful is contributed to any emergency by becoming the next victim yourself. So, think before you act, and *never* risk your life to bring out the dead. A hero may take a calculated risk—thinking carefully first. A fool plunges in without thought, becomes the next victim, and complicates the work of would-be rescuers. This anti-heroic message is very important: the need to think before acting will save many lives both by saving the would-be rescuer's life and by being able to contribute to first aid for others by remaining alive. So, to repeat, *priority one* is look after yourself. Then, if there is *immediate* danger, *priority two* must be to protect the scene of the incident and/or to remove any victims who are alive to a place of safety. Either or both may be appropriate. A fire can be fought, a highway can be blocked off to prevent further traffic from speeding along, a victim can be removed to a place of safety so that first aid can be carried out. *Priority three* will be to send for help if there are many victims and then do emergency first aid, or priority three will be to give first aid to save the lives of the victims and then to send for help if there are only a few victims. Remember that emergency first aid to save lives is what to do for someone who is unconscious, bleeding or not breathing. *Priority four* will then be what to do for victims whose lives are not in immediate danger. This will include first aid for fracture, burns, sprains and so on.

Experience shows that correct attention to priorities will ensure the best changes of survival for all as well as the least pain and suffering for all concerned. So, to summarize priorities:

1. look after yourself. Do not become a victim.
2. protect the scene of the incident, remove any victims who are in *immediate danger*.
3. give emergency lifesaving first aid for victims who are unconscious, bleeding or not breathing and send for help. Sending for help must have a high priority if there are many casualties.
4. give first aid for other conditions which do not threaten life immediately.

Some general points in first aid

If you are a victim or if you are going to give first aid to other people, try to stay calm. People who are hot and bothered, flustered and shouting, do not give of their best and do not get the best out of others. Think how it might feel if you were a victim and someone rushed up to you and shouted a remark about how bad you looked and then panicked. It is possible both to remain calm and cool in emergency conditions and to remain thinking logically and systematically. The need is great, the performance is difficult, but these things must be done. However, if the need is seen and if practice has been done and thought given before an emergency arises, there is every hope that calmness may prevail. Try to think now how you would and should behave in an emergency.

First aid for an unconscious victim

An unconscious person can be defined for first aid purposes as anyone who cannot speak to you in sentences. If a person is not conscious enough to speak in sentences he is not able to look after himself. Making grunting noises and/or moving are not indications of the victim being able to look after himself. If he cannot speak to you in sentences he may easily die from obstructed breathing. This is why most people who are unconscious die.

Obstructed breathing is easily prevented if the correct first aid for an unconscious victim is performed. First, the head of the victim should be tilted backwards as far as it will go. This is done by rotating the head backwards until it comes to a natural stop. The chin should be pushed upwards with the teeth clenched. In this position, the air passages are opened and if the brain is sending out signals to breathe, the victim will breathe. Breathing can be detected by listening with the ear over the nose of the victim. The air coming out will be felt in the ear. Even in loud noise the ear will detect the air movement because the ear is pressure sensitive. You should also watch the victim's chest as it rises and falls with each breath. Then, if the casualty is not breathing, proceed as described below in the section on not breathing.

If the casualty is *breathing but unconscious* the problem is to put him in a position so that he will not suffer from obstructed breathing.

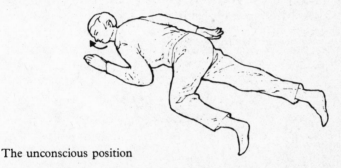

The unconscious position

To prevent obstructed breathing the victim must be put into the unconscious position and must be kept in that position until he can speak in sentences. To put a victim who is breathing but unconscious into the unconscious position, first turn him face down with the arms just out by the sides and with the face to one side or the other. Next, do three pulls—pull up the leg, the arm and the chin. The leg and arm which are pulled up must be the ones on the same side as the way the face is looking. When this has been done, the victim is in the unconscious position and will not die from obstructed breathing even if he vomits, because the nose and mouth are lower than the back of the throat. It does not usually matter whether the casualty faces one way or the other unless other injuries suggest that he may be better facing right or left.

When the casualty is placed in the unconscious position a check should again be made to ensure that he is still breathing. All that is now needed is to keep him in the unconscious position until help arrives or until he can speak to you in sentences. Lives have been lost because people have been allowed to move out of the unconscious position shortly before they recover consciousness. If an unconscious person vomits while lying on his back, obstructed breathing is almost certain to occur at once. Should he survive this, he will have about a 50/50 chance of dying of pneumonia from inhalation of vomit. These causes of death can be prevented by the proper use of the unconscious position.

First aid for a person who is bleeding

The rule is simple: press where the blood comes from and if possible lift up the part. This will stop the bleeding. Press where the blood comes from with the cleanest thing available. If you have nothing clean, press with something dirty, but press where the blood comes from. If you have nothing else, press with your bare hand. This will stop the bleeding.

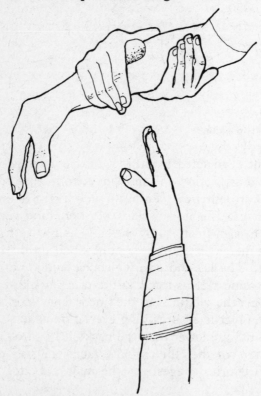

Press where the blood comes from and lift up the part

If bleeding is from a hand or arm, lift the part up. If bleeding is from a leg, tell the person to lie down and lift up the leg. The idea is to make it more difficult for the heart to pump blood to the part by making the heart pump uphill. If someone is bleeding from the head and/or neck and is conscious, he should sit up.

Self-help is very important and often very easy in bleeding. The simple rule to press where the blood comes from and lift up the part is easy. This will always stop the bleeding. It is often convenient to keep pressing where the blood comes from by tying something around the part and over the top of the cut or wound. A folded scarf, a torn sheet or a folded apron will do in place of a bandage. Whatever is used should be tied firmly in order to keep pressing where the blood comes from. If any blood comes through the dressing and wrapper, more material should be applied on the outside with firmer pressure. The part should also be lifted higher. This will always stop the bleeding. On no account should any dressing be removed from a cut or wound: this may only serve to disturb or rip off any clot which has already formed. Further dressings, further pressure and further lifting up will always stop the bleeding.

Foreign bodies in the cut or wound

Many people worry about what to do if there is a piece of wood, metal, glass or other material in a cut or wound. The rule is simple—if a foreign body is loose, lift it gently out. If it is stuck, leave it. Bleeding will occur around the edges of the cut and around the edges of the foreign body. So, press where the blood comes from, and this will stop the bleeding. Common sense will tell you not to press on the foreign body for fear of doing further damage.

Blood loss

Any blood which is not available for circulation is effectively lost. Anyone who bleeds internally is suffering from blood loss *from the circulation* even though the blood is still inside him. The greater the blood loss the greater is the need for immediate blood replacement by blood transfusion in a hospital. Adults who lose more than $2\frac{1}{2}$ pints (about 1 liter) of blood are in need of blood replacement. In children much smaller losses will require replacement.

Anyone who is or has been bleeding, looks pale and sweaty, and has a fast or rising pulse rate (count it, and write it down with the time, every 5 minutes) should be taken to a hospital without delay for he may need blood replacement. Internal bleeding can only be dealt with in first-aid by sending the victim at once to a hospital. In any case of severe bleeding—whether external or internal—blood replacement by blood transfusion may be needed so do not waste time treating trivial or non-life-threatening conditions.

First aid for not breathing

The brain needs a constant supply of oxygen to stay functioning. If the brain is deprived of oxygen for 4–6 minutes the person can easily die. The need therefore in someone who is not breathing is to get oxygen to the brain. This is done by blowing air into the nose (or mouth). The nose is easier and is less likely to be obstructed. In first aid, the person may be taken from the water or may have been electrocuted. Remember the priorities and look

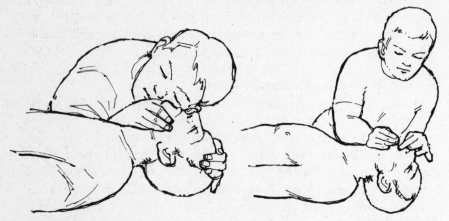

Listen for breathing   Head fully back

after yourself. Check for breathing by putting the head back as far as it will go with the teeth in clenched position. If no breath can be felt on your ear and no chest movements are seen, proceed at once to inflate the lungs. This is just like blowing up a balloon. You have to get an airtight seal at the neck of the balloon and then blow air in. As the balloon inflates, you can see it expand and you can feel the tension rising. Blowing through the nose is just as easy. Keep the head fully back with the chin pressed up and the teeth clenched to keep the air passages open. Now, making an airtight seal over the victim's nose with your lips, blow gently to inflate the lungs. When you see the chest rise and feel the tension rise, take your mouth away. The air will come out due to the elasticity of the lungs and the weight of the chest wall. Blow again, let the air out and keep on going with the head fully back, until the victim starts to breathe on his own. When he is breathing weakly, try to time your breaths with his. Then, when he is breathing and unconscious, turn him into the unconscious position and continue to check both that he continues breathing and that he stays in the unconscious position.

If the breathing does not begin soon, continue to give artificial respiration for an hour or until a doctor tells you to stop. If the victim has froth coming from the nose or mouth, wipe away what you can but blow the rest in and out because froth is mainly air.

Exhaled air contains 16 per cent oxygen, which is quite enough for an unconscious resting victim. If you see someone who is not breathing, waste no time in blowing air into his lungs. Delay may easily be fatal. Time is always short under these circumstances. Your reward may be to save a life.

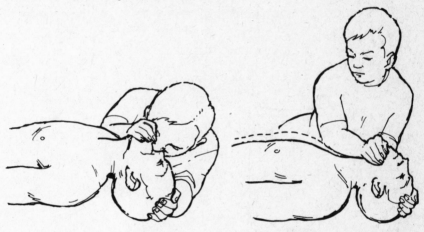

Inflate   Watch chest falling and repeat process

First aid for heat burns and scalds

In any heat injury, the first need is to *cool* the affected area. This is most easily accomplished by water from a shower, tap or bucket. If clothing is stuck, as in a heat burn, it should be left. In scalds, the clothing may trap a lot of wet heat and so should be removed as cooling proceeds. Cooling should be for ten minutes *timed by the clock*. Less will not be enough in serious burns. When cooling has been carried out the next need is to cover the burn to prevent infection. The covering used should be the cleanest non-hairy, non-fluffy material available. Pillow cases, sheets and smooth towels are ideal home coverings. If a sterile dressing is available it should be used. Cover the burn *and* an area beyond the edges of the burn. This completes first aid. No lotions, antiseptics, salves or creams should be put on burns. Cooling and covering is all that is required. The correct covering for skin loss is skin replacement. Burns cause skin loss. Skin grafts will not take on top of grease, ointments, hairy wool or fluff adhering to a burn—so these things must be avoided.

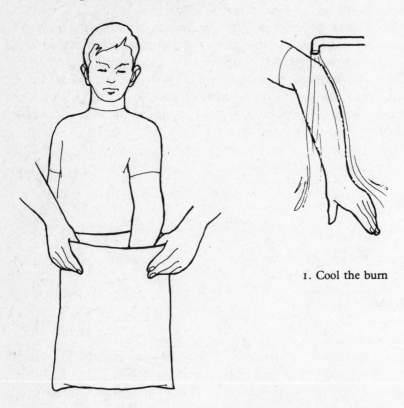

1. Cool the burn

2. Then cover the burn with cleanest non-hairy, non-fluffy material available.

In assessing the severity of a burn in first aid, the *area* of the burn is the best guide. A person's hand with the fingers together and the thumb close in will cover 1 per cent of that person's skin. Remember not to use *your* hand as guide to the area of someone else's burn—this will lead to errors, especially for a child. Burns of over 10 per cent in children and old people, and 15 per cent in fit adults, may need intravenous fluid. So, after you have cooled and covered the burn, send the victim to hospital for further treatment.

First aid for fractures

A fracture is a break in a bone. When any part of the body has been subjected to a heavy blow or other force and is painful, misshapen, swollen and cannot be used normally, it should be assumed that the bone is broken until proved otherwise. It is relatively easy to guess in many cases, but the only way of being *sure* that a bone is or is not broken is to take an X ray. So, if you have even a vague suspicion that a bone may be broken, treat the victim as if the bone *was* broken and then go to a hospital so that an X ray can be taken. Missed and untreated fractures will result if this suggested course of action is not followed.

Fractures are of two main kinds: open fractures in which there is a cut or wound at or near the fracture site, and closed fractures in which there is no cut or wound at or near the fracture site.

Open fractures have to be treated for bleeding by pressing where the blood comes from and by putting a cover on the wound to stop bleeding and prevent infection. When this has been done, the first aid for open and closed fractures is the same.

What follows is a simple guide to simple fractures. Always tell a person who has a fracture or suspected fracture to stay still. Movement will always increase pain and may increase damage. The aims in treating fractures are to stop movement and prevent further damage. This is often very easy. For example in the case of closed fracture of two fingers there is little need to do more than advise the person to keep still and go to a hospital. Broken ankles can be padded with pillows and cushions to keep the part still and at rest. Elaborate splinting and tying is not always necessary or desirable. Anything which makes a fracture or suspected fracture comfortable and pain-free is useful and good. Pain or its absence will usually indicate whether treatment is or is not effective in fractures (and dislocations).

HAND, WRIST AND FOREARM

Keep the part at rest. The good arm may be used as a rest and support for the bad arm—this is often known as the good arm sling. People will often do this for themselves. If they are comfortable they can be transported to hospital sitting up and holding their arm.

ARM AND COLLARBONE

A broad sling may be useful in arm fractures, or a collar and cuff to hang the wrist from the neck. People who need this will often clutch the opposite shoulder. If the victim is comfortable what you are doing for him is right. If pain is increased, then the first aid is probably not helpful. Simplicity of treatment designed to relieve pain is often the best.

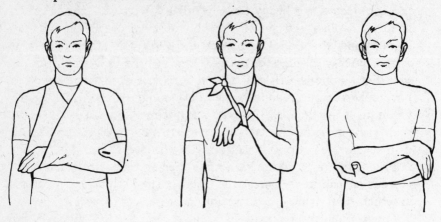

A broad sling   A collar and cuff   The good arm sling

ANKLE AND FOOT

Do not allow a person to walk on an ankle or foot which you think may be broken. Simple treatment to stop movement and relieve pain is usually all that will be required. Place the injured ankle on a pillow, cushion or rolled up clothing. This will usually be sufficient.

Use pillows and cushions for a fractured ankle

LEG AND THIGH

A good plan is often to tie the good leg to the bad one, thus using the good leg as a splint for the bad one. Begin by placing padding between the ankles and knees and then move the good leg to the bad one. Tie a figure-of-eight bandage around the feet and ankles to keep them together. Next bind the legs gently but firmly together taking care not to tie anything right over the site of the fracture or suspected fracture. The knots should also be tied so that the casualty does not lie on them. Sufficient ties should be used to keep the legs firmly together. If the break is near the upper end of the thigh bone, the victim should be told to lie down and he should be kept lying down when he is moved to minimize movement at the hip.

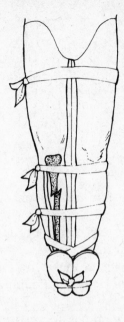

A fracture of the leg

NECK, BACK AND PELVIS

Fractures of the spine and pelvis are best treated by expert first-aiders. Make no attempt to move the victim. Tell him to lie still until expert help arrives. Make sure also that no one is allowed to move the victim. The price of movement could be paraplegia and double incontinence—so speed is not required. What is necessary is to make sure that the person is moved without increasing the spinal damage. Tragic and unnecessary paralysis has resulted from attempting to move a victim just to let the traffic go by. So, resist all attempts by unskilled people to move anyone who you think may have a spinal fracture. Tell the victim to lie still and keep him at rest until skilled help arrives.

DISLOCATIONS

A dislocation is present when a bone has been displaced from its normal position at a joint. NEVER attempt to manipulate or reduce a dislocation. Until an X ray has been taken it is impossible to be sure whether or not there may also be a fracture.

The first aid for a dislocation is the same as for a fracture—tell the victim to keep still, prevent movement and send the victim to a hospital for X-ray and further treatment. How to keep the part still and what to do is the same as for fractures.

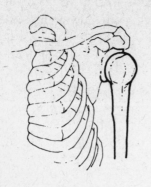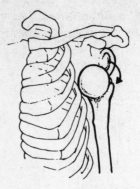

A dislocation at the shoulder

Poisoning by mouth

IF THE VICTIM IS UNCONSCIOUS, place him in the unconscious position and send him quickly to a hospital together with clues about what the poison could be. Send any empty bottles, pills, medicines, berries or whatever else you find.

IF THE VICTIM IS CONSCIOUS, it may help to make him vomit if *the poison is NOT a petroleum product and does NOT cause burning of the lips, mouth and tongue.*

The easiest way to make a person vomit is to get him lying face downward and head down over a bucket. Then, use his finger or yours on the back of the throat. This will usually make him vomit. 15 ml. of syrup of ipecac USP is also very good but you need to have it on hand. Do not use salt or mustard solutions. Then, after the casualty has vomited, give a drink of water or milk and send him to a hospital. Keep the vomited material and send it to the hospital. The doctors may wish to see it.

If the poison is a petroleum product or causes burning of the lips, mouth and tongue send the victim quickly to a hospital. Remember that unconscious people must be given *nothing* by mouth in case it chokes them.

Wet-cold exposure (hypothermia)

Many people who set out in temperate climates to walk, climb and adventure are ill prepared for the effects of wetting and cold. Under these conditions, a slight wind on wet clothing can result in a fall of the core temperature of the body to dangerous or even fatal levels. The signs of hypothermia in fit adults usually begin with lagging and stumbling, and this may be accompanied by complaints of cold and shivering. Loss of consciousness quickly follows in untreated victims. These people are in urgent need of warmth. Emergency measures to stop heat loss should include making a camp, sheltering, and putting the victim in a sleeping bag or polythene bag over blankets. Hot drinks should be given if the victim is conscious and if hot drinks can be prepared. If circumstances are such that the person can be given a hot bath this should be done and he should be kept there until recovered. Frequent reheating of the bath will be necessary. Then, the victim should be dried and put to bed in a warm place with plenty of blankets. Hot sweet drinks (nonalcoholic) should be given.

Prevention is really the important message for hypothermia. No one should set out without checking local weather forecasts, wearing or carrying adequate warm waterproof clothing and carrying dry changes of clothing. Weather conditions can often change rapidly and loss of life may be the price of lack of preparedness.

The definitive treatment of minor injuries

This section is not about first aid. It is about what to do if you are going to be the only one to deal with the condition. Before deciding to treat any condition, you should be sure that it is really a minor condition. Some examples of conditions which are often mistaken for simple or minor injuries are cuts near joints, small deep wounds or stabs with tiny skin entry wounds, wounds with foreign bodies in them, small deep cuts of the neck, abdominal and genital area and wounds near important organs such as the eye and ear. Discrimination is needed in every case. Training in discrimination is a lengthy process—so, if you have any doubt that

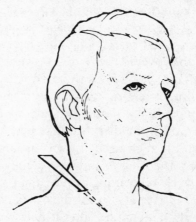

Stab and puncture wounds can be deep

a cut is not superficial or that the condition is not simple, carry out first aid to stop bleeding and prevent infection and then send the victim to a hospital or to a doctor.

MINOR CUTS, SCRATCHES AND WOUNDS

Two steps are required to deal efficiently and properly with any wound—first clean the wound thoroughly by removing all dirt, contamination and dead tissue; second cover the wound to prevent infection. The cover should be sterile if possible. A dry dressing is best unless there are raw areas when a non adhesive dressing will be required. No salves, ointments or medications are recommended on the cut. Good cleaning is *the* important step.

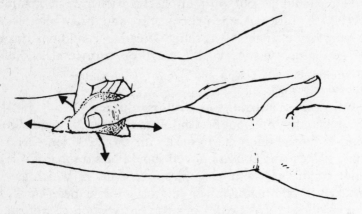

Cover the cut or wound and scrub dirt away from the wound

Begin by scrubbing and washing the hands. Next, the cut or wound should be covered while the surrounding skin is cleaned. A quaternary ammonium compound (1 per cent solution) is preferable because it is a good detergent and is non-irritating. If it is not available, soap and water will do very well. The skin is cleaned all around the covered area and the swabbing or scrubbing should aim to scrub dirt *away* from the covered area. Then, when the surrounding skin is clean, the cut is cleaned by repeated swabbing and rubbing. Time should be spent on this step because clean wounds heal well while dirty wounds heal badly. It is often a good plan to let children clean their own cuts and wounds. They can balance out for themselves how hard they scrub and how long they have to work at cleaning against the pain that they feel. As long as the child is kept at it until the cut is completely free of dirt it does not really matter how long it takes to get the desired result. But high standards must be set.

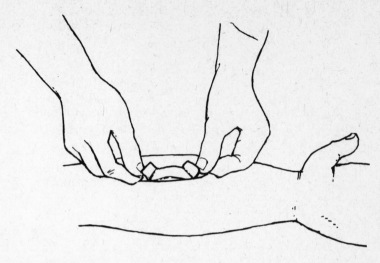
Put the dressing onto the wound without touching the surface which goes onto the cut or wound

When the wound is free of dirt, any dead skin is trimmed off and the area rescrubbed. Now, a dirt-free wound, free of dead tissue, remains. This should be dried and a suitable dressing applied. Adhesive patches with dry sterile dressings are often very useful. If raw areas are a problem, net or gauze petroleum jelly dressings can be used, or one of the varieties of non-adhesive shiny materials now available. The dressing surface which goes onto the wound should not be touched or handled to prevent infection of the area.

BURNS

After cooling, burns should be cleansed as for cuts and wounds. Any dead skin must be trimmed away. A dry dressing or a non-adhesive covering should then be applied. Only small-area burns should be treated—not larger than about a half an inch in diameter. Beware of burns near the eye and mouth or other vital organs. Such burns are best seen by a doctor.